KV-106-654

Defining Poverty in the Developing World

Defining Poverty in the Developing World

Edited by

Frances Stewart
Professor of Development Economics and
Director of the Centre for Research on Inequality,
Human Security and Ethnicity, Oxford University, UK

Ruhi Saith
Head of Research Programmes at the Public Health Foundation, India

Barbara Harriss-White
Director of Department of International Development,
Professor of Development Studies and Fellow of Wolfson College,
Oxford University, UK

MAGDALEN COLLEGE LIBRARY

Editorial matter and selection © Frances Stewart,
Barbara Harriss-White and Ruhi Saith 2007
Individual chapters © their respective authors 2007

All rights reserved. No reproduction, copy or transmission of this
publication may be made without written permission.

No paragraph of this publication may be reproduced, copied or transmitted
save with written permission or in accordance with the provisions of the
Copyright, Designs and Patents Act 1988, or under the terms of any licence
permitting limited copying issued by the Copyright Licensing Agency, 90
Tottenham Court Road, London W1T 4LP.

Any person who does any unauthorised act in relation to this publication
may be liable to criminal prosecution and civil claims for damages.

The authors have asserted their rights to be identified as
the authors of this work in accordance with the Copyright,
Designs and Patents Act 1988.

First published in 2007 by
PALGRAVE MACMILLAN
Houndmills, Basingstoke, Hampshire RG21 6XS and
175 Fifth Avenue, New York, N.Y. 10010
Companies and representatives throughout the world.

PALGRAVE MACMILLAN is the global academic imprint of the Palgrave
Macmillan division of St. Martin's Press, LLC and of Palgrave Macmillan Ltd.
Macmillan® is a registered trademark in the United States, United Kingdom
and other countries. Palgrave is a registered trademark in the European
Union and other countries.

ISBN-13: 978–0–230–51672–4 hardback
ISBN-10: 0–230–51672–6 hardback

This book is printed on paper suitable for recycling and made from fully
managed and sustained forest sources. Logging, pulping and manufacturing
processes are expected to conform to the environmental regulations of
the country of origin

A catalogue record for this book is available from the British Library.

Library of Congress Cataloging-in-Publication Data

Defining poverty in the developing world / Frances Stewart, Ruhi Saith,
    Barbara Harriss-White [editors].
        p. cm.
    Includes bibliographical references and index.
    ISBN-13: 978–0–230–51672–4 (cloth)
    ISBN-10: 0–230–51672–6 (cloth)
        1. Poverty – Developing countries – Evaluation. 2. Basic needs –
Developing countries. 3. Marginality, Social – Developing countries.
4. Quality of life – Developing countries. 5. Income distribution –
Developing countries. I. Stewart, Frances, 1940– II. Saith, Ruhi.
III. Harriss-White, Barbara, 1946–

HC59.72.P6D44 2007
339.4'6091724—dc22   2006048009

10 9 8 7 6 5 4 3 2
16 15 14 13 12 11 10 09 08
Printed and bound in Great Britain by
Antony Rowe Ltd, Chippenham and Eastbourne

Contents

List of Figures

List of Graphs

List of Tables

Acknowledgements

We are grateful to the Department for International Development in the UK (DFID) for supporting this research.

We have benefited greatly from cooperation with the National Council of Applied Economic Research (NCAER) in New Delhi, India and the Universidad del Pacifico in Lima, Peru. In the NCAER, we would particularly like to thank Abusaleh Shariff, Abhilasha Sharma and Rajesh Jaiswal for generously providing the NCAER/UNDP 1994 data, helping with field work and its analysis, writing background papers and organising a workshop in Delhi in 2002. We also thank the Academy of Science, Lucknow, which helped organise the field work in Uttar Pradesh. In Peru; we are especially grateful to Enrique Vasquez and the Universidad del Pacifico for their assistance with the research in Peru and in organising the workshop in Lima in 2001; the Instituto Cuanto for generously allowing us access to the ENNIV 2000 data and collaborating in the implementation of the surveys for the case studies; Araceli Roldán (CESA) and Francisco Díaz Canseco for their help with implementation of participatory techniques in Peru. Sincere thanks to Professor Amartya Sen for comments on the chapter on the capability approach, and also to Professor Arup Mitra, Institute of Economic Growth, Delhi University, for comments on the methodology used in the empirical work for India. We thank in Oxford, Karem Roitman, Emma Samman and Angela Ruiz-Uccelli for valuable research support and Nandini Gooptu, Taimur Hyat and Eri Taniguchi for useful discussions on destitution. Useful dialogue and support for the study on destitution were provided by Harsh Mander, Biraj Patnaik and Alok Chowdhury of ActionAid India, Indu Prakash Singh of Aashray Adhikar Abhiyan (Movement for Shelter for the Homeless) in New Delhi and Nilakantha Rath, A.K. Shiva Kumar, Frederic Landy and Denis Requier-Desjardins. The chapter on destitution was presented at the NCAER, New Delhi; WIDER, Helsinki; Maison des Sciences de l'Homme, Paris and Centre d'Economie de d'Ethique pour L'Environnement et le Developpement, Universite de Versailles and benefited from the discussions at these fora. An earlier version of Chapter 1 was published in *Oxford Development Studies* (see http://www.tandf.co.uk/journals).

An earlier version of Chapter 5 was published as Chapter 17 in J. Gonsalves, T. Becker, A. Braun, D. Campilan, H. de Chavez, E. Fajber,

M. Kapiriri, J. Rivaca-Caminade and R. Vernooy (eds.), *Participatory Research and Development for Sustainable Agriculture and Natural Resource Management: a Sourcebook*. Volume 1: *Understanding Participatory Research and Development* (International Potato Center – Users' Perspectives with Agricultural Research and Development, Laguna, Philippines and International Development Research Centre, Ottawa, Canada, 2005). An earlier version of Chapter 6 was published in *World Development*, vol. 33, no. 6 (2005): 881–92.

We would like to thank participants at four workshops for their valuable comments: at Queen Elizabeth House Oxford, 2000; at the Universidad del Pacifio, 2001; at the NCAER, New Delhi 2002; and at Save the Children Headquarters in London in 2003.

Notes on Contributors

Susana Franco (PhD Nottingham) is an economist who has specialised in development economics. She has worked as a lecturer at the University of Reading, UK, and as a research officer at the University of Oxford, UK. She has also worked as a consultant for the UNDP and UNRISD. Her research covers several areas, including the impact of foreign aid, the definition and measurement of poverty, and gender issues.

Barbara Harriss-White is Director of the Department of International Development (Queen Elizabeth House) and fellow of Wolfson College, University of Oxford. Trained in agricultural development economics, she has focused on two fields of research since 1969: the political economy of agrarian markets and aspects of deprivation. Her previous field research on poverty and deprivation appears in *Rural India Facing the 21st Century* (Anthem, 2004).

Caterina Ruggeri Laderchi holds a DPhil in Economics from the University of Oxford, UK, and is currently a poverty economist at the World Bank. Her research interests and publications are in the area of poverty and human development, participation, the distributional impact of reforms and poverty alleviation programmes, and labour market issues (the effects of internal migration in particular).

Ruhi Saith is qualified as a medical doctor and has a DPhil in Medicine from Oxford University. Her research interests and experience are in public health and multi-dimensional aspects of poverty. She has worked on projects with the UN, UNDP, UNRISD, the World Bank and worked at QEH, Oxford University and the Planning Commission of the Government of India. She is currently the Head of Research Programmes at the Public Health Foundation of India.

Abhilasha Sharma holds a postgraduate degree in Sociology from the Delhi School of Economics, India, and a PhD degree in Population Studies from the Jawaharlal Nehru University, India. She is currently an Associate Fellow at the National Council of Applied Economic Research (NCAER), New Delhi, India.

xiv   *Notes on Contributors*

Professor Frances Stewart is Director of the Centre for Research on Inequality, Human Security and Ethnicity (CRISE) and Fellow of Somerville College at the University of Oxford. She was director of the International Development Centre, Queen Elizabeth House from 1993–2003. She has written widely on issues of human development, poverty and conflict. Publications include *Adjustment with a Human Face* (OUP 1986) (with Andrea Cornia and Richard Jolly) and *War and Underdevelopment* (OUP 2001) (with Valpy Fitzgerald).

List of Abbreviations

AAA	Aashray Adhikar Abhiyan
BCB	Basic consumption basket
BFB	Basic food basket
BMI	Body mass index
BN	Basic needs
CA	Capability/capabilities
ENNIV	Encuesta Nacional de Niveles de Hogares sobre Medicion de Niveles de Vida
EU	European Union
FGD	Focus group discussion
FGT	Foster, Greer and Thorbeck
HH	Household
HPI	Human Poverty Index
IFI	International financial institutions
ILO	International Labour Organisation
IMF	International Monetary Fund
IN	Intermediate needs
NCAER	National Council of Applied Economic Research
NCHS	National Council of Health Statistics
NGOs	Non-governmental organisations
NSS	National sample survey
PA	Participatory Appraisal
PPA	Participatory Poverty Assessments
PRA	Participatory Rural Appraisal
PRSPs	Poverty Reduction Strategy Papers
RRA	Rapid rural appraisal
SC	Scheduled Caste
SE	Social exclusion
ST	Scheduled Tribe
UN	United Nations
UNDP	United Nations Development Programme
UNESCO	United Nations Educational, Scientific and Cultural Organisation
UNHCS	United Nations Centre for Human Settlements

UNRISD	United Nations Research Institute for Social Development
U.P.	Uttar Pradesh
UPPAP	Ugandan Participatory Poverty Assessment
WB	World Bank
WHO	World Health Organisation

1
Introduction: Four Approaches to Defining and Measuring Poverty

Frances Stewart, Caterina Ruggeri Laderchi and Ruhi Saith

1.1 Introduction

The elimination of poverty is a key concern of all those interested in the development of poor countries, and now provides the main justification for promoting economic growth and development. The central objective of the Millennium Goals, agreed by 149 countries at the UN Millennium Summit in New York, is the halving of poverty by 2015. In official discourse – for example, by the World Bank and major donors – almost every policy is currently assessed in relation to its impact on poverty, ranging from debt relief to macroeconomic stabilisation.[1] Ironically, however, while the objective of poverty reduction currently has overwhelming support, particularly among the donor community, there is increasing debate about what this objective *means*.

To devise policies to reduce poverty effectively, it is important to know precisely at what we are aiming. The current approach to the identification of poverty and to policy formulation is rather messy: on the one hand, there is acknowledgement of its multidimensionality, combined with a pick and choose approach in advocacy. On the other hand, in practice, the monetary approach largely retains its dominance in descriptions and analysis, both nationally and internationally. Clarification of how poverty is defined is extremely important as different definitions of poverty imply use of different criteria for measurement, potentially the identification of different individuals and groups as poor, and the use of different policy solutions for poverty reduction.

Different interpretations of reality translate into different poverty measures. These differences, in part, reflect different views of what constitutes a good society and good lives. Our main purpose in this book is to explore these differences and their implications, rather than assessing their merit. It is our view that clearer and more transparent definitions of poverty are essential prerequisites of any development policy that puts poverty reduction at its centre.

The aim of this book is to explore differences in approaches to poverty, both conceptually and empirically. We concentrate in particular on four alternative understandings of poverty: the monetary approach, the capability approach, social exclusion as defining poverty, and the participatory approach. We first explore the conceptual underpinnings of each approach, and then report on empirical work in India and Peru. The empirical work adopts the different approaches to identify who is in poverty, using both existing large data sets, and purposive surveys we carried out ourselves. The aim of this work is to see whether (and the extent to which) the different approaches identify the same or different people, since this will have important implications for poverty assessment and poverty reduction policies. If, despite conceptual differences, in practice the various approaches identify broadly the same people, then a single type of measure can be considered sufficient for these purposes. But if significantly different populations are identified, this indicates that a particular indicator (based on a particular approach) cannot be assumed to serve as a proxy to identify other types of poverty. This suggests different measurement strategies and different policies will be needed, according to the chosen concept of poverty.

Each of the following four chapters (Chapters 2 to 5) is devoted to the exploration of one of the four approaches, reviewing the history of the development of the concept, theoretical criticisms and problems of interpretation and measurement when implementing the approach in practice. Each chapter concludes by indicating the method to be followed in applying the poverty concept in the empirical work. This is followed by empirical analysis reported on in Chapter 6 (the Indian case) and Chapter 7 (the Peruvian case). In Chapter 8, we carry out an exploratory analysis of destitution in India and Peru. We assess the manner in which our analysis of the different approaches to poverty, maps on to the 'poorest of the poor' sections of the community. Chapter 9 contrasts the findings in the two countries, and reviews other empirical work in the area. This chapter comes to some conclusions, including implications for measurement of poverty and policies, as well suggestions for further work in this area.

The present chapter provides a brief overview and comparison of the four approaches, drawing on the material in Chapters 2 to 5, summarising the conceptual development of each approach, and then contrasting them. Readers who do not want greater detail on the approaches and their implementation may therefore read this chapter and proceed straight away to the empirical part of the work.

Section 1.2 of this chapter discusses some issues common to any approach to the definition and measurement of poverty. This is followed by a comparison of the conceptual underpinnings of the four approaches (Section 1.3). The concluding section points to the need for empirical investigations of which groups are identified as poor by the different approaches, and explains why we have chosen India and Peru for our empirical investigations.

1.2   Common problems encountered in defining and measuring poverty

There are a number of general questions about how to define and measure poverty that apply to all approaches, many of which were already apparent in the pioneering work of Rowntree in the late nineteenth and early twentieth century. It is helpful to discuss these in general terms before a detailed discussion of the different approaches.

First, a fundamental issue – which underlies the differences in the approaches we are considering – is the *space* in which deprivation or poverty is defined and how that space is captured by the indicators chosen. Different poverty definitions span different 'spheres of concerns', not all of which may be easily measured. For example, should the definition of poverty be confined to material aspects of life, or include social, cultural and political aspects? Is poverty to be measured in the space of utility or resources (broadly adopted by different versions of the monetary approach) or in terms of the freedom to live the life one values (as in the capability approach)? Depending on the space chosen, the choice of indicators to carry out measurements in this space raises its own set of dilemmas: e.g. with the monetary approach, should it be an indicator that measures income or one that measures expenditure? With regard to the capability approach, should indicators capture what *may be* achieved, given the resources available and the prevailing environment – that is the *ability* to be and do a variety of things – or what *is actually* achieved by individuals?

Secondly, there is the question of the *universality* of the definition of poverty. Should we expect definitions and measurement indicators applied in one type of society to be transferable to other societies, without serious modifications, or even at all? Two of the approaches we consider (the monetary approach and social exclusion) were initially devised for developed countries. In each, there are problems in translating their application to developing countries: in the monetary approach, for example, this involves heroic imputations of values for subsistence production; in social exclusion, substantial differences in societal norms lead to major differences in the defining characteristics of social exclusion.[2] In contrast, the capability approach and participatory methods were first devised with developing countries in mind, and the reverse question applies. Here again it is clear that the interpretation of the approaches will differ between societies with radically different characteristics – this is not just a matter of developed versus developing countries, but also other major societal differences (e.g. between socialist and capitalist societies). To some extent methods are context-specific, and may need to be reinterpreted for particular societies for operationalisation, which can make comparisons across contexts problematic.

Thirdly, there is the question of whether methods are *objective* or *subjective*. Most statements about poverty suggest objectivity: i.e. it is implied that there is a certain reality 'out there' which poverty statistics capture. To the extent that value judgements affect measurement then the methods are not objective, and the question then is who is making the value judgements: are they made implicitly by the researchers or statisticians who are measuring poverty? Are they made explicitly, and subject to sensitivity analysis, so that the effects of those value judgements can readily be evaluated? To what extent are these understood and shared by other stakeholders, for example, through the political process, or through a participatory process involving the poor themselves?

Fourthly, a crucial question is how to differentiate the poor from the non-poor through the use of one (or several) *poverty lines*. Two related issues arise: first, what is the justification for adopting any such line; and secondly, to what extent is the poverty line defined as relative to a given context or is intended to reflect some absolute standards of deprivation?

At a theoretical level, the possibility of identifying poverty relies on the crucial assumption that there is some form of discontinuity between the poor and the non-poor which can be reflected in the poverty line. Such a break can pertain to the behaviour of the poor, or to some salient feature which identifies the poor and which either moral or political considerations suggest should be addressed. For example, one approach, justified on political or moral grounds, is to define the poverty line at a level at which people can realise a full or decent life, or more ambitiously a good society. Essentially, rights-based approaches to poverty do this, and similar concerns animate the capability approaches (e.g. Nussbaum 2000b), while this type of argument is unusual in the monetary approach (e.g. Ravallion 1998). Other types of 'natural' breaks can be found: for example, evidence on the importance of social networks for provision of informal insurance and support mechanisms, as well as from participatory research, suggests there is a 'break' at levels of resources below which people are considered unworthy of community support as they would not be able to reciprocate their obligations if needed (see, e.g., Howard and Millard 1997).

Considerable attention has been devoted to the issue of whether the threshold between the poor and non-poor should be sensitive to the characteristics of the overall population. At one extreme, the poverty line between poor and non-poor is defined with reference to some summary measure of the overall distribution (as for example in the case of the member states of the European Union, where the poverty line is set at 60 per cent of the median of 'equivalised' income). At the other extreme a poverty line is set in terms of minimal requirements in the dimension of interest identified in absolute terms, for example on the basis of some needs of the individual deemed as essential for survival.

In reality it is difficult, perhaps impossible, to identify such absolute needs irrespective of societal standards. For example, in an era before the advent of writing, literacy could not be identified as an absolute require-ment, yet now any definition of capability poverty would include this dimension. Further, most apparently 'absolute' indicators of poverty contain some relative element, reflecting the need to maintain the relevance of a given definition over time. For example, although he did not take an explicitly relative approach, in his second study of York in the 1930s, Rowntree updated his minimum requirements for people to be non-poor to include having a bath and a garden. Sen has pointed out that even if requirements can be set as absolute in terms of needs anchored to some standards with intrinsic value, they would generally need to be inter-preted as relative in terms of resources. For example, if poverty is defined in absolute terms in relation to nutritional requirements, it is likely to some extent to be relative in income terms, since in richer societies people generally need more money to acquire the same nutrition – as cheaper foods are not available, transport is needed to shop, and so on.

Nonetheless, a conceptual difference remains in the choice – along a continuum – between an overtly relative approach and an intended absolute approach. This choice is ultimately a matter of political and cultural sensitivity. From a political point of view, a relative standard makes sense as people's toleration of poverty and governments' willingness to take action against it are generally relative to average standards in that society. It is also true that the sense of deprivation or unhappiness caused by poverty is greatly influenced by average societal standards. In general, relative standards are mostly adopted in countries where it is assumed that all have access to the means to ensure survival, while where the availability of a survival minimum is felt as a pressing issue (i.e. generally in developing countries), absolute standards are more often adopted.

A fifth issue concerns the *unit* over which poverty is defined – this is partly a question of whether poverty is defined at the level of the individual or the family, and also a matter of the geographical unit of analysis. While it is individuals who suffer or enjoy their lives, data, particularly of a monetary kind, normally pertain to households, and some resources (not only money income, but sanitation, clean water) come via the household and it is difficult to ascertain the distribution of services they provide to the individual. The geographic unit matters in three ways: first, for identifying the society with respect to which the relative poverty lines are drawn; secondly, for defining the boundaries of the relevant market, for example, to obtain prices for valuations; and thirdly, in terms of targeting, since when geographic areas are used for targeting, how the areas are defined will affect the efficiency of targeting.

Sixthly, a pervasive question is how to deal with *multidimensionality*: considering that individual well-being (and lack of it) manifests itself in multiple dimensions, should an aggregate index be developed, and how? The issue can be bypassed in a monetary approach by assuming that the monetary metrics either captures the essence of deprivation, or proxies all other deprivations. The proxying role of the monetary measures is reinforced to the extent that relevant heterogeneity between individuals can be adjusted for,[3] so that their monetary resources become comparable across individuals. The other approaches, however, incorporate what Sen labels the constitutive plurality of a welfare assessment, and therefore do not present themselves in the form of a single index. These approaches raise two questions: how each constituent dimension is to be measured; and how they are to be aggregated. Any aggregation requires a decision on whether and how the severity of deprivation in each of the basic dimensions should be included. However, in general there is no right way of aggregating. Moreover, aggregation, although helpful for summarising societal deprivation, implies a loss of information, whose influence on the final results should be appropriately tested for.

Seventh, the *time* horizon over which poverty is identified needs to be defined. This is commonly viewed as a technical issue concerning the period of time over which poverty should be measured, i.e. over a month, a year, or longer time. Many people move in and out of poverty over seasons and years, and therefore the longer the time perspective the less poverty will appear. Such variations are less likely the more the poor have access to income and consumption smoothing strategies (Morduch 1995), which suggests that in these cases there is a case for adopting longer time periods to arrive at less noisy accounts of living standards. Yet, these fluctuations can be of particular interest if they entail far-reaching consequences for the most vulnerable individuals (consider childhood poverty's consequences for future physical and cognitive development). If poor households are credit and insurance constrained, therefore, there is a case for shorter time periods that allow a greater differentiation between the chronic poor (variously defined as those always below a poverty line, or those, on average, below a poverty line (Hulme and Shepherd 2003) and the transitory poor). These considerations do not apply, however, to all approaches equally, as some capability and social exclusion measures, though observed at one point in time, by their nature indicate long-term deprivation either because they have long-term consequences (e.g. child malnutrition as revealed by low height for age) or because they are structural (e.g. some correlate of social exclusion, such as race).

Another aspect of the time horizon chosen relates to the concept of *lifetime* poverty. This could be seen as a statistical question concerning which and how many individuals are chronically poor throughout their lives. But it could also be approached in terms of life-decisions: what critical decisions or circumstances in a person's life – pre-birth, in their early childhood, in their school years, as an adult, for example – led to lifetime poverty (or avoided it). This approach could be useful for causal and policy analysis.

Finally, there is a general question about the extent to which a definition of poverty offers (or should offer) a causal explanation for poverty and points to policies towards its alleviation. Some of the approaches are built on causal analysis, while others aim only at providing a description. We believe, however, that even such descriptive exercises influence the broad thrust of policy-making. We shall return to this issue in the concluding section.

1.3 An overview of the four approaches

1.3.1 The monetary approach

As already noted, the monetary approach to the identification and measurement of poverty is the most commonly used. It identifies poverty with a shortfall in consumption (or income) from some poverty line.

The valuation of the different components of income or consumption is done at market prices, which requires identification of the relevant market and the imputation of monetary values for those items that are not valued through the market (such as subsistence production and, in principle, public goods) (Grosh and Glewwe, 2000). The assumptions needed for such imputation are generally somewhat heroic. The key assumption is that, with appropriately devised tools, uniform monetary metrics can take into account all the relevant heterogeneity across individuals and their situations.

For economists the appeal of the monetary approach lies in its being compatible with the assumption of utility maximising behaviour which underpins microeconomics, i.e. that the objective of consumers is to maximise utility and that expenditures reflect the marginal value or utility people place on commodities. Welfare can then be measured as the total consumption enjoyed, proxied by either expenditure or income data, and poverty is defined as a shortfall below some minimum level of resources, which is termed the poverty line.

The validity of the approach then depends in part on:

- whether utility is an adequate definition of well-being;
- whether monetary expenditure is a satisfactory measure of utility;[4]
- whether a shortfall in utility encompasses all we mean by poverty;
- the justification for a particular poverty line.

The use of a monetary approach to poverty can, however, be justified in two quite different ways: first, by the minimum rights approach, where a certain basic income is regarded as a right without reference to utility but rather to the freedom of choice it provides (Atkinson 1989; van Parijs 1992). This view has not gained much following, and faces much the same problems as the welfare-based view, for example in determining the level of basic income to be chosen as a universal right. Secondly, the use of a monetary indicator is often invoked *not* because monetary resources measure utility, but because it is assumed it can appropriately proxy other aspects of welfare and poverty. In this view, while lack of resources does not exhaust the definition of poverty, monetary indicators represent a convenient short-cut method, based on widely available data to identify those who are poor in many fundamental dimensions, not only lack of resources but also nutrition, health, etc. Empirical investigations are needed to explore the validity of this assumption. The work in this book provides one such empirical investigation, while other investigations are briefly surveyed in the concluding chapter.

The monetary approach to poverty measurement was pioneered in the seminal work of Booth and Rowntree, who studied poverty in London and York, respectively, in the nineteenth and early twentieth centuries. Booth's study of the East End of London, in 1887, was prompted by widespread rioting by the poor, which socialists explained at the time by the claim that one-third of the population was poor. This was a much higher proportion than the rate of poverty defined as those in receipt of poor relief, which amounted to about 5 per cent (Booth 1887). Booth used informants (school board visitors) not direct enquiry among the poor. He categorised people into eight social classes, four of which represented different degrees of poverty. His classification went beyond a pure monetary identification of the poor, encompassing more sociological concerns such as the 'conditions attaining in the home, and the nature and regularity of employment' (Marshall 1981: 145).

Rowntree explicitly followed in Booth's footsteps, though he adopted a different methodology, which in some of its fundamentals remains the methodology used today (Rowntree 1902). He defined a poverty line by estimating monetary requirements for a nutritionally adequate diet together with estimated needs for clothing and rent. Those below this line were defined as in *primary poverty*. The interviewers also classified households who were seen to be living in 'obvious want and squalor': those who fell into this category despite being above the defined poverty line were classified as being in *secondary poverty*. On the basis of interviews of people around York, Rowntree identified 30 per cent of the population as in poverty (including both primary and secondary). Both Booth and Rowntree agreed on some important issues – views which are shared by most economists adopting a monetary approach today. First, they believed their assessment was an *objective* one: i.e. that an objective condition termed *poverty* existed, which they were measuring. Secondly, their assessment was an *external* one, i.e. carried out by social scientists and others, not by the poor themselves; thirdly, they took an *individualistic* view of poverty, i.e. that poverty should be defined with respect to individual circumstances and behaviour, rather than as a social phenomenon. These three elements remain central to the current practice of the monetary approach.

Some outstanding issues concerning the definition and
measurement of monetary poverty

As noted, the modern monetary approach contains many elements already present in those early analyses, especially Rowntree's method of identifying the poverty line. Nonetheless, there have been many methodological advances in the development and standardisation of this approach (e.g. Grosh and Glewwe 2000), although some issues remain contentious, leading to theoretical and methodological choices that undermine the claims of objectivity of the approach.

The welfare indicator. Monetary poverty has been argued to be better measured by consumption data as it approximates welfare more closely than income (Deaton 1997). Consumption also comes closer to a measure of long-term income, avoiding some of the short-term fluctuations in income and access to resources – under the assumption that individuals have access to credit and saving instruments. On the basis of a minimum rights perspective, however, a case has been made for the use of income (Atkinson 1989). It is theoretically possible to incorporate measures of non-marketed goods and services in estimates of either consumption (which is approximated by expenditure data, sometimes with adjustments for the use of services from durables) or income. In practice however, these measures almost invariably only include *private* resources, and omit *social* income (i.e. a variety of goods and services provided publicly, e.g. schools, clinics, the environment). This can lead to an implicit bias in policy choices in favour of the generation of private income as against public goods provision, and similarly, a bias in the identification of the poor for targeting purposes towards those lacking private income.

The monetary poverty line. A key issue – noted earlier – is how to differentiate the poor and non-poor, and whether there is an objective way of doing so. In the case of the monetary approach various technical solutions have been suggested for this differentiation, notwithstanding the fuzziness of the theoretical framework that in principle should justify it. At a fundamental level, in fact, problems in identifying a poverty line stem from the fact that there is no theory of poverty that would clearly differentiate the poor from the non-poor.

Relative poverty lines can be determined by political consensus. In fact, in many developed countries, a pragmatic way of determining the poverty line is to define as deprived those who receive support from public sources. This simply leaves the decision on the poverty lines to those responsible for social policy and budgetary decisions.[5]

Attempts to find an objective basis for an absolute poverty line aim at identifying behavioural breaks between the poor and non-poor. The most common basis for such a break is provided by estimates of the nutritional needs for survival, and/or efficiency wages. An efficiency wage argument has been put forward by Dasgupta (1993) and others. Yet there is considerable ambiguity about what constitutes an efficiency wage; questions about whether this should be applied to those outside the workforce (e.g. the old or disabled); while it also raises the moral question of the appropriateness of defining poverty in such an instrumental way.

Ravallion has suggested that the poverty line should be defined as the 'the cost of a reference level of utility' (Ravallion 1998: ix). Yet this does not get one much further as the concept of a 'reference level of utility' is itself not well-defined. More emphasis is generally given to the methodological, rather than the theoretical, issue of how to calculate this minimum. Ravallion suggests two methods: one is the Food Energy Intake Method, which essentially amounts to a nutritionally based poverty line; the other is a 'cost of basic needs' line, either starting with food and adding a non-food component (a method similar to Rowntree's), or starting with list of basic needs (which of course themselves need to be defined) and costing them.

For the most part, nutritional requirements form the fundamental justification of, and practical basis for, defining the poverty line in the monetary approach. Yet there are problems about nutritionally based poverty lines. Differing metabolic rates, activities, size, gender and age among people mean that what is adequate varies among them (Sukhatme 1982, 1989; Dasgupta 1993; Payne 1993). Then differing tastes, food availability and prices affect how much money income is needed to secure any particular level of nutrition. Moreover, poverty lines are often drawn up at the level of the household, yet the way resources are distributed within the household affects the nutrition levels of individuals within it (see below). All this suggests that it is not possible to draw up a unique poverty line based on nutritional requirements, but rather a range of income, from a minimum line below which everyone is certainly in poverty (Figure 1.1), to a line above which no one would be in poverty, in nutritional terms. Such a practice is akin to the fairly common approach of adopting two poverty lines, identifying 'poverty' and 'extreme poverty'. Lipton has suggested that there is a natural break in behaviour justifying a distinction between what he calls 'the poor' and 'the ultra-poor', defining the latter as households spending at least 80 per cent of their income on food, and yet receiving less than 80 per cent of their calorie requirements (Lipton 1988). He argues that empirical work identifies 80 per cent as a maximum that people can spend on food because of other essential needs. However, others have questioned whether the 80/80 per cent lines hold, and whether there is such a natural break that is universally valid (Anand et al. 1993). Others have used household perceptions to differentiate poverty and core poverty (see Clark and Qizilbash 2002).[6]

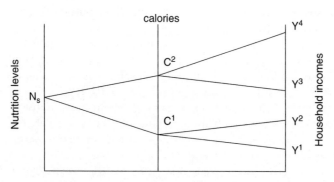

Figure 1.1:   Two poverty lines

Let N_s be a minimum 'adequate' nutrition level for any individual.

C^1, C^2 is the range of calories that may be needed to achieve this nutrition level which varies among individuals according to metabolic rate, age, gender and activity.

In order to achieve calorie consumption for an individual, C^1, household income of from Y^1 to Y^2 may be needed, varying according to numbers in the household, and household consumption and allocation patterns. For calorie consumption, C^2, household income of between Y^3 and Y^4 may be needed. Below household income Y^1, malnutrition is certain; above household income Y^4, adequate nutrition is certain.

Individuals versus households. Economists' approach to welfare is essentially individualistic – i.e. welfare pertains to individuals, and hence poverty (as a welfare shortfall) is a characteristic of individuals too. Income and consumption data, however, are normally collected by household, so that at the very least some adjustment is needed in translating a household's resources into individual poverty. Such an adjustment has three aspects: one is to estimate the needs of different individuals; the second is to estimate the extent of economies of scale enjoyed; the third is to consider how household resources are allocated to the different individuals within the household.

The issue of estimating individual resource needs involves both theoretical and practical problems. If a minimum rights perspective is adopted and all individuals have the same rights, then it would be wrong to weight individual needs differently. However, if those rights are seen as relating not to resources but to outcomes (e.g. the right to a certain standard of living, or the right to certain achievements in terms of nutrition), or, alternatively, adopting a utility-based perspective, adjustments that take different individual characteristics into account are justified. Mostly, rights-based approaches assert that each individual has the right to the same resources as every other individual, so do not allow for variations in how these resources are translated into life conditions.

Equivalence scales are designed to take into account both differences in needs and economies of scale in consumption. Estimates of equivalence scales are normally derived from empirical comparisons of incomes needed among households of different size to achieve a given nutritional outcome (Banks and Johnson 1993). In practice there are considerable variations in the estimates, which are sensitive to the specific methods adopted. Since they are based on patterns of consumption of the 'average' household they do not fully take into account power or bargaining considerations which play a role in the way resources are allocated within the household, implying different allocation of household income according to the bargaining situation.

The importance of various adjustments for the empirical estimation of poverty has been powerfully illustrated by Szekely et al. who have shown that the poverty rate varies between 13 per cent and 66 per cent of the population in seventeen Latin American countries, according to the methods adopted towards calculating equivalence scales, assumptions about the existence of economies of scale in household consumption, methods for treating missing or zero incomes and adjustments to handle misreporting (Szekely et al. 2000). Given the magnitude of this variance, adopting stochastic dominance techniques to test the robustness of poverty estimates to varying assumptions on where the poverty line is set or how differences in needs are taken into account, as suggested by Lipton and Ravallion (1995), would indicate that many monetary estimates of poverty are not robust.

Aggregation issues. The issue of how to translate the identification of poverty at an individual level into an aggregate value is closely linked to the literature on social valuation. Following Sen's (1976) pioneering contribution, which applied a similar approach to poverty measurement to that used in the measurement of inequality, the literature generally adopts an axiomatic approach in setting the desirable properties of a poverty index. Foster, Greer and Thorbeck (FGT) (1985) is a fundamental contribution offering a general formulation[7] including a valuation parameter of choice, alpha, which incorporates some of the most widely used indexes.[8] It has become standard practice to compute FGT indexes for values of alpha ranging from 0 to 2 in order to test the sensitivity of the poverty assessment to the distribution of resources among the poor.

Some conclusions on the monetary approach

The following conclusions emerge from this brief review of the monetary approach.

- At a theoretical level it has been shown that different theoretical interpretations can underpin the approach. All of them have their weaknesses. The welfarist view, for example, assumes that all relevant heterogeneity between individuals can be controlled for, but this requires rather strong assumptions. Further, this approach disregards social resources that are of great importance in determining individual achievements in some fundamental dimensions of human well-being such as health and nutrition. The alternative rights-based approach generally also fails to capture effective achievements in terms of human lives.
- While the monetary approach has benefited from significant methodological developments in terms of measurement, these technical adjustments require numerous value judgements. Despite their apparent 'scientificity', the estimates of poverty the approach provides, therefore, are open to question – an example is the debate on the one dollar a day poverty line (Reddy and Pogge 2002; Ravallion 2002). It should be noted that while many of the methodological elements, which are part of a monetary poverty assessment, are derived from economic theory (e.g. the literature on equivalence scales) poverty in itself is *not* an economic category. Though efforts have been made to identify natural breaks between poor and non-poor based on some behavioural characteristics, none is fully satisfactory in pointing to a unique poverty line.
- It has also been emphasised that this approach is fundamentally addressed to *individual* achievements; social interactions and interdependences are considered only from the mechanical point of view of appropriately scaling household resources to take into account different household structures.
- The value judgements that form an intrinsic aspect of much of the methodology – for example, about what should constitute an essential consumption basket – like many other aspects of the methodology, are generally performed 'externally', i.e. without the involvement of poor people themselves.

The three other approaches to deprivation reviewed in this chapter each address some of the perceived defects of the monetary approach.

1.3.2 The capability approach

According to Sen, who pioneered this approach, development should be seen as the expansion of human capabilities (CA), not the maximisation of utility, or its proxy, money income (Sen 1985, 1999). The capability approach rejects monetary income as its measure of well-being, and instead focuses on indicators of the freedom to live a valued life. In this framework, poverty is defined as deprivation in the space of capabilities, or *failure to achieve certain minimal or basic capabilities*, where 'basic capabilities' are 'the ability to satisfy certain crucially important functionings up to certain minimally adequate levels' (Sen 1993: 41).

The capability approach constitutes an alternative way of conceptualising individual behaviour, assessing well-being and identifying policy objectives, based on the rejection of utilitarianism as the measure of welfare and of utility maximisation as a behavioural assumption. It is argued that utilitarianism implies that individuals' mental disposition plays a critical role in social evaluation while their physical condition and other such aspects influencing their quality of life are neglected. As a result, people can be 'satisfied' with what is a very deprived state (e.g. ill-health, termed 'physical condition neglect'), while their desires are constrained by what seems possible (described as 'valuation neglect'). Furthermore choices are influenced by the social context not only in terms of its influence on expectations but also through strategic interactions, making observed behaviour in the market of dubious value for social valuation (Sen 1985).

In the capability approach well-being is seen as the freedom of individuals to live lives that are valued (termed the capabilities of the individual), i.e. the realisation of human potential. This emphasis on the 'outcomes' characterising the quality of life of individuals implies a shift away from monetary indicators (which at best can represent an indirect measure of those outcomes) and a focus on non-monetary indicators for evaluating well-being or deprivation. In this context, monetary resources are considered as a means to enhancing well-being only, rather than the actual outcome of interest. Moreover, monetary resources may not be a reliable indicator of capability outcomes because of differences individuals face in transforming those resources into valuable achievements (*functionings*), differences which depend on varying individual characteristics: for example, differences between individuals in terms of metabolic rates; differences between able-bodied and handicapped individuals; or differences in the contexts in which individuals live (e.g. differences between living in areas where basic public services are provided and areas where those services are absent). If the emphasis is on final outcomes, poverty (and more generally well-being) assessments should take into account the fact that some people need more resources than others to obtain the same achievements.

The instrumental role of monetary resources in the achievement of well-being is illustrated in Figure 1.2. With their income individuals acquire commodities and the utilisation of these commodities' characteristics and those of publicly provided goods and services allows individuals to achieve certain functionings. Besides private monetary income and publicly provided goods and services, an individual's own personal

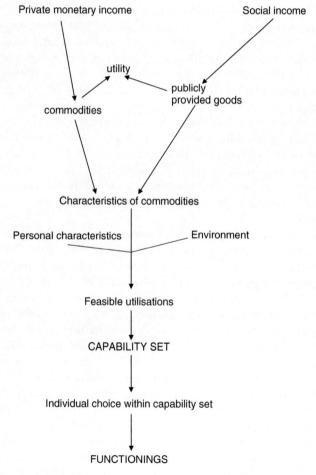

Figure 1.2:   Capability approach – the links

characteristics (including, for example, age, gender, physical capacities) and the general environmental context help determine the capability set of the individual and the use made of this set, or the individual's functionings. Monetary resources, therefore, remain instrumentally related to the achievement of well-being (or, conversely, poverty), but do not exhaust the causal chain.

Operational issues in measuring poverty as capability failure

Translating the capability approach into an operational framework for poverty evaluation raises a number of issues. Most fundamental is the definition of basic capabilities and of the levels of achievement that are to be considered as essential.

Defining basic capabilities. In his work Sen does not provide a specific list of minimally essential CA (though he suggests that basic concerns such as being well-nourished, avoiding preventable morbidity etc. should be part of such a list) nor guidelines for drawing up a universal list. Alkire has argued that the lack of specification was deliberate in order to allow room for choice across societies and to ensure the relevance of the approach to different persons and cultures (Alkire 2002).

The problem of identification of basic CA is similar to that of the identification of Basic Needs (BN).[9] Doyal and Gough attempted to define an objective and non-culturally sensitive list of BN using as a fundamental criterion avoiding serious harm (Doyal and Gough 1991). They include physical health and autonomy (which covers a person's level of understanding, mental health, and a range of opportunities) as BN. Satisfiers to achieve these needs, or the actual goods and services required, are argued to vary across societies. Several attempts have been made to define basic capabilities specifically. An important effort in this regard is that of Nussbaum, who has argued that there is an 'overlapping consensus' between different societies on the conception of a human being and what is needed to be fully human. She hopes to arrive at a theory which is not 'the mere projection of local preferences but is fully international and a basis for cross-cultural attunement' (Nussbaum 2000b: 74).

Nussbaum's list (see Table 3.1) seems to represent a Western late-twentieth-century conception of the 'good life', including such elements as 'play', 'respect for other species', 'property', raising doubts on how far it truly reflects an 'overlapping consensus'. Moreover, the list defines characteristics of a full human life at a very general level, and does not specify cut-off points for defining deprivation. Other attempts to define the essential capabilities have been conducted by Alkire (2002), Qizilbash (1998), and

MAGDALEN COLLEGE LIBRARY

Desai (1995). Each arrives at similar lists. These lists, and practical applications of the CA approach (e.g. by Dreze and Sen 1995), generally interpret the minimal essential CA as being constituted by health, nutrition and education – broadly the same as the list of basic needs identified in BN approaches (see e.g. Stewart 1985; Streeten et al. 1981).

Measurement of capabilities. A second issue, in making a CA approach to poverty operational, is the translation of the concept of capabilities (i.e. all the possible achievements an individual may have, which together constitute the capability set) into something that is measurable. The crucial issue is, of course, that capabilities represent a set of *potential* outcomes and as such are problematic to identify empirically. Arguably, however, if the capabilities considered are basic enough individuals will not be willing to forgo them so that assessing their actual achievements, or functionings should reveal the constraints they face. The identification of the capability set with the set of achieved functionings can be conceptualised as performing the evaluation of a set through one of its elements, in much the same way as economists value budget sets by considering the bundle of goods actually chosen (Sen and Foster 1997). But this risks losing the key insight of the CA which is its emphasis on freedom.[10] In practice, there has been a strong tendency to measure functionings rather than capabilities (i.e. life expectancy, morbidity, literacy, nutrition levels) in both micro and macro assessments. Using such functionings makes the approach virtually identical with the BN approach to the measurement of poverty.

The poverty line. As in the other approaches, there is a need to identify breaks in the distribution of capabilities, to differentiate the poor and non-poor. The choice of such breaks – which is necessary for each CA separately – appears to be context-dependent and somewhat arbitrary. The Human Poverty Index (HPI) developed by the United Nations Development Programme (UNDP) can be taken as an example since the concept of 'human poverty' was primarily derived from the CA approach. UNDP defined human poverty as 'deprivation in three essential elements of human life . . . longevity, knowledge and decent standard of living' (UNDP 1997: 18). The indicators adopted in the 2001 *Human Development Report* for the three elements were: having less than 40 years' life expectancy at birth, adult illiteracy, and an average of not using improved water sources and under-five mortality. It is clear that both choice of dimensions and cut-off standards are somewhat arbitrary and are likely to be revised according to the general standards attained in the world, the region, or the country where poverty assessments are being made. This is exemplified by the fact that UNDP adopted a different HPI for developed countries which includes life expectancy of below 60, lack of functional literacy among adults, the long-term unemployment rate, and the population below an income poverty line of 50 per cent of median disposable household income in the country being assessed.[11] Whether a universal conception of poverty from a CA perspective can be reconciled with such changing measures has not been much discussed (Ruggeri Laderchi 2001).

Aggregation. The multidimensional emphasis of the capability framework makes the issue of aggregation particularly pertinent. It is arguable that since each of the different capabilities is intrinsically valuable, no trade-offs between achievements in one or the other dimensions should be introduced. This severely limits the type of aggregative strategies that can be adopted.[12] Yet, aggregation can be desirable for political purposes, and to reduce a large amount of information to manageable proportions, for example, for inter-country comparisons. And for policy purposes fully aggregative strategies (i.e. those which arrive at full orderings by providing explicit trade-offs in terms of achievement in each dimension) are likely to be more useful than strategies that arrive only at partial ones (consider, for example, the case of having to identify regions to be given priority for poverty alleviation expenditure). Such fully aggregative strategies include, for example, the use of factor analysis to obtain data driven weights in aggregating deprivations, the use of fuzzy sets applications, borda rankings or the more familiar averages (popularised by the work done by UNDP in constructing its human development and human poverty indexes).[13] The use of concepts of union (a comprehensive approach, by which an individual deprived in *any* dimension is considered poor) or intersection (an overlapping approach, by which only individuals deprived in *all* dimensions are considered as poor) are also possible approaches to aggregation.[14]

A further issue is whether and how the severity of deprivation in each of the basic dimensions should form part of the aggregation procedures. Bourguignon and Chakravarty (2003), for example, provide a formula that allows for varying rates of trade-off across dimensions. Individuals' deprivations in each dimension can be weighted by the *distance* from each cut-off line, for example, differentiating and giving more weight to the extremely malnourished as against the malnourished.

Some conclusions on the capability approach

The CA approach represents a major contribution to poverty analysis because it provides a coherent framework for defining poverty in the context of the lives people live and the freedoms they enjoy. This approach draws attention to a much wider range of causes of poverty and options for policies than the monetary approach. The shift from the private resources to which individuals have access to the type of life they lead addresses the neglect of social goods in the monetary approach and its narrow vision of human well-being. Yet, like the monetary approach, arriving at operational measures poses a number of methodological choices. Though decisions on these too are somewhat arbitrary, the choices made are arguably more visible, and therefore more easily subject to scrutiny than in the monetary approach.

There are some features common to both CA and monetary approaches. First, in principle, both take an individualistic perspective since both utility deprivation and capability failure is a characteristic of individuals, even though, in both cases, communities and households are important determinants of achievements, especially for children and the old. Secondly, both typically represent external assessments, though, in principle, as we shall suggest below, both could be adapted, by using the participatory methods, to include more internal inputs. Thirdly, neither approach captures fundamental causes or dynamics of poverty. Fourthly, they aim to describe the situation at a point in time, providing data for, but not themselves directly involving, fundamental analysis of the causes of poverty, although some studies, of course, do follow up measurement with investigations of the causes of, or processes leading to, monetary and/or capability poverty (e.g. Dhatt and Ravallion 1998; Baker 1997). Social exclusion and participatory approaches differ from the monetary and capability in each of these respects.

1.3.3   Social exclusion

The concept of social exclusion (SE) was developed in industrialised countries to describe the processes of marginalisation and deprivation that can arise even within rich countries with comprehensive welfare provisions.[15] It was a reminder of the multiple faces of deprivation in an affluent society. The concept now forms a central aspect of EU social policy; several European Council decisions (starting with the Lisbon Council of March 2000) have adopted strategic goals and political processes aimed at countering the risk of poverty and social exclusion. The concept of SE has been gradually extended to developing countries through the activities of various UN agencies (especially the International Labour Institute), and the Social Summit (Clert 1999).

The definition of SE is contested (Hills et al. 2002). The EU defines SE as a 'process through which individuals or groups are wholly or partially excluded from full participation in the society in which they live'

(European Foundation 1995: 4).[16] This echoes the earlier work of Townsend who defined deprivation as referring to people who 'are in *effect excluded* from ordinary living patterns, customs and activities' (Townsend 1979: 31; our italics). Somewhat more precisely, Le Grand has defined SE as occurring when a person is excluded if he/she is (a) resident in society; (b) but for reasons beyond his/her control cannot participate in normal activities of citizens in that society; (c) would like to do so.[17] Others have argued that a person is excluded if conditions (a) and (b) hold, whether or not they actually desire to participate or not (Barry 1998).

Atkinson has identified three main characteristics of SE: *relativity* (i.e. exclusion is relative to a particular society); *agency* (i.e. they are excluded as a result of the action of an agent or agents); and *dynamics* (meaning that future prospects are relevant as well as current circumstances) (see Atkinson 1998; Micklewright 2002). Room concurs with the relational and dynamic aspects and adds three others – the multidimensionality of SE; a neighbourhood dimension (i.e. that deficient or absent communal facilities are in question); and that major discontinuities are involved (Room 1999).

The dynamic focus and an emphasis on the processes that engender deprivation are distinguishing features of this approach, compared to the approaches reviewed earlier. It has been noted for example that SE is 'a dynamic process, best described as descending levels: some disadvantages lead to some exclusion, which in turn leads to more disadvantages and more exclusion and ends up with persistent multiple (deprivation) disadvantages' (Eurostat Taskforce 1998: 24). While the other approaches can study causes and interconnections between different elements of deprivation, such investigation is not part of the process of identifying the poor. In contrast, the *definition* of SE typically includes the process of becoming poor, as well as some outcomes of deprivation.

SE also contrasts with the two previous approaches in making a social perspective central – that is to say SE is socially defined. For example, Burchardt et al. define exclusion as occurring if an individual 'does not participate in key activities of the society in which he or she lives' (Burchardt et al. 2002: 30). Moreover, SE is often a characteristic of groups – the aged, handicapped, racial or ethnic categories – arising from discrimination (overt or not) against particular groups. The relational and group emphases open up a different policy agenda from the individualistic approaches – e.g. policies addressed to groups, such as eliminating discrimination and various forms of affirmative action. While other approaches can be extended to include these considerations, such as for example the recent developments in the studies of vulnerability in a monetary perspective, SE is the only approach where these considerations play a constitutive role.

Multidimensionality is an intrinsic feature of SE. Indeed, in general being deprived in *more than one*, and perhaps many, dimensions is a key feature of SE, which raises aggregation issues similar to those of CA.[18] Furthermore, there can be causal connections between different dimensions of exclusion, e.g. between employment and income; housing and employment; formal sector employment and insurance. SE generally is found to have a strong connection with monetary poverty. For example, lack of monetary income is both an outcome of SE (arising from lack of employment) and a cause (e.g. of social isolation and low wealth).

In order to apply SE empirically to particular societies, these rather general statements about SE need to be interpreted more specifically. The precise characteristics of SE tend to be society-specific, since they identify exclusion from *normal* or *key* activities. The concept of SE thus necessarily involves a *relative* approach to the definition of poverty. In industrial countries the indicators adopted in empirical work normally include unemployment, access to housing, minimal income, citizenship, democratic rights, and social contacts.

The application of the concept of exclusion to developing countries raises difficult issues. Characteristics of SE are likely to be different from those in developed countries. On the one hand, the defining features noted by Atkinson and Room are clearly highly relevant. But, on the other, it is difficult to identify appropriate norms to provide the benchmarks of exclusion, since exclusion from formal sector employment or social insurance coverage tends to apply to the majority of the population. Lack of formal sector employment or social insurance coverage therefore does not imply exclusion from normal social patterns or relationships. However, to the extent that the normal may not be desirable, what is 'normal' may not be satisfactory in defining the benchmarks of exclusion. Consequently, there is a serious problem in deciding what would be appropriate SE characteristics. A further complication is that exclusion is part of the social system in some societies, as with the caste system. Various solutions to the interpretation of SE in particular societies are possible: one is to take norms from *outside* the society, e.g. from developed countries. Some of the work on the marginalisation of whole societies in the process of globalisation implicitly does just that (Room 1999). Another is to derive the characteristics through consultation in participatory approaches. A third approach is to derive the characteristics empirically, by exploring what structural characteristics of a population (such as race, or caste, or region where one lives) are empirically correlated with multiple deprivations defined in other approaches.

Empirical work in developing countries has adopted just such a variety of approaches to the definition of SE – mostly it seems taking definitions which seem relevant to the reality being studied, but without providing much justification for their particular choice, and rarely making any explicit reference to what is actually normal in the society. Some have defined SE as exclusion from various social services (e.g. Appasamy et al. 1996). Another approach is to define social and political rights and then interpret SE as not having these rights (e.g. Figueroa et al. 1996). Others define certain categories of people as socially excluded, on the basis of prior knowledge of the society (e.g. in Tanzania, poor urban households and the rural landless (Rodgers et al. 1995)). Finally, some base their definition on perceptions of local people (Bedoui and Gouia 1995).

Some conclusions on social exclusion

SE is perhaps the least well-defined and most difficult to interpret of the concepts of deprivation under review. Indeed, according to Micklewright (2002: 3) 'exclusion is a concept that defies clear definition and measurement'. Problems of definition are especially great in applying the concept to developing countries because 'normality' is particularly difficult to define in multipolar societies, and because there can be a conflict between what is normal and what is desirable. The question of whether there exist relevant discontinuities also arises in a particularly difficult form, since the characteristics defining SE are society-specific and therefore researchers in each country need to devise their own methods for identifying dimensions and appropriate breaks.

Nonetheless the approach is the only one that focuses intrinsically, rather than as an add-on, on the processes and dynamics which allow deprivation to arise and persist. Moreover, the analysis of exclusion lends itself to the study of structural characteristics of society and the situation of groups (e.g. ethnic minorities or the landless) which can generate and characterise exclusion, whereas the two individualistic approaches (the monetary and CA) tend rather to concentrate on individual characteristics and circumstances. SE also leads to a focus on distributional issues – the situation of those deprived relative to the norm generally *cannot* improve without some redistribution of opportunities and outcomes – whereas monetary poverty (defined in absolute terms) and capability poverty can be reduced through growth without redistribution. The agency aspect of SE, noted by Atkinson, also points to *excludors* as well as *excludees*, with the main responsibility for improving the situation on the former, again a contrast to the monetary and capability approaches which describe a world without analysing or attributing responsibility.

1.3.4   Participatory methods

As pointed out above, conventional poverty estimates, including both monetary and capability ones, have been criticised for being *externally* imposed, and not taking into account the views of poor people themselves. The participatory approach – pioneered by Chambers – aims to change this, and get people themselves to participate in decisions about what it means to be poor, and the magnitude of poverty (Chambers 1994a, 1994b, 1997).

The practice of participatory poverty assessments (PPA) evolved from participatory rural appraisal (PRA) defined as 'a growing family of approaches and methods to enable local people to share, enhance and analyse their knowledge of life and conditions, to plan and to act' (Chambers 1994a: 57). Initially intended for small projects, PPA were scaled up by the World Bank as a complement to their poverty assessments. By 1998 half the completed World Bank poverty assessments included a participatory element. An extensive multi-country exercise (23 countries were covered) was also carried out as background to the WB 2000/1 *World Development Report*, published as *Voices of the Poor* (Narayan-Parker and Patel 2000). Poverty Reduction Strategy Papers (PRSPs) of the World Bank and IMF, which form an important element in IFI lending to poor countries, have further institutionalised the use of participatory methods.[19]

Cornwall (2000) differentiates three types of PPA: (1) exercises intended to promote self-determination and empowerment; (2) those primarily intended to increase the efficiency of programmes; and (3) those emphasising mutual learning.

The use of participatory exercises by the World Bank, especially in their poverty assessments, has tended to be instrumental, i.e. adopting PPA primarily so that the poor would cooperate with the programmes, rather than to change the nature of the programmes themselves (type 2), while *Voices of the Poor* emphasises type 3. There is not much self-determination and empowerment in most of this work.

Method and tools

Contextual methods of analysis are involved, i.e. data collection methods which 'attempt to understand poverty dimensions within the social, cultural, economic and political environment of a locality' (Booth et al. 1998: 52). The methods derive from and emphasise poor people's ability to understand and analyse their own reality.

A range of tools has been devised, including the use of participatory mapping and modelling, seasonal calendars, wealth and well-being ranking. The large variety of methods can be used flexibly, according to the situation. Using more than one method helps in triangulation, i.e. verifying the information that has been obtained. This contrasts with the other approaches, where a more rigid framework and methodology is involved. For example, a PRA in Zambia used wealth/well-being grouping, social, resource and institutional mapping, focus group discussions, and semi-structured interviews to get information on well-being and poverty, household and community assets, coping strategies, community support mechanisms and environmental trends (de Graft Agyarko in IDS 1998). The example shows not only the variety of methods but also the range of questions addressed, by no means confined to assessing the extent of poverty, but looking beyond this to mechanisms of support for the poor and coping strategies.

Some challenges in truly operationalising PPAs

In principle, people themselves conduct PPAs – but inevitably it is nearly always outsiders who conduct the assessments and interpret the results. For example, *Voices of the Poor* identified five types of well-being – material, physical, security, freedom of choice and action, and social well-being – a classification which emerged at least partly from subsequent rationalisation of the materials gathered in the various studies. An evaluation of PPAs in Africa noted that certain themes were not emphasised in the analysis, and many were omitted altogether. There was obvious 'selectivity' due to pressures to highlight what were considered to be policy relevant conclusions (Booth et al. 1998).

Although the participatory methods are intended to determine the nature of projects and to allow poor people's views to help shape plans and contribute to development strategies, in practice their impact on projects or plans are often remote. For example, the Poverty Reduction Strategy Papers, prepared before debt relief can be agreed under HIPC, require participatory exercises as inputs. Yet 39 organisations and regional networks in 15 African countries agreed at a meeting in Kampala, in May 2001, that PRSPs 'were simply window dressing'.[20] The statement concluded that 'the PRSP process is simply delivering repackaged structural adjustment programmes and is not delivering poverty focused development plans and has failed to involve civil society and parliamentarians in economic policy discussions'. A review of processes adopted in PRSPs revealed very limited time given to consultations, heavy representation of NGOs rather than poor people, under-representation of rural populations and of women, all of which limited the potential contribution of the poor (Stewart and Wang 2003).

A foundational problem for such methods arises from heterogeneity within the community: the question, in that case, is whose voices are being heard. Where there are conflicts within a community, the PPA has no agreed way of resolving them to arrive at a single community view. Moreover, certain groups are likely to be fearful of voicing opposition to powerful members of the community. It has been argued that Participatory Appraisal (PA) tends to condone and reinforce existing social relations (da Cunha and Junho Pena 1997). Furthermore, some people are structurally excluded from 'communities'. This is shown, for example, by the fact that groups often identify others, outside the group, as being really poor. These outsiders generally consist of people who no longer have social relations with the rest of the community – typically the poorest who have fallen through the cracks of the reciprocity network (Howard and Millard 1997 provide poignant examples). The method, by focusing on 'the community', does not compensate for such exclusions. Furthermore, the intensive process involved in participatory poverty assessment often means that only small numbers are included, who tend to be gathered on an ad hoc basis and rarely constitute representative samples of the population.

There is a deeper problem about exclusive reliance on participatory methods, which goes back to Sen's criticisms of the utilitarian approach. People's own assessment of their own condition can overlook their objective condition and therefore can be biased as a result of limited information and social conditioning (i.e. these methods also suffer from 'valuation neglect'). The generally public aspect of assessments may also make it difficult to get honest assessments, and could involve participants in some risk.

Some conclusions on the participatory approach
to poverty measurement

The major advantage of this approach is that PPAs go some way to getting away from externally imposed standards. They also provide a way of solving some of the problems encountered with the other methods, for example helping to define: an appropriate minimum basket of commodities for the monetary approach; a list of basic capabilities in the capability approach; and whether the concept of SE can be applied in a particular society, and what its main elements might be.

There are two major differences from the other approaches: the main one is that the perspective is that of the poor, who, at least in theory, make the judgements which in other approaches are imposed from outside. The other is in the small samples – even in the scaled-up version – relative to other methods. It is therefore difficult to carry out statistical significance tests on material gathered in this way. The method is complex and invariably contains multidimensional analysis. Like the SE it includes processes, causes and outcomes of poverty, as perceived by the poor. The method is apparently cost-effective, but the community spends much more time on these exercises – estimated at five times in one study (de Graft Agyarko in IDS 1998) – which is not usually costed.

1.3.5 A comparative overview

Each of the different approaches to poverty discussed above derives from a different perspective on what constitutes a good life and a just society. For operationalisation, each requires a set of methodological assumptions, which are often not transparent. Table 1.1 provides an overview of comparisons between the approaches, on a number of criteria that we have discussed earlier.

Two important issues which have not been discussed earlier are data availability and policy consequences. Currently, for many countries data are available at regular intervals for the measurement of monetary poverty – from household consumer surveys or sometimes national income data;[21] moreover, the data are usually available on a continuum so it is possible to vary the poverty line, and to measure the depth of poverty. In contrast, data for different types of capability poverty are often unavailable on a regular basis and rely on one-off surveys, with some capabilities not measured at all, and others with deficient indicators. There are similar data deficiencies with respect to dimensions of social exclusion. These deficiencies reflect prior preoccupation with monetary poverty, not any intrinsic property of the data. Participatory data is different in this respect. By its nature it requires intensive dialogue with groups of the poor, and is difficult to organise nationally or at short intervals. However, a modified form of consultation can be carried out comprehensively and regularly, along with other surveys.

With regard to the question of policy consequences of different approaches, the way one defines and measures poverty inevitably influences the emphasis given to different types of policy. Thus if poverty is defined as lack of household income, then policies towards it are likely to be primarily directed towards correcting this – e.g. by income generation programmes or monetary transfers. In contrast, if a capability approach is adopted, policies would tend to focus more on provision of public services, while a social exclusion approach leads to anti-discrimination and redistributive policies and, more generally, policies to promote the

Table 1.1: A comparison of the four approaches to poverty

	Monetary poverty	*Capability approach*	*Social exclusion*	*Participatory approach*
Unit of analysis	ideally, the individual, de facto the household	the individual	individuals or groups relative to others in their community/society	groups and individuals within them
Required or minimum standard identified by	reference to 'external' information (defined outside the unit); central element food requirements	reference to 'lists' of dimensions normally assumed to be objectively definable	reference to those prevailing in society and state obligations	local people's own perceptions of well-being and ill-being
Sensitivity to social institutions	none, but assessments can be broken down by group	emphasis on adequacy rather than sufficiency leaves space for (non-modelled) variations	central element	reflected in the way poor people analyse their own situation
Importance of processes	not essential, but has increasing emphasis	not clear	one of the main thrusts of the approach	critical for achievement of satisfactory methods
Major weaknesses conceptually	utility is not an adequate measure of well-being; and poverty is not an economic category	elements of arbitrariness in choice of basic capabilities; problems of adding up	Definition unclear, framework susceptible to many interpretations and therefore difficult to compare across countries	whose perceptions are being elicited, and how representative or consistent are they? how does one deal with disagreements?

Major weaknesses for measurement	needs to be anchored to external elements. Arbitrary	impossibility of set evaluation. Problems of dealing with multidimensionality even if only of basic functionings	problems with multidimensionality. Challenge of capturing processes	how comparable? how representative?
Problems for cross-country comparisons	comparability of surveys; of price indices; of drawing poverty lines	fewer problems if basic capabilities are defined externally; but adding up difficulties make comparisons difficult with inconsistencies according to adding up methodology	lines of social exclusion essentially society-specific; also an adding up problem	cultural differences can make appropriate processes differ across societies; results may not be comparable
Data availability	household surveys regularly conducted; omitted observations can be important. Use of national income data – but requires assumptions about distribution	data less regularly collected, but could easily be improved	currently have to rely on data collected for other purposes. If agreed on basic dimensions, data could be regularly collected.	generally only small purposive samples. Never available nationally; would be difficult to extend method for regular national data collection
Most obvious policy implications	emphasis on economic growth and distribution of monetary income	investment in extending basic capabilities/ basic needs via public services as well as monetary incomes	foster processes of inclusion, inclusion in markets and social process, with particular emphasis on formal labour market	empowerment of the poor

inclusion of marginalised groups. These policy alternatives will be discussed more fully in Chapter 9.

1.4   The need for empirical research on alternative approaches to poverty measurement

A critical issue is whether the four approaches identify broadly the same people as poor when applied empirically, as if they do the theoretical differences may be unimportant in policy or targeting terms. Where all approaches identify broadly the same people as poor, monetary poverty could be used as a proxy for other types of poverty despite its theoretical deficiencies, and addressing policy towards reducing monetary poverty could then be expected to reduce poverty according to the other approaches to definition and measurement.

One way of approaching this issue is to see how far there is consistency between the different measures across countries. Taking data for countries as a whole[22] we find that there is a correlation between monetary poverty and the Human Poverty Index (HPI) of the UNDP, but there are also major differences to be observed. The Spearman rank correlation coefficient between national poverty lines and the HPI is 0.54, but the correlation with the internationally set lines of those falling below $1 or $2 a day is much higher at 0.707 and 0.779 respectively (see Graphs 1.1–1.3). What is striking is that low levels of poverty

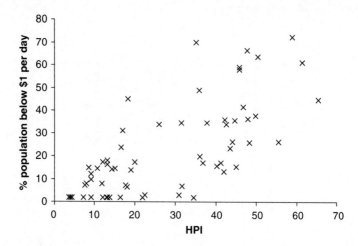

Graph 1.1: Relationship between Human Poverty Index and monetary poverty (international, $1 a day)

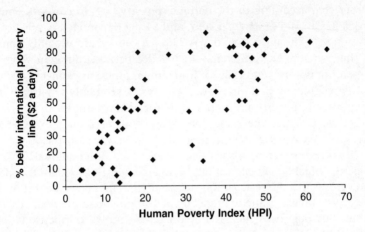

Graph 1.2: Relationship between Human Poverty Index and monetary poverty (international, less than $2 a day)

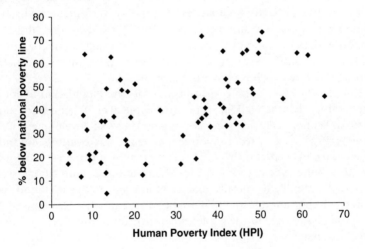

Graph 1.3: Relationship between Human Poverty Index and monetary poverty (national poverty line)

according to one measure are compatible with high levels of poverty according to another. Some countries have low human poverty relative to monetary poverty For example, Nicaragua with an HPI of around 18 per cent, although at the lower end of the HPI scale, has a high percentage of individuals who are identified as being in monetary poverty – 45 per cent using the $1 a day line, almost 80 per cent using $2 a day and around

48 per cent according to the national poverty line. In contrast, South Africa has an HPI of 31.7 per cent, and $1 per day monetary poverty is just 7.1 per cent and $2 per day is 23.8 per cent. This variability points to the potential lack of overlap in practice between different ways of measuring poverty, and calls for in-depth empirical assessment of what is driving different performances. Moreover, it is not only a matter of the magnitude of poverty, but importantly for policy purposes and poverty targeting, whether the same people are poor according to different measures. We can get no indication of this from the global data.

Cross-country comparisons are relevant to international policy-making, notably aid allocation between countries, which the data indicate would differ according to whether a monetary definition of poverty – and what kind of monetary definition – were adopted, or some other. But our focus here is not on cross-country comparisons, but on within-country analysis because it is at this level that poverty reduction policies operate. Hence the focus of the research reported on in Chapters 6–8 is an investigation of how far there is overlap (or lack of it) between the different approaches to poverty measurement in two national cases, India and Peru. We chose these two very different countries because we wanted to see whether the results would be similar in two quite different settings, viz. a higher income, higher inequality setting and one which is poorer but more equal.

In terms of geographic distribution of the population, Peru is predominantly urban (about two-thirds) while over 70 per cent of India is rural. Economically, they are at different stages of development. Peru is generally characterised as a lower middle income country, and India as low income. Peru, however, is characterised by much greater inequality (the Gini coefficient for India for 2000 was 0.325 while that for Peru was 0.498). In Peru, socially and economically indigeneity and race plays an important role in differentiating the population. Analysis of the large databases used in the book for comparison of the four approaches gives estimates suggesting that 70 per cent of the population speaking indigenous languages was in monetary poverty compared to 51 per cent in the case of Spanish speakers. In India, the major differentiation is by caste with those belonging to the scheduled caste/scheduled tribe (SC/ST) groups estimated as having a higher likelihood of being monetary 'poor' (around 50 per cent compared to 33 per cent for non SC/ST). With regard to economic policies, Peru has undergone a sweeping process of liberalisation, while India has introduced liberalisation measures slowly and selectively.

It is clear from the review of the alternative approaches at a theoretical level that each requires a number of methodological decisions in implementation – and different results will occur according to these decisions. This is also evident from the international data. While the two international monetary lines give similar rank estimates, the national monetary lines often generate radically different results. In fact the rank correlation between the national monetary poverty estimates and the $2 per day is just 0.602. None of the methods gives a unique measure, even before considering the consistency of alternative approaches. This points to the general fuzziness in the definition of poverty, as well as the need for care and transparency in taking the decisions needed for implementation. Each of the chapters that follow, reviewing each approach in more depth, concludes by presenting the basis for the implementation in the India and Peru studies, deciding how to deal with some of the difficult issues raised above. In the comparisons we adopt, we try to use commonly assumed solutions to these issues, since the aim is to explore differences that occur in practice when alternative methods are used.

Notes

1. Of course, poverty has not always been the prime concern of the 'development community'. In the 1950s and 1960s, the main objective was economic growth. Recognising that growth alone had not eliminated poverty, a series of poverty-reducing strategies were adopted in the 1970s, including Basic Needs Strategies. But these concerns were again forgotten in the 1980s when stabilisation and adjustment policies and the advance of the market dominated official discourse and policies. The poor economic performance and sharp rise in poverty in many countries in the 1980s led to renewed interest in poverty. Following UNICEF's *Adjustment with a Human Face* in 1987 (Cornia et al. 1987), UNDP's first *Human Development Report* in 1990, and the World Bank's 1990 *World Development Report* on poverty, poverty reduction once more became central to the development agenda. In the early 1990s, the World Bank President, Lewis Preston, declared that 'poverty is the benchmark against which we must be judged'.
2. See Silver (1995) for a discussion of how societal characteristics translate into different definitions of social exclusion.
3. For example scaling household resources according to household composition to take into account different needs of different types of household members, as well as the possibility of enjoying economies of scales in consumption or using market prices to compare quantities over space and time.
4. These two arguments have been amply discussed in the literature (see Sen 1993 for a summary of the main arguments) and will not be further illustrated here.
5. An early example of how this approach could lead to different estimates of poverty than those which correspond to other concerns was noted above: in the

nineteenth century the poor relief standards led to a poverty rate of just 5 per cent, while Booth and Rowntree came up with estimates of around 30 per cent.

6. Clarke and Qizilbash use 'fuzzy' multidimensional measures. Chiappero-Martinetti (2000) uses fuzzy measures in the context of the capability approach.

7. The Foster-Greer-Thorbeck formula is $P_\alpha = \frac{1}{n}\sum_{i=1}^{q}\left(\frac{z - y_i}{z}\right)^\alpha$ where P_α is the poverty index for value α which is the weight given to the depth of poverty, n the total number of individuals in society, q the number below the poverty line, z the poverty line, y_i the income of the ith individual – Foster et al. (1984).

8. A value of alpha equal to 0 corresponds to the headcount ratio, or the percentage of individuals living in poverty, capturing the incidence of poverty; a value of alpha equal to 1 is the income gap index, and is therefore sensitive to the depth of poverty; a value of alpha equal to 2, which is commonly used, is more sensitive to the severity of poverty.

9. See Alkire (2002: Chapter 5) for a discussion of similarities and differences between the BN and basic capability approaches.

10. A particular problem in this context is provided by the existence of other objectives that might either be deemed irrelevant for the assessment at hand, or might be hard to measure, whose relation with the dimensions of interest is unknown. Consider for example the case of a malnourished individual who might be fasting but 'scoring high' in terms of the capability to lead a life which respects religious principles, versus an individual who is starved and does not have the option to be better nourished.

11. UNDP (2001), *Human Development Report 2001*. There have been minor changes in the constituent elements of both HPI-1 (human poverty among developing countries), and HPI-2 (human poverty among developed countries) since the initiation of the HPI in 1997.

12. Brandolini and D'Alessio (1998) provide a comprehensive review of different aggregation strategies and the trade-off between obtaining complete orderings and imposing structure in the aggregation.

13. These are methods that have been adopted to aggregate capabilities.

14. Clarke and Qizilbash adopt a union approach in which anyone who is 'core' deprived in any 'core' dimension is considered as poor.

15. The first use of the term, SE, has been attributed to Lenoir, French Secretary of State for Social Action in Government in 1974, referring to people who did not fit into the norms of industrial societies, were not protected by social insurance, and were considered social misfits. It included the handicapped, drug users, delinquents and the aged, among others, and was estimated to account for one-tenth of the French population.

16. A report from the EU uses the terms social exclusion and poverty together, defined in the following way: 'Throughout this report the terms poverty and social inclusion refer to when people are prevented from participating fully in economic, social and civil life and/or when their access to income and other resources (personal, family, social and cultural) is so inadequate as to exclude them from enjoying a standard of living and quality of life that is regarded as acceptable by the society in which they live. In such situations people are often unable to fully access their fundamental rights' (European Commission 2001: 11).

17. At an early meeting of the Centre for the Analysis of Social Exclusion at the London School of Economics – see Burchardt et al. (1999: 229).
18. Some empirical work in the UK, however, indicated that a relatively low proportion of people excluded on one dimension were also excluded on more than one other dimension. For example, of those without production activity, almost 40 per cent also had low income, but less than a fifth were politically disengaged or socially isolated (Burchardt et al. 1999: 237).
19. Poverty Reduction Strategy Papers (PRSP) are prepared by the member countries through a participatory process involving domestic stakeholders as well as external development partners, including the World Bank and International Monetary Fund (IMF website, 29 January 2003).
20. 'PRSPS are Just PR say Civil Society Groups' (http://www.BrettonWoodsproject. org/topic/adjustment/a23prspsstats.html).
21. There are severe disadvantages to the use of national income data – an assumption about the distribution of income is required to derive poverty lines (see Deaton 2002).
22. Data come from UNDP, *Human Development Report 2004*. The data relate to a range of years (2000–5) for the HPI, 1990–2002 for the international poverty lines, and 1990–2001 for the national poverty lines.

2
The Monetary Approach to Poverty: a Survey of Concepts and Methods

Caterina Ruggeri Laderchi

2.1 Introduction

This chapter briefly surveys the monetary approach to poverty measurement – a set of techniques and methodologies, widely adopted by economists, which identifies poverty with a shortfall from a certain level of resources, measured in monetary terms. This level of resources is known as the 'poverty line' and is arrived at by 'objective' investigation.[1]

In order to describe the methodologies, the underlying rationale and the factors which have contributed to the current shape of this 'approach', we will start by discussing its origins. This will allow us to substantiate the view that this approach to the measurement of poverty is driven by measurement concerns, and to assess critically the extent to which the 'objectivity' of the methods makes the results independent of value judgements. Further, it allows us to identify some crucial features of the approach, which will be discussed with respect to current developments in the literature. Particular emphasis will be placed on identifying the key issues which need to be addressed for comparisons of empirical investigations across place and time.

2.1.1 The 'monetary approach' as an analytical category

At the outset of this critical review we need an explanation of what we mean by a 'monetary approach' to poverty measurement. In short, it implies the identification of poverty with a shortfall in a monetary indicator, as generally adopted by economists in measuring poverty. Though economics does not provide us with a definition of poverty, relevant definitions and values are embedded in the methodology. We intend to go beyond a narrow discussion of methods and issues arising when performing such an identification to encompass a discussion of concepts and values.

The main problem with the identification of the 'monetary approach' as an analytical category is that different conceptual reconstructions might underlie similar practices, so that equating them with a single homogeneous category is not only artificial but possibly even misleading. Nevertheless, defining the approach by the common denominator of measurement based on monetary indicators is useful for comparative purposes. It reflects the apparent homogeneity of current mainstream practices, and the underlying tension between theoretical complexity and diversity, on the one hand, and the simplicity of adopting standard measurement practices on the other. Further, adopting a definition emphasising measurement captures the greatest 'selling point' of the set of practices we are referring to, especially to economists, as will be illustrated below. We are aware, however, of the fundamental ambiguities underlying the monetary approach which are sometimes concealed by the simplicity and apparent authority of the results, and will point to these in the following discussion, highlighting where they arise and where they have a bearing on the kind of results obtained.

2.2   Monetary poverty: the undefined yet measurable thing

The pioneering of empirical social investigation, in Britain as elsewhere (Stigler 1954), owes much to poverty, or rather to the philanthropic or intellectual interest that poverty triggered. While first examples of 'political arithmetic' started appearing at the end of the seventeenth century, the identification of poverty as a problem (Marshall 1981), and one to which a scientific method could be applied, gave impetus to large-scale efforts of fact gathering at the end of the nineteenth century – a time when both sociology and economics were starting to take their current shape.

Some important features of current poverty analysis already emerged in those early studies (see more below): these include the absence of a definition of poverty, closely linked to the emphasis on methodological issues, and the, at times ambiguous, relation with political values (searching for objectivity on the one hand and wanting to inform political processes on the other). For example, when Charles Booth gave his first address to the Royal Statistical Society – the success of which led him to compile the massive 'Life and Labour of London' study – he affirmed that 'The *a priori* reasoning of political economy, orthodox and unorthodox alike, fails from want of reality. At its base are a series of assumptions very imperfectly connected with the observed facts of life' (Booth 1887: 376). What he thought was needed was 'a large statistical framework which is built to receive accumulations of facts out of which is at last evolved the theory and the basis for more intelligent action' (Simey and Simey 1960: 77).

We will discuss Booth and Rowntree's pioneering studies at greater length below, but it is worth noting here that by emphasising the statistical, orderly and scientific aspect of the analysis, for them the definitional issue became one of creating a method of identifying the poor which would lend itself to quantification and would make objective analysis possible. The deeper definitional issue about what poverty is, as opposed to what poor people do, or have, or are, which makes them identifiable and countable, was not raised. In the study of a stratified society, lifestyle[2] was a powerful identifier of the lower classes, and poverty had something of the obvious. The focus of investigation was not therefore on how to identify the poor but rather on 'the physical condition and moral character of the working classes' (Kent 1985: 61), and in those an understanding of the immediate causes of poverty was to be found.

These initial contributions started a fertile tradition of poverty studies which, when consolidated later with the new developments in statistics (Bowley's contributions on sampling and Pearson's and Yule's contributions on correlation representing the major ones) provided a rather standardised way of measuring poverty empirically. The measurement rather than the social analysis part of this approach, though developed outside economics, suited economists well as it was compatible with the welfarist roots of microeconomic analysis. And until the breakthroughs in the measurement of inequality were applied to poverty indices (Sen 1976) no major conceptual change affected the way economists measured poverty.

While such continuity might appear as surprising, it is even more surprising that almost a century had to pass without any systematic analysis within economics of the concept of poverty underlying standard practices of poverty measurement. When it did appear, in various contributions by Sen on the welfaristic roots of economic analysis, it was in critical assessments which were more constructive at the philosophical than at the empirical level. Though there are examples of authors who have used some definition of poverty as an explicitly economic category (e.g. Lipton's work on ultra-poverty, or Dasgupta's version of the efficiency wage theory) such conceptualisations have not been absorbed in the core of mainstream economists' poverty analysis.

Paradoxically, however, though poverty is a peripheral concept in economics, without any independence from what is measured, i.e. the shortfall in a monetary indicator, the way economists measure it is considered orthodox and authoritative and is the most influential approach in terms of policy.

2.2.1 In the beginning there were rich men . . .

Though the first budget studies which appeared in England in the 1790s arose from 'the distress of the working classes at this time' (Stigler 1954: 95), the two major empirical studies of poverty appeared about a century later and are linked to the names of Charles Booth and Seebohm Rowntree. Both men appeared to share a modern belief in an objective scientific method to guide action for poverty reduction, though their works were methodologically quite different. The influence they exerted, especially the latter, on current practice of measuring poverty makes a more thorough description of their work of relevance.

Charles Booth's first study of London's East End (1887) was prompted by widespread rioting in the city by the poor, and by the desire to check whether the claim made by socialists that one-third of the population was living in poverty was indeed true (which could not be checked otherwise as there were no data available). In the tradition of Royal Commissions of inquiry (Bulmer 1985) Booth relied on the information provided by 'informants' (School Board visitors in his case) rather than on direct inquiry (Bulmer 1985). His research covered all aspects of how people lived, but of most relevance for us was the identification of eight social classes. Four of these classes were considered as above the 'the poverty line' – a concept which Booth has generally been credited with inventing (Marshall 1981: 37). It has been suggested that he derived his standard for the poverty line from the level of income which district school authorities adopted to waive pupil fees,[3] which explains why the standards he adopted were higher than those at which poor relief (aimed only at the most destitute) was granted (Gillie 1996).

Whether Booth invented the poverty line or not, it is undisputed that 'poverty for him, as for his predecessors, was not a matter of income only, but of the conditions attaining in the home and of the nature and regularity of employment' (Marshall 1981: 37). He was interested in the qualitative differences between the classes. Factors like 'aspiration' and the standards adopted in defining one's own condition therefore played a role in differentiating the classes more than the 'poverty line itself'.

Rowntree's first survey of York explicitly referred to Booth's work, but adopted a number of different methodological solutions. This study, undertaken in 1899, is generally described as the first scientific study of poverty, mostly because of the high level of sophistication applied in deriving a 'modern' poverty line, and, in particular, in estimating the minimal food requirements for maintaining efficiency on the basis of nutritional standards which had recently been estimated. Such minimal requirements, together with those necessary for the purchase of clothing and rent, were added up to identify a poverty line, so that households whose income level fell below it were deemed to be in 'primary poverty'. Rowntree's interviewers (who collected information on about two-thirds of York's households, i.e. those living in areas identified as where the working-class population[4] resided) were asked to note down which households appeared to be living in 'obvious want and squalor'. This gave rise to a further concept of poverty: 'secondary poverty', i.e. the poverty of those who, despite having enough income to maintain minimal efficiency appeared to the investigators to be living in poverty.

The methodology adopted to measure primary poverty came to dominate Rowntree's later analyses, as well as those of his successors. It has been convincingly argued (Veit-Wilson 1986), however, that the emphasis that it was given by contemporaries and successors alike did not reflect Rowntree's original intentions. The poverty line he derived was not meant to be a normative device prescribing intended patterns of expenditure. It was rather a heuristic device to show that, contrary to long-held beliefs, not only improvidence and vice but also low incomes accounted for the poverty of the working classes. As such, the line that he devised was meant to be based on conservative estimates of needs, for example choosing to price the required nutrients according to a diet even less appealing than the one offered to poor people in workhouses. Rowntree's emphasis throughout his book is on poverty *overall*, which he stated, without further qualification, was a situation in which nearly 30 per cent of the population of York was to be found. He went to great lengths to show that his results were comparable with Booth's London study (i.e. by publishing a letter from Booth stating as much), and indeed they both adopted a concept of poverty as something that is perceived by external observation. The aim was to challenge common perceptions about the distribution of poverty within England, showing that it was a country-wide phenomenon linked to urbanisation and not a pathological feature of the capital city (Hennock 1987).

2.2.2 ... and the legacy of their 'fact based' methodology

Booth and Rowntree's legacies have been quite different. While Booth succeeded in enlarging the terms of the debate on the 'poverty question' beyond a moral interpretation of poverty, as well as impressing the public opinion of his time with the wealth of information he produced (Marshall 1981), it is Rowntree's work which is generally acknowledged as the first scientific study of poverty. Both authors were aware of the importance of their own contributions whose undertaking they financed themselves, as well as of the methodological and informational void in which their studies were taking place.

From a methodological point of view, despite the differences illustrated above, some important similarities can be identified. Both Rowntree and Booth adopted definitions of poverty which were based on the different lifestyle of the poor, as externally assessed, against a standard on which there was 'general agreement' (Veit-Wilson 1986: 81), though they showed different degrees of sensitivity to the qualitative differences between classes. Both also shared a faith in objectivity and in the importance of the scientific method in elucidating *facts* (almost touching when considering the amount of literature which has been dedicated to eviscerating the beliefs, values and stereotypes which their definitions reflected or contributed to creating!). Rowntree and Booth were united as well in adopting an individualistic conception of poverty. In their static view of a stratified society they did not investigate the social dynamics of poverty, inclusion or exclusion from society, nor the forces behind them. The poor were part of the lower classes, and their poverty was seen as a series of repeated individual circumstances rather than the outcome of some social process. Though their poverty was seen as a problem to be solved, denoting a break with a previous tradition stressing its functional role (Marshall 1981), a view which is echoed in Marxist thought, it was perceived as a problem of a number of individuals.

Booth and Rowntree also showed a high degree of flexibility (by some interpreted as lack of accuracy) in making do with the kind of information and instruments which were available. Both adopted an eclectic approach: Booth by using a variety of approaches (e.g. producing a variety of tables with the same data presented in different ways), believing in the benefits of cross-checking. In Rowntree's case, flexibility was shown in the kind of data that he used (mostly from questionnaires, but also from neighbours and other informants; using wage data from his own factory for his employees but also using estimates of wages by trade and other sources to interpolate the gaps).

An important feature in the interpretation of the work of Booth and Rowntree has been the debate on how far their analysis was influenced by Victorian values. Such an influence has been seen, for example, in their explanations of poverty based on moral weaknesses of the poor (e.g. betting and drinking as well as thriftlessness), in Rowntree's concern with the plight of poverty preventing the creation of a healthy army and labour force, and in the imaginative solution for poverty offered by Booth – i.e. deporting the poor into 'industrial or labour colonies', to be 'well housed, well fed, and well warmed; and taught and trained, and employed from morning to night'[5] (quoted in Bales 1999: 155).

While current thinkers are concerned with discussing the values implicit in Booth and Rowntree's methodologies for identifying poverty, contemporaries were clearly aware of the political message which they conveyed. Indeed both of them were interested in the living conditions of the poor out of concern for improving it. They both saw the value of a scientific method to collect 'facts' in order to inform and justify action.

2.3   The monetary approach: a critical view

The approaches adopted by both Booth and Rowntree were broadly adopted and then further developed by both economists and sociologists interested in the quantification and analysis of poverty. In what follows we will concentrate on the use that economists make of money metrics.[6] First, we review technical steps taken in the measurement of poverty. We then examine the deeper conceptual issues which underpin this approach, and in particular how well its claimed objectivity stands the test of critiques of its philosophical foundations. Although we discuss these issues separately, it is clear that they are intrinsically related.

We have emphasised that faith in the scientific objectivity of the method characterised early attempts at measuring poverty. This became obvious in the shift from Booth's social classification based on the convergence of various criteria to Rowntree's poverty line explicitly derived from 'objective' calculations and 'scientific' knowledge. The methodology seemed to open a new avenue which would allow objective quantification of poverty as a purely technical issue, rather than a normative, analytical or prescriptive matter. In the words of Bowley and Hogg, who acknowledge the similarity of their method to Rowntree's: 'It is not part of our plan to discuss remedies, but only to provide the detailed numerical setting out of the problem' (Bowley and Hogg 1925: 47).[7]

2.3.1   Getting to a number: different steps in poverty measurement

As earlier researchers found, the 'numerical setting out of the problem' posed enough questions to keep them busy, without having to worry about any underlying normative values. Issues such as the precise definition of variables,[8] the derivation of the minimum needs for efficiency,[9] and developments in the understanding of nutritional requirements in the following decades, including exploring the complexities and implications of differing metabolic rates,[10] were to challenge the idea that one standard of poverty could easily be set. A helpful way of organising this brief review of these issues is to follow Sen (1976) in dividing poverty measurement into two phases – identification and aggregation.

Issues related to data collection, however crucial for the measurement process and its comparability over time and place, will not be explicitly reviewed here, though they have important consequences for measurement. It is worth noting, however, that data are generally collected through household surveys, normally with complex structures, characterised by stratified non-random samples and clustered observations, with efforts made to standardise practice by sharing and discussing what has been learned in running surveys (see for example the comprehensive discussion in Grosh and Glewwe 2000). Nonetheless, data quality remains a key concern for poverty analysis in general, with issues ranging from sample design,[11] the breadth of the questions asked,[12] the consistency of the questionnaires over time, the choice of the price indices to be used, the institutional features determining the recruitment and the motivation of the enumerators, and practical issues like the choice of whom to interview.[13] While these problems plague estimations of poverty and their comparability in ways which are hard to overcome *ex post* (even when researchers are aware of the problems in their data) it is worth stressing that these are not weaknesses of monetary data only. Challenges are presented, for example, even by measuring supposedly more 'clear-cut' indicators such as literacy (e.g. Lavy et al. 1995).

Identification

The *identification* issue is concerned with identifying who the poor are. It involves the choice of a criterion of poverty (e.g. the selection of a 'poverty line' in terms of a certain monetary income), and then finding out who falls below the defined 'poverty line' and who does not (Sen 1976). The choice of a criterion for the determination of the poverty line can be divided into several steps: the choice of an indicator, the choice of a unit of analysis, and the choice of a poverty line.

The choice of an indicator. The issue of what it is that is lacking which identifies someone as poor is a very broad one which can be discussed at very different levels. In the common practice of the monetary approach, however, practitioners do not dwell too much on the philosophical positions underlying alternative possibilities.[14] Data availability generally restricts the possible indicators of monetary poverty into either expenditure or income since the use of wealth as the criterion is generally ruled out by problems in the observability and valuation of assets. Arguments can be found in favour of either income or expenditure, as expenditure can be considered as effective spending and income as potential spending. It is often claimed that theoretically expenditure is preferable to income, either because it can be seen as a proxy for consumption and hence of utility, or as a proxy for 'permanent' income, or long-term living standards.[15] And this argument is reinforced in the light of the difficulties in obtaining reliable income data especially in developing countries, while expenditure data is generally regarded as more reliable.[16]

A rather stringent set of assumptions are needed in order for the money metric of either income or consumption to capture individual welfare – for example, on the completeness and non-rationed nature of the markets. Moreover, further problems in such an interpretation arise from the way the methods are put into practice. For example, whether the consumption indicator includes the benefits from subsistence production and public goods by using shadow pricing and imputed values in the methodology depends on data availability and the inclinations of researchers (Deaton and Zaidi 1999). It seems that the homogeneous definitions across investigations which were advocated by Bowley have not yet been achieved. In practice, important determinants of welfare such as social income and subsistence production often enter into the indicators in rather limited way, if at all.

The choice of a unit of analysis. As discussed above, from the beginning of poverty measurement, poverty was seen as a problem pertaining to an individual, even though many of the causes of poverty seemed to operate at the household or community level. Despite the emphasis on poverty as being a characteristic of individuals, it is difficult to get individual income or expenditure data since much income is pooled within the household and much expenditure made on behalf of the household as a whole, and some consumption is done collectively by the household as a whole. The simplest way of dealing with this is to take the household as a unit of observation, and then take into account its size (and possibly its composition) to determine whether the household is poor.[17]

An important issue then is how to allow for households of different sizes in calculating the resources a household needs to avoid poverty, since households with different size and composition have different needs and also may satisfy them differently, because of some economies of scale in meeting some needs. For this purpose equivalence scales have been devised whose aim is to allow for differences in needs and efficiency of expenditure of households of different size and composition. Equivalence scales are coefficients representing the cost to a household of reaching a certain welfare level expressed as a proportion of some standard, reference, household (Banks and Johnson 1993). There is considerable debate about the best method to arrive at such scales[18] while several authors have stressed the sensitivity of poverty estimates to the way household composition is accounted for (e.g. Lanjouw and Ravallion 1995; White and Masset 2003). While equivalence scales are standard practice in the analysis of developed country data, their use in developing countries analysis is much less common.

It is important to stress that deriving individual well-being from household data is intrinsically difficult as individuals living together have interdependent standards of living. This is partly a problem of observability, due to the difficulty or cost of observing the resources to which the individual has access.[19] But it also may depend on the dimension or space in which poverty is defined: for example, if it is a matter of individual freedoms rather than utility, then control over income may be important as well as the total level.

The choice of a poverty line. The derivation of a poverty line is central to the monetary approach to poverty measurement. One of the most long-standing debates on the nature of poverty is whether poverty is absolute or relative, i.e. whether the poverty line is to be defined and measured independently of the standards prevailing in the society in question (as with absolute poverty) or depends on average living standards (relative poverty). This debate obviously has implications for the determination of the poverty line and for the methodologies adopted to update it over time (the latter is a problem whose importance is often overlooked). Attempts have been made to tackle the issue of the choice of the poverty line in a framework explicitly based in welfare economics (Ravallion 1998), in which the poverty line is defined as 'the minimum cost of the poverty level of utility' (ibid.: 3). This leaves open the issue of how to define such a minimum.

Perhaps the most serious challenge to the 'objectivity' of the monetary approach is the arbitrary basis for the level of utility which represents the poverty minimum. As already noted, this is a foundational problem for the monetary approach to poverty. While a sophisticated literature has developed in measurement of monetary poverty, the problem of the intrinsic economic significance of any welfare threshold remains unresolved.

Standard practices[20] take different starting points on this issue, identifying the poverty line either with respect to a list of basic needs to be fulfilled or with respect to some characteristic of the distribution of the welfare indicator chosen. Methodologies which build on basic needs can generate either 'objective' or 'subjective' poverty lines: absolute poverty lines using 'objective' definitions are based on external observers' estimates of the goods required to meet basic needs, while 'subjective' poverty lines are based on what the poor themselves identify as being minimally adequate, or as necessary to getting by.[21] Relative poverty lines derive the poverty line as some ratio of the average (mean or the median) of the societal income distribution. The absolute poverty lines, adopted in the analysis of poverty in most developing countries (and, a significant exception among the industrial countries, adopted as the national poverty line in the US), are very similar to those in Rowntree's approach as they take food energy requirements as the hard core around which the line is constructed.

There are various ways of estimating these food energy requirements. To use Ravallion's (1998) terminology, there is the Food Energy Intake method which identifies the level of income or expenditure at which food energy requirements are met; and there are different versions of the Cost of Basic Needs method: writing down a full-blown list of basic needs and the expected costs of achieving them (à la Rowntree), or starting from the cost of achieving the minimal food energy requirements, and adding a non-food component in a way which is aimed at being compatible with household behaviour (e.g. scaling the food requirements up according to the average food share, or the food share of some particular group, or adding to the minimal food expenditure the non-food expenditure of those whose overall consumption is equal to the minimum food expenditure). Food requirements (and conceivably other basic needs) therefore operate as a way of identifying the poverty line, bringing in additional information to solve the problem of a lack of a firm anchor in welfare economics itself. To reiterate, the core issue is that economics does not in itself provide indications of or criteria for a minimum level of either welfare or consumption or income, unless either some link is made to efficiency-type arguments by which food intakes are justified with respect to the working capacity of the individual, or some link is made to an explicitly normative – and non-economic – theory of a just society.

In sum, while it is helpful to anchor the definition of a minimal level of welfare to the level of welfare enjoyed when certain basic needs are satisfied (or at least when the expected value of need satisfaction is above a minimum level), it is by no means a given of economic theory that it be so, and that the range of needs entering the determination of a poverty line is so restricted. More specifically, while a concern with nutritional achievement and efficiency – traceable already in Rowntree's analysis of the risk posed by poverty to the creation of a healthy work-force and army – makes sense in terms of not depleting one of the poor's most important assets (i.e. their working capacity), there is no intrinsic reason why the analysis of welfare (in static or dynamic terms) should be so narrowly restricted to the consumption of one particular kind of good, where the restriction consists both in focusing on the consumption of goods rather than on the consequences of that consumption and on the range of goods considered.[22]

In the face of these structural weaknesses in the concept of the poverty line, a constructive interpretation centres on the idea that the poverty line acts as an indispensable device to focus attention on the lower end of the distribution, as well as to make comparisons over time and place. Such a view, which de-emphasises the importance of a single poverty figure, fits well with the practice of adopting more than one poverty line to test the robustness of the results (see Chapter 1).[23]

A different logic underpinning the adoption of two poverty lines concerns differences in the behaviour of poor and very poor people. This lies behind Lipton's (1988) identification of the ultra-poor, defined as a group of individuals who devote more than 70–80 per cent of their income to food but do not manage to cover 80 per cent of their caloric needs, whose behaviour contrasts with that of the poor. At the centre of this definition is the idea that different groups among the poor show differences in their production and consumption behaviour due to the severity of the constraints they face (Lipton 1988).[24]

Aggregation

Having identified all those who fall below the agreed poverty line (drawn in the chosen indicator, income or expenditure), the second phase of poverty measurement involves the aggregation of all the information on individual poverty into a single index. Early approaches adopted statistical indices like the headcount (the percentage of people living in poverty) and the income gap ratio (the shortfall between poor people's average income and the poverty line, divided by the poverty line). However, a seminal paper by Sen (1976) developed the principles of an axiomatic approach to the measurement of poverty following similar axioms to those in the literature on inequality. Sen also developed a new index (Sen's index), which incorporated a measure of the distribution of income of people below the poverty line, as well as the numbers of people falling below the line. Three key axioms (Patrizi 1990) according to which poverty indices are to be devised and judged are: (1) the axiom of the irrelevance of the non-poor, i.e. the incomes of those lying above the poverty line should not affect the poverty index; (2) the monotonicity axiom, stating that 'given other things, a reduction in income of a person below the poverty line must increase the poverty measure' (Sen 1976: 219); (3) the transfer axiom stating that 'given other things, a pure transfer of income from a person below the poverty line to anyone who is richer must increase the poverty measure' (ibid.).

This axiomatic approach has focused attention on the desirable characteristics of a poverty index.[25] By far the most popular of ensuing efforts is the FGT family of indices (Foster, Greer and Thorbeck 1984), which respects all of the three axioms mentioned above, and which encompasses three important poverty indices: the headcount ratio, the poverty gap ratio and an index for the severity of poverty. The headcount ratio can be obtained by substituting with 0, for the value of α in the formula below, while the poverty gap index involves substituting 1 in the formula and a common approach to measuring the severity of poverty is when $\alpha = 2$. The last measure is often termed the FGT measure of poverty.

$$P_\alpha = \frac{1}{n} \sum_{i=1}^{q} \left(\frac{z - y_i}{z} \right)^\alpha$$

Comparability of results

Given the variety of issues that have to be faced in order to arrive at an estimate of the extent of poverty, the comparability of results over time and location may often be questionable. While it is easy to calculate the same indices in different contexts, they do not necessarily reflect the same kind of information, even when calculated over variables that are defined in the same way – including the same components[26] – and in the absence of verbal confusion on what is meant by similar questions posed in different surveys.

This problem was already faced squarely by Rowntree when replicating his York surveys and updating the poverty line. He chose to maintain a standard which bore some reference to the general context in which individuals lived. In analysing his 1936 survey, for example, he updated the items included in his previous calculations, considering the availability of a dwelling with a bath and a garden (not regarded as luxury items for working-class households by 1936) and no longer considering goods such as second-hand boots and jacket appropriate (Atkinson 1989).[27]

But the solution adopted by Rowntree is just one interpretation of the concept of comparability, as it takes Rowntree's own interpretation of the norms prevailing in society, as the reference against which poverty is defined. This procedure means that different poverty lines could arise in different parts of the same country, or in different countries. Hence there is no sense of equal rights nationally or globally, which might be morally or politically unacceptable.

2.4 Beliefs beyond numbers?

Our discussion of the methodology to assess poverty in a monetary poverty perspective has shown that a number of choices have to be faced, potentially affecting the results, all motivated by serious theoretical considerations. In this light, the objectivity of the method and its ability to portray an undisputed reality, a feature which emerged strongly as a claim made about the approach in the discussion of its origins, is undermined. Yet in most policy discussion, the numbers identified by monetary poverty assessments are regarded as important and objective facts justifying particular policies. Moreover, the apparently obvious choice of a monetary indicator seems to bias policy advice towards the key role of growth in monetary income as a solution to poverty, a factor which might seem obvious to many practitioners of this approach, but which is often questioned by those holding wider views on what poverty means.

2.4.1 Towards an economic definition of poverty

It is apparent that for most practitioners of the monetary approach, poverty is regarded as an objectively measurable phenomenon, albeit rather undefined, though theorists sometimes recognise its weak foundations. As already discussed, the monetary approach does not offer a widely accepted 'self-contained' (i.e. not anchored to some normative theory) definition of poverty. Similarly, the big questions on the mechanisms responsible for poverty and determining its intensity – questions to which the classics devoted a good amount of thought – are generally not on the agenda as they cannot be approached from an exclusively microeconomic and individualistic perspective. Hence there have been attempts to improve the foundations, two of which we illustrate here.

In response to this unsatisfactory situation, Lewis and Ulph (1988: 120) propose a model incorporating 'two critical features that should be present in any coherent account of poverty at the individual level': first, that there is a strictly positive minimum of expenditure required on one or more specific commodities to escape poverty, and, secondly, that this minimum consumption also provides indirect consumption benefits in the form of participation in certain activities or social participation.[28] This model allows the authors to show why poverty matters for the utility of the individual and how it matters for society in as much as societal welfare is a reflection of individual preferences. While the Lewis and Ulph model does not seem to have shifted the way poverty is modelled generally, it provides an interesting example of the way the concept of poverty can be integrated into microeconomic analysis. Such a way of proceeding is, however, quite reductionist as it is focused on individual utility and on a view of society as composed by 'the sum of individuals acting rationally' (Bürgemeier 1994: 343). In the next section we will briefly summarise how these basic foundations of welfarism have been criticised, and this will be discussed in greater depth in the next chapter, while the popularity of Sen's critique makes it superfluous to dwell on this in much detail.

2.4.2   Of philosophers and values

Two alternative philosophical systems have been identified as justifying the use of monetary indicators in the measurement of poverty. The first is the welfarist one, and applies when poverty is conceptualised as lack of economic welfare, measured in terms of achieved standard of living. This view is explicitly linked to the assumptions of microeconomics, crucial among them that individuals have consistent preferences. In this framework it is the concept of utility as inferred from market behaviour that becomes the indicator supposed to capture economic welfare. The second view, less widespread, adopts a rights-based approach, and assumes that households or individuals are entitled to a minimum income, the disposal of which is a matter for them (Atkinson 1989).

In various contributions (usefully synthesised in Sen 1997) Sen has offered a thorough review of the welfarist approach, by criticising in a sequence the different 'steps' which link market behaviour to individual welfare. He emphasised the distinction between well-being and welfare where the former pertains only to purely self-seeking behaviour,[29] and also includes the consideration of agency (which includes other goals, values and ideals that are important in an individual life despite not increasing an individual's well-being). While well-being can be arguably proxied by utility, agency goals cannot, so that utility stands as a very imperfect approximation of welfare. As for inferring utility from market behaviour, market choices might be determined by factors other than pure utility maximisation (e.g. strategic interactions). He then questioned the significance of utility maximisation, as he argued it would be foolish (rather than rational) to define the whole of a person's well-being on the basis of the same criteria adopted to determine market choices. Further, even if the utility outcome was the only thing that mattered for the individual, subjective and objective elements would contribute to it, therefore making utility a rather noisy indicator.

To prove this, Sen criticised alternative interpretations of utility, in turn. If utility stands for desire fulfilment or happiness, then adopting a utility-based framework entails neglecting factors which might not be desirable in an objective valuation of well-being, for example, neglecting what people can effectively do by focusing only on their mental disposition ('physical-condition neglect') as well as neglecting the way that valuation is influenced by what appears reasonable or possible (the 'valuation-neglect'). If utility is taken instead as a description of choices without reference to the underlying psychological conditions, i.e. the Revealed Preference definition of utility, it provides an even weaker basis for ethical judgement since the act of choosing, involved in revealed preference, does not imply greater utility or value to be attributed to the chosen position.[30]

It can be noted, however, that Sen's critique does not extend to approaches based on rights. They offer a non-welfarist alternative ethical justification to monetary-based poverty measurement with the advantage of avoiding the issue of interpersonal comparisons. For example Von Parijs (1995) suggests an approach based on 'real freedom' – not only the formal freedom of 'doing what one might want to do' but also having the minimal means for doing it. It is interesting to note that, unlike in Sen's rights-based capability approach, the actual space in which satisfaction of minimum rights is to be verified in Von Parijs' approach is the space of resources.

2.5   Conclusions

From a mission of a few enlightened minds, poverty measurement has now become a sophisticated and professional endeavour. Its developments have closely followed those of many disciplines, from sociology to economics and statistics, and a set of standard procedures has now been identified. Still, in this survey we have reminded ourselves that there are many unpleasantly vague details and questions which require solutions (often ad hoc), often requiring decisions of a rather normative nature. Be it in the definition of the poverty line, or in the decision of the space in which it has to be drawn and for which unit of analysis, vagueness surrounds any given estimate of monetary poverty. The ideal objective assessment in which early studies believed seems therefore to have been proved unachievable. Another aim of the early pioneers, however, has been extremely successful. Estimates of monetary poverty have entered into the political debate and become policy targets across the globe, and their reduction has even occasionally been enshrined into constitutional law (for example, in the case of Ireland). While these developments are in one way a reason for optimism, knowing what the numbers mean and what they hide has consequently become even more of an important issue.

Notes

1. As will be discussed below this definition consciously omits other important ways (both within and outside economics) in which monetary indicators of poverty have been constructed in order to focus on what can be considered 'mainstream poverty measurement'.
2. On the debate on whether the definition of poverty adopted by Booth and Rowntree was based on lifestyle (hence relative) or was absolute, see Veit-Wilson (1986).
3. The way those standards was derived seems not to have been very 'scientific'. It is interesting to note that though mention of the poverty lines can be found in the minutes of the meetings of various school authorities, their existence was kept secret to prevent people from declaring lower incomes and having fees waived.
4. Defined as households not keeping servants.
5. Such a plan was defined by Booth himself as 'limited socialism'; the plan was received with 'condemnation by those on the political right, cautious acceptance by moderates and the centre-left, and with complete apathy from socialists' (Bales 1999: 158).
6. We disregard other important approaches which have developed using monetary indicators in very different ways, such as the methodology associated with Townsend's contributions in deriving a relative poverty line.

7. And the claim of aseptic scientificity of the procedure was reinforced by a footnote letting the reader know that the data are kept at the London School of Economics, and are available for detailed study (Rowntree 1902).
8. Bowley in 1915, in a paper on 'The Measurement of Social Phenomena' (quoted by Bulmer 1985), highlighted the need for standard definitions of variables such as income, poverty and household.
9. Already in the second edition of his 1900 study Rowntree lamented that the meagre diet he used to calculate his food poverty line had been attacked as 'extravagant'.
10. See for example the debate on the 'small but healthy hypothesis', e.g. Seckler (1982).
11. And some of these problems are rather fundamental: for example, it is not uncommon for surveys to be run in urban areas only.
12. It has been found, for example, that focusing the food modules of the questionnaires on meals eaten and failing to record the amount of snacking can significantly underestimate the amount of food consumption, at least by certain household members.
13. It is customary to interview one member per household, often the head or the person deemed to be better informed on the issue on which a certain module is centred, but this practice overlooks the possibility of different members of the household having autonomous streams of income which they control.
14. An example of the pragmatism which characterises the construction of indicators is the inclusion of socially disapproved goods such as alcohol in the welfare indicator. While defensible on the grounds that such expenditure reflects household choices, doubts could be raised on whether such expenditure really contributes to household welfare.
15. This requires strong assumptions on the existence and functioning of credit markets. 'Permanent income' is the constant annual income which would be sustainable over a person's lifetime in contrast to actual income in any year which represents the particular circumstances of that year.
16. It has been noted, however, that if, as is often the case, one measures levels of expenditure and contrasts them with the minimum required to face fundamental needs, there is no certainty that expenditure has effectively been allocated to these needs. In practice this amounts to adopting a hybrid between a focus on effective and on potential spending (Nolan and Wheelan 1996).
17. Whether the results are presented in terms of poor households or poor individuals, though changing the results, does not matter from the procedural point of view as the assessment is still performed at the household level.
18. A fundamental critique, made by Pollak and Wales (1979), is the impossibility of identifying equivalence scales from observed behaviour *conditional* on household demographics (since different preferences over demographic composition can be consistent with the same behaviour). This does not seem to be addressed by the most common methods of estimating equivalence scales.
19. Recent analysis has tried to unpack what happens within the household in terms of production and allocation of resources (e.g. Haddad et al. 1997), thereby helping to address the issue of lack of direct observability.
20. We are here consciously omitting a discussion of the poverty lines which are derived as minimal income levels below which state benefits can be claimed.

These, in fact, have the peculiar characteristic of suggesting that the best way to lower poverty is to lower the threshold at which benefits can be claimed and do not seem to be rooted in an explicit theoretical framework.

21. 'Subjective' enquiries have used different questions to identify poverty (e.g. 'adequacy', 'minimal adequacy', 'just enough to get by', or 'enough for survival'); each can be expected to get different results.

22. As an example of the arbitrary nature of the choice of caloric requirements to anchor the poverty line consider the case of India, where these were changed from 2400 to 1900 calories.

23. At the limit this practice leads to testing for stochastic dominance (e.g. Bishop et al. 1993) when comparing different situations (countries over time, different regions etc.). By plotting the density functions one can test whether one distribution entails less poverty than another independently of the poverty line chosen.

24. In particular, their overriding concern is to increase their caloric intake when income rises so that – unlike the case of the other poor people – their food-outlay ratio rises and they do not substitute cheaper for more expensive calories. Another distinguishing feature is that despite the high proportion of outlay going to food, ultra-poor people show the physical signs of malnutrition in severe impairments in their anthropometric measurements. The consequences in terms of malnutrition and disability also affect the supply of labour.

25. Foster (1994: 367–8), however, offers a convincing discussion on how the axiomatic characterisation of an index needs to be tempered with other practical considerations: 'A researcher's time might be better spent identifying important aspects of the phenomenon to be measured and showing how a particular index captures them, rather than erecting axiomatic structures around measures which will never be used.'

26. An interesting question in this respect is what to do when in different contexts different goods are considered necessary to avoid poverty. Note for example that the practice of deriving context-specific poverty lines using local consumption baskets (e.g. in the urban context, Satterthwaite 1995) while justified in terms of, for example, local availability of certain goods or local customs, might be seen to implicitly reward 'expensive tastes', as for example when the food baskets in certain areas include more expensive calories such as those derived from proteins.

27. He presented both a definition of 'abject poverty' (with the poverty line updated only by valuing it at new prices) and an entirely new poverty line, based on his work for the book *The Human Needs of Labour* aimed at capturing the minimum necessary for a healthy life rather than bare subsistence.

28. These critical features are derived models (e.g. Sen's) developed quite outside the standard monetary approach.

29. Altruistic concerns for others are not excluded, but are part of well-being inasmuch as they are reflected in the individual utility function: they do not matter in themselves.

30. If choice between two options is not directly linked to an individual attaching any particular value to one choice compared to the other, the fact of that choice does not provide grounds for attributing greater social value to the chosen option (Sugden 1993).

3
Capabilities: the Concept and its Implementation

Ruhi Saith

3.1 Introduction

Amartya Sen first introduced the capability approach in the essay 'Equality of What?' delivered as the Tanner Lecture on Human Values in 1979. At the time, the two popular theories offered by moral philosophy with regard to equality (be it social, economic or political) were utilitarianism and the Rawlsian theory of justice. Sen (1980) proposed the thesis that the space of 'capabilities' is more appropriate to an evaluation of inequality than the space of utilities or that of primary goods as suggested by Bentham (1789) and Rawls (1971) respectively.[1] Sen's approach has subsequently gained popularity in its use in the context of addressing poverty.

In the research presented in this book, we compare at empirical and theoretical levels the application of the capability approach with the monetary-based, social exclusion-based and participatory approaches to poverty analysis. In this chapter, we present first a brief background to the capability approach (Section 3.2) followed by a discussion on possible methods of implementation of the approach (Section 3.3) for poverty analysis. We concentrate on developing countries and try to arrive in the concluding section (Section 3.4) at a capability approach implementation framework that can be used by us for the comparative analysis (between different approaches to poverty), in later chapters.

3.2 Background of the approach

Central to the development of Sen's capability thesis are criticisms of Rawls' theory of justice (and particularly the commodities-based approach in the context of poverty) and utilitarianism (and particularly, the utility-based approach in the poverty context). The crux of these criticisms is briefly reproduced below. Details may be found in Sen (1980, 1982 and 1985).

Rawls' theory concentrates on obtaining equality in the space of 'primary social goods'. Sen's criticism of this approach is directed towards the emphasis on the goods and their equal distribution – 'commodity fetishism' – rather than the relationship between goods and persons. Sen suggests that the possession of commodities may not necessarily translate into well-being given the large interpersonal variations of personal characteristics or the disparities in the natural/social environment that affect the 'conversion' of commodities to particular ends. A common example is that of fulfilling the nutritional demands of an individual who suffers from some intestinal parasitic infestation. Other things being equal, such an individual would require higher quantities of the commodity, food, than those of someone without such an infestation.

As with a commodity basis of poverty analysis, Sen also finds utilitarianism, which has greatly influenced welfare economics, problematic. With regard to equality, the utilitarian objective is the maximisation of the total sum of the utility (seen as satisfaction or happiness in classic utilitarianism, or desire fulfilment in modern utilitarianism), irrespective of the manner of distribution. Sen (1973, 1997) suggests that this particularly raises problems if some individuals are better 'utility producers' than others. The approach would in fact discriminate against individuals who are handicapped in the conversion of resources into utility (for example a physically handicapped individual). This is because such individuals would be considered inefficient in terms of utility generating ability and instead more resources would be given to more efficient producers so as to increase the sum total utility. Using utility as the guide, an individual who is mentally in a 'happier' state having reconciled herself to her lot although malnourished and uneducated ('physical condition neglect') and valuing a particular kind of life over another ('valuation neglect'), may well be ranked higher than one who is well nourished and educated but is unhappy and aspires for more.

As an alternative to the commodities-based and utility-based approaches, Sen proposes the capability approach. Here it is not the possession of the commodity or the utility that it provides that proxies for well-being, but rather what the person actually succeeds in doing with the commodity, given its characteristics and his or her own personal characteristics and external circumstances. This achievement is referred to as the *functioning*. Thus for example, for the commodity (*sack of rice*) with its characteristic (*nutrition*), some individual may achieve the functioning (*moderately nourished*). Some other individual, utilising the same quantity of rice, but having a parasitic infection, may achieve the functioning (*poorly nourished*). Thus, while the characteristics of commodities (here the characteristic *nutrition* of the commodity *rice*), do not alter depending on the person possessing it and the external circumstances, the functionings do.

While functioning refers to the actual achievement, *capability* refers to the potential. Thus given the commodity *rice* and her personal characteristics and external circumstances, the individual has the *capability to be moderately nourished*, although she may choose not to be. While a functioning (here *moderately nourished*) therefore is an actual achievement, and directly related to living conditions, capability is a notion of freedom in the positive sense.

Given the commodities available to the person, a list of functionings may be achieved. This is a *functioning vector*, giving a snapshot of the person's state of being. For example, the commodities, rice and a bicycle, may result in the following functioning vector (*moderately nourished, transported*). Other modes of utilisation by the same person (for example, choosing not to use the bicycle and therefore not expending this additional energy, but at the same time not having any other means of transportation) might result in a different functioning vector like: (*well-nourished, stationary*).[2]

A *capability set* is the set of all possible functioning vectors that a person can achieve. The capability set is obtained by applying all feasible utilisations to all possible choices of commodity characteristic vectors. The person can then select a preferred functioning vector from this set to lead his/her life. This is thus the person's 'chosen state of being'.[3] A capability set, defined in the space of functionings, is thus a set of various alternative combinations of functioning vectors, any one of which a person can choose. In the restricted example above therefore, the capability set is ([*moderately nourished, transported*], [*well-nourished, stationary*]). This freedom to choose between existing options constitutes an important aspect of the capability approach.

It is not the purpose of this chapter to arbitrate between Rawls, Bentham and Sen. The emphasis is on issues pertaining to the operationalisation of the capability approach in the context of developing countries and it is this discussion that is pursued in the sections that follow.[4]

3.3 Implementation of the capability approach

Before proceeding to implement the capability approach for the comparative analysis in this book, we discuss below issues related to implementation. These can be broadly classified as follows: (a) The first issue that needs to be addressed is whether interpersonal comparisons would require to be done between 'capability sets' or between 'chosen functioning vectors' (Section 3.3.1). (b) The second issue pertains to deciding on the subset of capabilities/functionings that the comparison would be concerned with in the context of poverty analysis in developing countries (Section 3.3.2). (c) The third issue relates to the methodology to be followed for interpersonal comparisons of this restricted set of capabilities/functionings (Section 3.3.3). Each of these issues is discussed below.

3.3.1   Comparison of 'capability sets' or 'chosen functioning vectors'[5]

With regard to interpersonal comparisons, for purposes of poverty analysis, an implementation of the capability approach ideally ought to involve evaluation and comparison of capability sets. The freedom to choose is thus taken into account. Beginning from the present 'state of being' of the person, obtaining counterfactual information as to what a person might have been or done, as an assessment of the capability set requires, is quite difficult however. One possibility is to collect information about hypothetical choices. This, however, would be expected to be less reliable than that of actual choices (Brandolini and D'Alessio 1998). People are being asked to imagine and place themselves in scenarios and this is quite a difficult task. The other possibility is to try and construct or estimate the capability set from observed achievements (Ysander 1993). This, however, requires an a priori behavioural model, which spells out the probability that a particular capability or capability set will manifest itself in certain observable achievements. Ysander gives the example of a certain degree of political capability indicating a certain probability that an individual will get politically organised, make speeches, or write to newspapers. The reliability of the results would require (1) the construction of a priori models that incorporate joint probabilities to account for the interdependence of individuals' choices in different areas (for instance, whether or not an individual uses their options for political action, could be dependent on their capabilities in other areas like education) and (2) an a priori model that takes into account the current social and institutional setting (for example, although the functionings may remain the same, options may shrink dramatically in situations of political regulation or social sanctions).

Given the extensive information required to perform interpersonal comparisons of capability sets, empirical work is usually restricted to interpersonal comparisons of the chosen functioning vector. Under the assumption of maximising behaviour, this would coincide with the maximally valued element of the capability set. It is, however, important to remember that this assumption may not hold. The motive for a particular choice may not necessarily be that of maximising one's own well-being. A person's choice may be guided by other considerations or requirements (Sen (1985) gives the example of one's obligation to others), in which case a functioning vector which does not give the highest well-being value may be chosen.

Thus an evaluation of just the 'chosen functioning vector' can be criticised as disregarding the options the person has and the freedom to choose from these. Having the functioning x when one has no other alternative would surely be viewed differently to choosing x when other substantial alternatives do exist (Sen 1997). While the 'well-being' assessed in this manner remains the same for each situation (for example well-being for a well fed, well clothed prisoner compared to a free person), the 'advantage' or the value of the capability set of the free person would certainly rank higher than that of the imprisoned person.

Yet, due to data constraints, comparisons of the chosen functioning vector may be all that is practically possible. Some notion of the freedom to choose can, however, still be obtained under the following interpretations of the chosen functionings:

1. By looking at the chosen functioning vector, we are in some way 'assessing the options a person had, *through* judging the option-collection by the alternative the person actually chose to use (what was the most selected functioning combination that the person had the opportunity to choose?)' (Sen 1994: 340). The nature of the chosen vector thus reflects indirectly the capability set the person could choose from.

2. Choosing itself can be considered a valuable functioning incorporated 'among the doings and beings in the functioning vector' (Sen 1985: 44).[6] The problem of characterising and evaluating the 'choosing' remains. Sen suggests that it need not be detailed, but can just be a broad notion which assesses whether substantial alternatives were available to choose from.

3. In Sen's later work this broad notion of 'choosing' is taken further to refining elements within the functioning vector itself. This is the notion of refined functionings, which takes note of the alternatives available with regard to each functioning. Thus, 'Choosing to do x when one could have chosen any member of a set S' is defined to be a 'refined functioning' (Sen 1988: 18). Thus, for example, if a person

was fasting and therefore under-nourished despite having access to the commodity *rice* and the conversion ability to achieve adequate nourishment, the functioning under-nourished would be considered a refined functioning (Sen 1987). In case of refined functionings therefore, alternative opportunities figure in the characterisation of the functionings themselves. A possible way of taking such freedom of choice into account may be to incorporate questions in surveys that ask individuals whether a shortfall in or lack of a particular functioning is perceived by them as a privation. Similarly an enquiry may be made as to whether the individual chose something in particular despite having alternative choices available. In a study conducted in Belgium by Schokkaert and Van Ootegem (1990) information for 46 'refined functionings' was obtained using a questionnaire. The notion of refined functionings, with regard to developing countries, does not, however, appear to have been explored. A possible reason for this may be that in countries where under-nutrition and ill-health are rife, it would be unrealistic to hypothesise that these functionings were chosen despite alternative options being available.

To sum up the discussion in Section 3.3.1, an ideal implementation of the capability approach involves interpersonal comparison between capability sets. Given practical difficulties with obtaining such data, however, in practice the comparison is usually carried out between 'chosen functioning vectors'.

3.3.2   Selection of capabilities/functionings

Irrespective of whether the assessment of well-being is done at the level of the capability set or the chosen functioning vector, assessment and interpersonal comparison of well-being would involve considering an extremely large number of capabilities/functionings related to different aspects of the individual's life. Their selection would, however, depend on the context of the particular investigation. If the main concern, as in this chapter, is to do with interpersonal comparisons with regard to poverty, a subset of capabilities/functionings may be adequate.

In an industrial country, it would be expected that capabilities/functionings concerned with basic nutrition, basic health, primary and secondary school education would not show much variation between individuals. Other functionings (for example involving literary, cultural, and intellectual pursuits, vacationing, and travelling related to the ability to entertain friends and such), would, however, vary considerably between individuals, and being sensitive as indicators of relative poverty, may form the focus of poverty investigations (Sen 1985). In a developing country, however, even 'basic capabilities', i.e. 'the ability to satisfy certain crucially important functionings up to certain minimally adequate levels' (Sen 1993: 41), may not be possessed by all individuals. Their assessment could thus reveal much inter-individual variation. Since this chapter is concerned mainly with implementation of the capability approach with regard to developing countries, such an assessment is discussed in some detail.

An assessment of 'basic capabilities' first involves developing a list of what these 'basic capabilities' and the consequent 'basic functionings' include. Sen (1985) gives examples of some basic functionings like being adequately nourished, being healthy, avoiding escapable morbidity, etc. Alkire (2002) argues that a lack of specification was deliberate on Sen's part, so as to ensure the relevance of the approach to different persons and cultures. She draws on Sen's own work and statements to support the 'incompleteness' of the capability approach. For guidelines to developing a specific list of 'basic capabilities', we have therefore to look at other work (see Table 3.1). Fundamental discussions of basic values, needs, etc. have taken place in a range of disciplines. The discussion below is restricted to research that has evolved in parallel with and has been linked explicitly with the capability approach.[7]

(1) *Basic needs.* Although initiated by the International Labour Organisation (ILO), the basic needs approach was developed during the subsequent World Bank programme launched in 1978. The programme was to study operational implications of meeting basic needs of the whole population, by national development efforts, within a short period of possibly one generation (Streeten et al. 1981). Table 3.2 lists the basic needs and their indicators used in the implementation of this approach (list taken from Streeten et al. 1981: 93).

The indicators in this list allow an assessment of the satisfaction of the basic needs of a group of individuals or a population within particular geographically defined areas. If the indicators identify a shortfall, this would indicate the necessity of concentrating on the provision of goods and services to satisfy the basic needs.

The indicators in Table 3.2 could be of assistance in the selection of basic functionings. However, since 'functionings' pertain to individuals, indicators in the basic needs list that relate to groups will have to be replaced with indicators that can be assessed with respect to individuals, for instance substituting an indicator of education like 'literacy percentages' with an indicator of individual education like 'level of education of

Table 3.1: 'Basic capabilities' as identified using differing criteria

Basic needs	Doyal & Gough[a]	Qizilbash	Desai	Nussbaum
Health[b]	Physical survival – i.e. physical health (BN)	Health, basic physical capacity	Stay alive	Life
Food	Mental health (BN)	Nutrition	Healthy living	Bodily health
Water supply	Understanding (BN)	Shelter	Ensure (biological) reproduction	Bodily health (nourishment)
Sanitation	Having opportunities (BN)	Sanitation	Knowledge, freedom of expression and thought	Bodily health (shelter)
Education (including freedom of expression and religion)	Appropriate health care (IN)	Education	Social interaction	Bodily integrity (free movement; security against assault; opportunities for choice in matters of reproduction)
	Food (IN)	Basic mental capacity		Senses, imagination, thought
	Protective housing (IN)	Basic level of aspiration and self-respect		Emotions
	Water (IN)	Rest		Practical reason
	Non-hazardous work environment (IN)	Security		Affiliation
	Non-hazardous physical environment (IN)			Other species
	Safe birth control and child bearing (IN)			Play
	Appropriate education (IN)			Control over environment (political and material)
	Security in childhood (IN)			
	Significant primary relationships (IN)			
	Physical security (IN)			
	Economic security (IN)			

a Doyal and Gough classify needs into basic needs (BN) and intermediate needs (IN). The latter are considered necessary to achieve the former. Thus intermediate needs have also been included.

b Although many approaches mention the capability 'health', the indicators that are used are often indicators of 'life' (e.g. life expectancy and mortality rates).

Table 3.2: Basic needs and their indicators

Basic need	Indicator
Health	Life expectancy at birth
Education	Literacy Primary school enrolment as a percentage of the population aged five to fourteen
Food	Calorie supply per head or calorie supply as a percentage of requirements
Water supply	Infant mortality per thousand deaths Percentage of population with access to potable water
Sanitation	Infant mortality per thousand births Percentage of population with access to sanitation facilities

individual'. Besides, indicators like calorie supply, suggested for food in the basic needs approach, are 'input' indicators, rather than 'output' indicators as an assessment of functionings would strictly require. Anthropometric measurements such as height, weight and/or mid-arm circumference would be considered more appropriate for the assessment of functionings for food as these take into account the role of personal characteristics. This neglect of interpersonal variations in the conversion of commodities into functionings has been identified as one of the major differences between the functionings and the basic needs approach. Another major difference is the absence of the notion of choice or freedom in the basic needs approach as compared to the capability approach (Balestrino 1991, 1994).[8] Thus, although the parameters identified in the basic needs approach may be useful as guidelines to define the basic functionings to be assessed, freedom to choose may have to be included as an additional functioning or the functionings refined to take this into account. As discussed in Section 3.3.1, however, implementation of the capability approach in developing countries, which concentrates on basic functionings and does not usually assess the notion of choice or freedom does in practice come quite close to the basic needs approach.

(2) *Doyal and Gough's theory of human need.* Doyal and Gough (1991) argue that basic needs are linked to the avoidance of serious harm, are objective and universal, and do not alter based on cultural differences. In trying to identify such basic needs, these authors define serious harm as 'dramatically impaired participation in a form of life' (1991: 55). They identify physical survival (more specifically physical health) and

personal autonomy as constituting the most basic human needs – 'those which must be satisfied to some degree before actors can effectively participate in their form of life to achieve any other valued goals' (1991: 54). They emphasise that although the basic needs of physical health and autonomy are considered universal, the basic goods and services that are needed to satisfy these needs ('satisfiers' as Doyal and Gough label them), may differ between different cultures. They introduce the concept of characteristics of these satisfiers and suggest that there may in fact be certain 'universal satisfier characteristics' (or intermediate needs) which are *'those properties of goods, services, activities and relationships which enhance physical health and human autonomy in all cultures'* (1991: 158). While the nutrition property of food would thus be universal, the specific types of foods that provide this may be culturally specific. They draw up a list of such intermediate needs (see Table 3.1) and propose to measure need-satisfaction by concentrating on them.

Evidence on what is universally necessary to achieving physical health and autonomy is derived from technical as well as anthropological knowledge. The indicators to assess need (basic and intermediate) satisfaction proposed by Doyal and Gough do not pertain to individuals but rather to allowing comparisons between countries, or groups. The indicators could, however, be suitably modified for use at the level of the individual.

(3) *Qizilbash's prudential values for development.* The problem as Qizilbash (1998) presents it, is not just with that of the notion of 'basic' (need, value, capability, etc.) but that of specifying the precise level at which it is considered basic. Although this requires a sensitivity to cultural, social and historical contexts, Qizilbash also argues for the absolute view of poverty in that 'there is some notion of a distinctively *human* life, which crosses culture and time, and this must guide us in formulating the precise standards for what is basic to any human flourishing' (1998: 12). He draws on the work of James Griffin on prudential values to suggest a list of 'basic prudential values' which are instrumental values and necessary requirements for the pursuit of any good human life (see Table 3.1).

Qizilbash clarifies that these things are removed from commodities and the approach cannot thus be accused of commodity fetishism. They are rather values that commodities can help to realise. With regard to a comparison with the capability approach, certain minimal intellectual and physical capacities are included which Qizilbash considers capacities necessary for the pursuit of any good life, but instrumentally rather than intrinsically valuable.

(4) *Desai's capabilities*. Desai's (1995) list of capabilities is not divided into separate basic or non-basic capabilities. The propositions guiding the capabilities included in the list are:

(a) capabilities should be few and common to all individuals;
(b) they must be co-realisable, i.e. that it is essential for all capabilities to be realised irrespective of the extent to which some are fulfilled;
(c) the *level* at which the capability can be guaranteed is expressed in terms of the commodities/resources required to obtain that capability. While capabilities are therefore absolute, the *level* expressed in this manner can be different for different societies; and
(d) while the number of capabilities may be limited, these allow for a large number of functionings. Achievement of the functionings would, however, be dependent on the actual resources the person has.

The capabilities listed by Desai (1995: 193) are shown in Table 3.1. Implementation involves assessing the minimum resource requirement to guarantee these capabilities. The actual functioning achieved, however, is not taken into consideration.

(5) *Nussbaum's 'basic human functional capabilities'*. Nussbaum (1995) argues for a 'universalist' and 'essentialist' position, which sees some capabilities as being more important and at the core of human life than others. Nussbaum's idea is that there is an overlapping consensus between different societies of a general outline of the conception of the human being. She develops a list of certain capabilities, with a threshold below which a life will be so impoverished as not to be human at all. The second threshold is defined with respect to a list of 'basic human functional capabilities', below which a life may be considered human, but not a good one. Nussbaum suggests public policy should not just aim to bring its citizens to the bare minimum, but ought to be committed to at least bringing all individuals above this threshold. Further, her argument is that capability (and not actual functioning) should be the goal of public policy – thus, for instance, governments need to ensure that people have enough to eat, though they may still choose to starve. Nussbaum's list of these 'basic human capabilities', which has progressively evolved during the course of her research is shown in Table 3.1 Nussbaum emphasises that all the capabilities in her list are of central importance and trade-offs may not be permitted. Further, the list is deliberately general to leave room for further negotiations.

(6) *Alkire's criteria for basic capabilities*. Generalising from Sen's arguments in defence of life expectancy measures as capability indictors, Alkire (2002: 184) suggests six criteria that achieved functionings must satisfy to be considered possible indicators of basic capabilities:

(a) The functioning belongs to the capability set (is itself valuable) OR the functioning is directly associated with the capability set (highly correlated, etc).

(b) The functioning pertains to a basic human need, i.e. that without which one's life may be blighted.

(c) The functioning is not significantly dependent on any non-basic prior functioning.

(d) The functioning is not dependent on the presence of uncommon ability or interest.

(e) A level of achieved functioning which is widely recognised to be 'basic' can be specified and empirically observed.

(f) Provision of the functioning does not necessarily compromise freedom to pursue other significant functionings in the long term.

Although a list is not provided, the guidelines may be used to decide whether a functioning does or does not qualify as an indicator of a basic capability.

Table 3.1 shows different authors, approaching the issue of identifying 'basic capabilities' from different perspectives and criteria. Basic capabilities common to all lists are identifiable as those related to health, nutrition and education.

As with theoretical work, most empirical work on basic capabilities also concentrates on health, nutrition and education. In empirical work in developing countries, the functionings approach has mainly been implemented in the restricted sense of assessing the chosen functioning vector and certain basic functionings within it. The assumption is that at the level of 'basic functionings' one can reasonably assume that people who show a shortfall did not have any alternative choice. The number of people who could afford to eat but were fasting (or on a hunger strike) and thus functionally under-nourished is likely to constitute an insignificant minority. The comparison of capability sets or the notion of refined functionings are not explored.

The functionings assessed are further restricted by data availability, which is not an unimportant consideration. In effect, therefore, most empirical work concentrates on indicators similar to those used in studies related to the basic needs school. The similarity is further increased because the assessment of these functionings is usually restricted to that of the 'living standard' rather than that of 'well-being'.[9]

Examples of empirical work include the following. Sen (1985) presents inter-country comparisons performed at the level of functionings, like education and health. In the same book, comparing data for Bombay and West Bengal in India, Sen looks at indicators of the functionings of health and nutrition to investigate the issue of gender bias. Drèze and Sen's monograph on India (1995) proposes to analyse economic development in India in terms of the expansion of basic capabilities. As detailed by Alkire (2002), however, the sustained attention given in the analysis to inequalities in health and education (using indicators like literacy rates, life expectancy, infant mortality and fertility) results in a narrowing of the focus, as with the other studies, to specific basic functionings.

Other studies, such as Ruggeri Laderchi using data for Peru (1999) and for Chile (1997), compare the monetary approach to poverty analysis with the capability approach. Here too, the data used for the capability approach include indicators on functionings related to nutrition, health and education. Similarly, the indicators used in the Human Poverty Index introduced by the UNDP in the 1997 *Human Development Report* relate to achieved functionings.[10]

Most operational work in developed countries has also been done at the level of functionings rather than capabilities (Erikson 1993; Razavi 1996; Brandolini and D'Alessio 1998). Schokkaert and Van Ootegem (1990), in a study on data for Belgium, do, however, try to capture the notion of freedom to choose, with the inclusion of refined functionings.

To sum up Section 3.3.2, theoretical arguments and practical restrictions suggest that interpersonal comparisons of poverty in developing countries may be assessed by a comparison of 'basic functionings'. An overview of previous theoretical attempts to develop a list of 'basic' criteria and empirical attempts to assess basic functionings suggests that in most studies, health, education and nutrition have been included as basic functionings.

3.3.3 Method of comparison of capabilities/functionings

Irrespective of the finite dimensions that are selected, whether basic or more extensive, the issue of performing comparisons between different individuals for this finite list of capabilities/functionings remains. Comparisons that involve single functionings (for example a comparison between the values for the functioning 'being educated') are fairly straightforward. If the chosen indicator is the extent of education, the comparison between individuals would be between different levels of achieved education, such as education until class five, until class ten, or university education. Values for *each* of the selected functionings are thus compared between individuals, without trying to develop any overall measure of well-being.

An interpersonal comparison of the overall combination of functionings, i.e. the chosen functioning vector or the capability set, is more difficult, however. Recall that depending on their evaluation the person will choose one of the vectors out of the capability set. He or she thus has a particular level of well-being in this 'chosen state of being'. Since the process of evaluation varies from person to person, it would appear to confound any straightforward comparisons of well-being – what one person may consider the highest well-being may not be considered so by another. For example, an individual A with the functionings vector (*educated, comfortably housed*) may be considered by some as having a higher well-being than individual B with functionings vector (*uneducated, luxuriously housed*), while others may insist that person B has a higher level of well-being than person A. Nevertheless, as pointed out by Sen (1985), it may be possible to agree on some minimal constraints on the different states of well-being. This is particularly the case when dealing with basic functionings. For example, all personal evaluations might agree (thus allowing 'complete' ordering) that the well-being of a person with a functioning vector (*ill-nourished, transported*) will be less than one with the vector (*well-nourished, stationary*). A personal evaluation may be 'partial' in the sense that it is unable to pass any judgement on the ordering between some vectors, for example (*well-nourished, being stationary*) and (*moderately nourished, transported*). This 'partial' nature also extends to the minimal constraints that are agreed upon by a group.

Some procedures that allow a partial or, under some conditions, a complete ordering of interpersonal comparisons are as follows:

(1) *Partial ordering.* Two possible procedures are recommended here:

   (a) Dominance partial ordering: here an individual may be considered better than another if the value for one of the functionings in the functioning vector is higher than that of the other, provided the value of none of the remaining functionings is lower, which is similar to a Pareto criterion. Although this method does not rank all individuals in relation to each other, it can be useful to some extent and is recommended by Sen as a plausible approach for limited interpersonal comparisons. For an example see Table 3.3.

Table 3.3: Dominance partial ordering

Individuals	Functioning		
	'Being healthy' *days well previous year* *(maximum: 365)*	*'Being educated'* *level of education* *(maximum: 12)*	*'Being nourished'* *mid-arm circumference* *(maximum: 8)*
A	360	8	4
B	330	6	4
C	365	7	5

Assessed on the basis of dominance ordering, both A and C rank higher than B; but A and C cannot be ranked against each other. That is, all we can say is that the well-being of A and C are higher than that of B; no conclusions are made on the comparative well-beings of A and C.

(b) Sequential dominance: This technique has been used by Atkinson and Bourgignon (1987) and Jenkins and Lambert (1993) for the comparison of income distributions when family needs differ. Although these empirical applications have focused on the space that includes income and needs, Brandolini and D'Alessio (1998) suggest that the technique might also be used to obtain partial orderings within the capabilities framework.

(2) *Complete ordering.* If a complete ordering is required, some decision will have to be taken on the extent to which each functioning is important.[11] Conflicts can arise when subjectively deciding on weights. While being nourished may be considered most important (and therefore worthy of a higher weight) by some individual, being housed may be regarded as more essential by another. Listed below are some methods suggested by Martinetti (1994), Chakraborty (1996) and Brandolini and D'Alessio (1998), as being useful to decide on weights to be allotted:

(i) The choice is made by the investigator or decision-maker and reflects his/her preference system.

(ii) A weighting system that reflects the value system prevailing in the society under consideration is used. In a small enough group, participatory techniques too could possibly be of use to arrive at a consensus.

(iii) Data-driven methods which are independent of any value judgement have been used. Possibilities are the use of standard statistical techniques like Principal Component Analysis or Factor Analysis to derive the relative weights.[12] Alternatively, a weighting system that is based on observations of the data can be used, so that the weights are decided based on the relative frequencies of the attributes in the data. Martinetti (1994) gives the example of an individual lacking a widely available facility like a lavatory as opposed to a television set, which many people may not have. Lacking a toilet would then be given a higher weight than not owning a television set.

(iv) An equal weighting system is used where the same weight is attached to each functioning. This can be viewed as being adopted to reduce interference at the minimum, or when there is no consensus view (Brandolini and D'Alessio 1998).

If we take the weights as given (i.e. any one of the methods suggested above is used to decide on the weights), methods suggested in the literature for interpersonal comparisons to assess overall well-being and allowing complete ordering are the following:

(a) *Borda rule ranking*: The Borda rule uses ordinal information, in the form of rank order positions (for an application to international comparisons of poverty, see Qizilbash 1998). Thus, each of the N individuals to be compared are ranked with regard to the values for each individual functioning, such that the alternative with least well-being scores 1 and the one with most well-being scores N. For each individual, the rank order positions for each functioning are added to give the Borda score. The individuals are then ranked according to the score with the lowest scoring 1 and highest N. If two individuals tie they are given the same number, and the rank given to the next score is one higher to account for the replication. The advantage this has over the dominance ranking is that it can give a complete ordering, although it only allows for ordinal comparisons.[13]

Considering the same example as in Table 3.3, values for three functionings, assumed to be of equal weight are given in Table 3.4.

Table 3.4: Borda rank

Individuals	'Being healthy' Rank	'Being educated' Rank	'Being nourished' Rank	Total Rank value	Borda Rank
A	2	3	1	6	2
B	1	1	1	3	1
C	3	2	3	8	3

According to the Borda rank, the well-being of C is highest, followed by A and finally by B. However, we cannot determine whether the difference in well-beings of C and A is the same as that between A and B.

(b) *Composite index*: The values for the different functionings are combined to give a scalar measure, which is then used to make the interpersonal comparisons. The advantage this has over the Borda ranking method, which only allows ordinal comparisons to be made, is that it also gives an indication of the extent by which an individual's well-being is higher or lower than another.

When indicators of different dimensions are combined together to develop a scalar measure, the different measurement units have first got to be standardised. The possible solutions are detailed in Brandolini and D'Alessio (1998).

The same example used in Tables 3.3 and 3.4 is used in Table 3.5 to perform interpersonal comparisons of well-being using a composite index. The composite index has been constructed based on the fuzzy set methodology.[14]

The three functionings are assumed to be of equal weight for each of the three individuals. The entries here are 'normalised' versions of those in Table 3.3 (denoting the fraction of the maximum value attained). The composite index – here simply the arithmetic mean – assigns the highest well-being to C, followed by A and then by B. Unlike the Borda rank, it is evident that the difference between C and A is much smaller than between A and B.

Comparisons that are made using scalar measures of well-being have, however, been criticised for concealing more than they reveal. A simple example would be that of an individual considered the best with regard to his or her overall well-being. It may, however, be possible that the individual performs very poorly on one of the functionings and this information would be disregarded (in the example here, this

Table 3.5: Composite index (based on fuzzy set methodology)

Individuals	'Being healthy' (normalised value)	'Being educated' (normalised value)	'Being nourished' (normalised value)	Composite index (arithmetic mean)
A	0.99	0.67	0.50	0.72
B	0.90	0.50	0.50	0.63
C	1.00	0.58	0.62	0.73

would correspond to the variance in the normalised entries). Therefore, whenever an interpersonal comparison of overall well-being is done, it is important to present information about the component functionings as well.

To sum up Section 3.3.3, interpersonal comparison of single functionings is easier to perform than that of 'functioning vectors' which include more than one functioning. Methods have been suggested in the literature which allow partial or complete ordering. Developing a composite index of the different functionings in the 'functioning vector' makes interpersonal comparisons amenable to complete ordering (for example with the Human Development Index). Such composite indices can, however, conceal a lot of information. It is thus necessary to present data on individual functionings together with the composite index.

3.4   Conclusion

The main features of the capability approach and its implementation in the context of poverty analysis have been discussed in this chapter. Review of the literature suggests that practical considerations usually restrict evaluation to the 'functionings' that have been achieved, rather than covering the capability set. This is especially the case for poverty analyses in developing countries, where the notion of 'refined functionings' or 'freedom to choose' would not be a very meaningful exercise in the context of the assessment of basic capabilities.

A comparison of lists of 'basic' capabilities developed by different researchers using differing methodologies indicates that capabilities related to health, nutrition and education consistently appear in all the lists, despite the different criteria for inclusion, reflecting their importance for any investigation of poverty. Further, most empirical studies using the capability approach to poverty analysis have also explored basic functionings related to health, nutrition and education.

In the comparative study between the four different approaches to poverty analysis that we explore in this book, we propose comparing empirical results between commonly employed methods of implementation of each of the approaches. Thus with regard to the capability approach, based on the theoretical and empirical work discussed in this chapter, we propose assessing basic functionings related to health, nutrition and education. Further details on the indicators used and the methodology adapted for the interpersonal comparisons of well-being are given in Chapter 6, the empirical results chapter for India.

Notes

1. Other ethical theories dealing with the question of inequality in spaces other than utility and commodities also exist, e.g. Nozick's 'entitlement theory' and Dworkin's 'liberal conception of equality'.
2. For simplicity, in the example used here, the commodity vector has only two commodities, each with only one characteristic. The commodity vector for any individual would, however, include all the commodities in the set the person has access to. The corresponding commodity characteristic vector would be quite large and would include all the characteristics of each of these commodities. The corresponding set of functioning vectors that are possible based on the different utilisations of the commodity characteristic vector would also, in reality, therefore be correspondingly large, rather than comprising just two functionings as shown in the example.
3. Two individuals with the same capability sets could end up choosing different functioning vectors, while two individuals with different capability sets could choose the same functioning vector.
4. This chapter is concerned with issues related to the implementation of the capabilities approach. For issues related to its conceptualisation see Muellbauer (1987), Kanbur (1987), Williams (1987), Crocker (1992, 1995), Cohen (1993) and Qizilbash (1998) amongst others.
5. Alternative ways of implementing the capabilities approach have been attempted. One of these involves supplementing traditionally used measures of poverty in the income space with either information on functionings themselves or variables which may be considered instrumental in the determination of the capability set. This could be seen as a way of enriching the overall understanding of the prevailing poverty or inequality. The measures developed by the UNDP in its *Human Development Report*, particularly the Human Development Index, can be seen as an implementation of such a suggestion. The indicator 'per capita income adjusted for purchasing power parity' (as a measure of access to resources to enable a decent living standard) is combined with the indicator 'life expectancy at birth' (to measure the functioning 'being healthy') and the indicators 'adult literacy' and 'average primary, secondary and tertiary enrolment' (to measure the functioning 'being educated'). Normalised values for indicators are obtained and averaged to give the Human Development Index.

   Another suggestion on implementation of the capabilities approach involves evaluation in the income space itself. Individual specific income lines are obtained, taking into account each individual's respective conversion ability. Sen (1993) suggests that different amounts of income may be required for different individuals (or communities) to reach the same levels of capabilities, given differences in their social and personal characteristics. Income lines may therefore be adjusted taking these differences in conversion ability into account. Sen (1997) gives the example of adjusting the income level of a family downwards by illiteracy and upwards by high levels of education so that they become 'equivalent' in terms of capability achievement.

   Since our intention, however, is to compare the capability approach, in the manner it is commonly implemented, with other approaches to poverty analysis, we decided not to combine an assessment with incomes, as in most practical implementations of the capability approach, this has not been done.

6. Note that if choosing itself is regarded as a valuable functioning, then choice becomes *one* of a number of valuable functionings while if one looks at capabilities, choice is a more fundamental element.

7. Thus, for example, the work of Maslow, Max-Neef and Finnis amongst others is not discussed. Inclusion does not, however, suggest an agreement with the research. A critical assessment of the included work is beyond the scope of this chapter.

8. Sen (1994), however, suggests that the basic needs approach may be seen as incorporating some notion of freedom since the person is left free to decide what to do with the opportunity provided by the possession of the basic goods and services.

9. As Sen (1987) defines it in this specialised sense, 'living standard' is a narrow notion, taken to relate to the individual while 'well-being' is broader including 'sympathy' for other individuals. For instance, it may be possible for somebody to feel sorry for another individual, and thus reduce their well-being, without in any way reducing their living standard. In empirical work, assessment of well-being would be more difficult than that of the living standard. It could involve psychological assessments. Besides, in the policy-oriented context, it gives rise to additional risks of paternalism and increased difficulty in reaching a consensus on the pertinent functionings (Brandolini and D'Alessio 1998).

10. The Human Poverty Index was designed to focus on deprivation in three essential dimensions of human life: longevity (or 'being healthy') represented by the percentage of people expected to die before age 40; knowledge (or 'being educated') measured by the percentage of adults who are illiterate; and access to resources to enable a decent living standard. The third dimension is itself measured using a composite of three variables, namely the percentage of people with access to health services, the percentage of people with access to safe water and the percentage of malnourished children under five. Details of the Human Poverty Index can be obtained from technical notes 1 and 2 in the UNDP's *Human Development Report* for 1997.

11. An implicit valuation has already been done in some sense when certain functionings are selected over others for investigation.

12. A detailed explanation of these procedures can be found in the Statsoft electronic textbook (1984–2001) as in other major statistical textbooks.

13. Further, it is of use only when there is a consensus on the weights to be used for the individual components. If it is not possible to achieve a consensus on the weights to be applied to the different components, Qizilbash (1998) proposes the use of a method which combines the 'Borda' score and the 'dominance ranking' which he refers to as the 'intersection Borda ranking'.

14. Here we give an example related to individuals. An example with regard to comparing countries is discussed by Qizilbash (1998). He compares country rankings (based on the UNDP's composite capabilities-based poverty index) when the dominance ranking, Borda rank or intersection Borda rankings are used.

4
Social Exclusion: the Concept and Application to Developing Countries

Ruhi Saith

4.1 Introduction

'Social exclusion' (SE) refers to a state of exclusion from the normal activities of society, and is often of a multidimensional nature, including access to the welfare state, lack of employment, of housing and poor social relationships.

In the nineteenth century, modernisation and industrialisation resulted in a new type of poverty that affected the working class – overcrowding, squalor, poor sanitation, overwork – all contributing to malnutrition, poor physical and mental health and occupation-related illnesses. Various measures – like the enforcement of factory legislation, social insurance, and institutionalisation of industrial relations – were introduced in industrial countries to address this. These measures constituted the origins of the modern welfare state (Bhalla and Lapeyre 1999). The first use of the term 'social exclusion' (attributed to Lenoir) referred to those who were not protected by the welfare state and were considered social misfits (Lenoir 1974). The 'socially excluded' included the mentally and physically handicapped, the aged and invalid, drug users, delinquents, and so on. In the later part of the 1970s and in the 1980s, however, the term 'exclusion' was extended beyond the earlier French definition. In addition to exclusion from the welfare state, the extended version took into account the rising unemployment in Europe and precariousness affecting those who formerly enjoyed secure jobs and associated social networks (Bhalla and Lapeyre 1999). These changes were attributed to globalisation and the new trend to privatisation, deregulation and reduction of public services, a shift towards targeted assistance and deregulation of the labour market. This extended version of the social exclusion approach to addressing socio-economic problems people faced, gradually became popular in other countries in Europe and was adopted by the European Community.[1]

In the sections that follow, definitions and core features of the social exclusion approach are presented first (Section 4.2). This is followed by a discussion of research studies that explore the implementation of social exclusion in industrialised countries (Section 4.3). In Section 4.4, we look at attempts to implement the concept in developing countries. Following a discussion of previous studies, we decide on the methodology to be used by us to compare social exclusion with other approaches to poverty analysis. Some concluding remarks are made in Section 4.5.

4.2   Description of the approach

We do not attempt to develop a new definition of 'social exclusion'. Rather, some definitions that have been proposed are presented (Section 4.2.1) followed by a discussion of the main features of the approach (Section 4.2.2).

4.2.1   Definition

Social exclusion has been defined in European documents such as the 1992 *Second Annual Report* of the European Commission's Observatory on National Policies to Combat Social Exclusion, 'in relation to the social rights of citizens . . . to a certain basic standard of living and to participation in the major social and occupational opportunities of the society' (Gore, with Figueiredo and Rodgers 1995: 2).

Le Grand has argued that the definition should take into consideration the difference between voluntary and non-voluntary exclusion (Burchardt et al. 1999). An individual is defined as being socially excluded, if (a) he or she is geographically resident in a society but (b) for reasons beyond his or her control he or she cannot participate in the normal activities of citizens in that society and (c) he or she would like to so participate. A refinement of Le Grand's definition has been attempted by Barry (1998). Barry suggests that although people's decision of no participation is supposedly voluntary, the decision may in fact often be the result of their perceiving that their participation is not desired in the first place, for instance, blacks not wanting to go to 'whites only' clubs in South Africa during the apartheid regime. Barry thus suggests that groups be considered socially excluded if they are denied the opportunity of participation, whether they actually desire to participate or not.

While appearing quite broad, such definitions implicitly relate to activities and standards considered the norm in industrial societies, like participation in the welfare state or being part of the organised employment force. An examination in Section 4.3 of some of the studies that investigate 'social exclusion' in industrial societies makes this apparent.

4.2.2 Main features of the 'social exclusion' approach

Major characteristics of social exclusion which distinguish it from monetary definitions of poverty, are its multidimensional, relational, relative and dynamic approach, with an emphasis on process as well as outcomes.

Multidimensional

The SE approach arose out of dissatisfaction with the monetary approach to poverty. In industrial countries this seems to have been prompted by the realisation that the problems of people excluded from the social welfare system or secure employment could not be addressed just by monetary compensation. Atkinson (1998), investigating the relationship between income poverty and unemployment in eight European countries in the late 1970s and the 1980s, showed that although there had been a rise in unemployment, it had not been accompanied by a rise in income poverty, except in the UK. It would therefore appear that there was no cause for concern from an income perspective. Governments in Europe were, however, gravely concerned with rising unemployment. It was recognised that employment was not just about income, but also about social networks and a sense of self-worth. It was towards addressing all these aspects (including income and access to state benefits), that the 'social exclusion' concept was directed.

The multidimensional aspect of 'social exclusion' is not just about looking at a number of dimensions individually, but also at the links between them (Clert 1999). The broader concept of 'social exclusion' thus began adding to and sometimes replacing the narrow monetary approach to poverty assessment in Europe. Formulation of poverty alleviation policies was similarly influenced.

Relational

Monetary poverty has traditionally focused primarily on households as a unit, assessing deficiencies in resources at the disposal of the household or the individual. The 'social exclusion' concept shifted the focus to social relationships. The vulnerability of an individual or household to 'social exclusion' is seen to depend not just on their own resources but also on the community resources that they can draw on (Room 1999). Some examples are ties with family members, local traditions of mutual aid, self-help organisations and the state. This has been attributed by some researchers to the different intellectual traditions underlying the two approaches (Room 1999; de Haan 1999). Research on poverty having its roots in Anglo-Saxon – specifically British – thought in the nineteenth century (Booth 1887; Rowntree 1902; and more recently Townsend 1979) was associated with a liberal view of society, which viewed individuals as producers or consumers, as the basic unit of interest. The market governing the economy consists of free individuals volun- tarily entering into contracts. In line with this, poverty was therefore viewed as an individual problem (de Haan 1999). In this context, the goal of social policy was primarily to ensure that each person had sufficient resources to be able to survive in such a competitive arena. The notion of 'social exclusion' on the other hand, is rooted in continental – particularly French – discourse. In this case, society is seen 'by intellectual and political elites, as a status hierarchy or as a number of collectives, bound together by sets of mutual rights and obligations which are rooted in some broad moral order' (Room 1999: 169). In this context 'social exclusion' is viewed as the process of becoming detached from the moral order, the task of social policy being to reintegrate people into society.

Relative

'Social exclusion' by definition involves the 'exclusion' of people from a particular society. One cannot therefore explore whether people are socially excluded in isolation but must look at their circumstances in the context of the rest of the society they live in, to judge whether a person is excluded or not (Atkinson 1998). 'Social exclusion' thus essentially incorporates a relative element, in contrast to monetary poverty, which may be defined in absolute or relative terms.[2]

Dynamic

Most early poverty studies both in industrial and in developing countries were largely static, relating to 'outcomes'. In parallel with the recognition of the multidimensional nature of poverty, however, the importance of the time dimension became obvious. With implementation of the social exclusion approach in Europe, studies were directed towards investigat- ing long-term unemployment and prospects over longer time frames. People are considered 'excluded', not just because they do not have a current job or income, but also because they have few prospects of alter- ing the situation, not only for themselves but also for their children (Atkinson 1998). Atkinson (1998) thus suggests that social exclusion may apply across generations for the future. The recent focus on chronic poverty with regard to developing countries (*Chronic Poverty Report, 2004–2005*) has also helped take into account long-term changes.

Emphasis on process

Poverty alleviation policies based on the monetary approach have generally concentrated on the uplift of targeted groups, rather than on rectifying the processes that have resulted in poverty. The 'social exclusion' approach, however, originated in relation to concerns regarding the welfare state. From the start, the approach was therefore concerned with institutions and their role in the processes leading to poverty, causing a shift in emphasis from outcomes to processes. It is suggested in the literature that adopting the concept of social exclusion shifts the emphasis from outcomes to that of processes and 'causal analysis of various paths into and out of poverty, getting beyond the unhelpful lumping together of diverse categories of people as "the poor" ' (Gore and Figueiredo 1997: 10).

At the European level, the concept of 'social exclusion' has led to an improvement in the conceptual framework underlying the approach to poverty assessment, which had previously concentrated on a static description of income deficiencies. As indicated above, it has prompted the enlargement of analysis and policy in two main directions – namely the encompassing of a multidimensional set of living conditions and a focus on the dynamics and processes leading to poverty or deprivation (Berghman 1995). Around the same time as SE was taken up in Europe, in developing countries, different concepts like basic needs, entitlements, capabilities, vulnerability and human development emerged. These too have had the impact of widening the scope of poverty assessment and poverty alleviation policies beyond a narrow monetary base. In social exclusion, however, investigating the process of exclusion is inherent to the approach. In contrast, studies looking into processes (including structural and institutional constraints) that lead to monetary/capability poverty/chronic poverty/basic needs poverty (Chambers 1992; Harriss 1992; Agarwal 1992; Dhargamwar 1992) have remained incidental to mainstream analyses that focus on outcomes. Taking note of the emphasis on process and structures in the 'social exclusion' approach might well help correct this.

4.3   Research studies in industrial countries

In this section some empirical explorations of the 'social exclusion' concept in industrial countries, which help to illuminate its definition and interpretation, are reviewed. Most take employment status as a starting point.

Correlations between employment or unemployment status and exclusion along a number of dimensions are then investigated.

Whelan and Whelan (1995) distinguish between three classes (based on occupation) – the middle class, the non-marginalised working class, and the marginalised working class (these are people who are unemployed) – and focus on looking at the impact of labour market marginalisation. They examine correlations between class and income, savings, house value, deprivation of basic items (like food, clothes and heat), secondary deprivation (involving absence of items like car, telephone or participation in leisure activities), and housing deprivation (involving absence of items relating to housing quality and facilities). Their findings indicate that households exposed to labour market marginalisation are associated with the lowest levels of income, savings and net housing values and the highest levels of primary, secondary and housing deprivation. The non-marginalised working class does better in all respects though lagging behind the middle class. Whelan and Whelan also examine the relationship between belonging to one of these classes and certain aspects of physical and mental health. They note that it is possible that with regard to health relationships, the direction of causality may run from ill-health to marginality and exclusion. The marginalised group is found to have higher psychological distress compared with the non-marginalised working class who fare less well in turn than the middle class. The incidence of self-reported physical illness was found to be markedly lower amongst middle-class people compared to working-class people (irrespective of their labour market marginalisation). The authors suggest, however, that the influence of marginalisation (if any) on physical ill-health would be likely to occur over a longer time period than in relation to psychological distress, and suggest that marginalisation would be likely to contribute to physical health inequalities in future generations.

Paugam (1995) conducted an analysis on data for France, to identify the group with the highest accumulation of social disadvantages and therefore most likely to spiral into 'social exclusion'. Again as its starting point, this study used five groups based on their employment status and looked at the relationship between individuals in each group and their conjugal relationship, income and social life. The analysis suggests that even amongst those with stable jobs, there are small percentages (about 3 per cent) of individuals who are in poverty with regard to income and social relationships. Such individuals would thus be vulnerable to 'social exclusion' on losing their jobs. The percentage increases to around 22 per cent amongst those who are unemployed. Even this group, however, has people who are not in monetary poverty or poverty of social relationships, despite not having a job.

In a comparative research project covering seven Western European countries, Paugam (1996) similarly looks at the relationship between precariousness in the labour market (defined as unemployment or lack of job security) and a range of indicators that reflect social links, material poverty and other forms of social disadvantage (like dependence on welfare and ill-health). Precariousness in the labour market was found to be correlated with marital problems, low incomes, poor housing conditions, increased dependence on state welfare benefits, and increased risk of health problems in all seven countries. While precariousness was associated with impoverished social relationships in France, Germany and Great Britain (the three largest industrial countries) it was not significantly correlated with weak family connections and the absence of private support networks in Spain, the Netherlands and Denmark. In fact, in Italy social relationships were found to be stronger. The author suggests that here (especially in the South) the unemployed participate in the black market and are thus able to remain fully integrated within the social system.

In their empirical study, Burchardt et al. (1999) define exclusion in relation to lack of participation in what would be considered 'normal activities' for the society under study (Britain) for that particular time period (1991–5). They go on to identify five dimensions, which they consider as representing the normal activities in which it is most important that individuals participate. These are (a) consumption activity (being able to consume, at least up to some minimum level, goods and services considered normal for that society); (b) savings activity (accumulating savings, pension entitlements or owning property); (c) production activity (engaging in economically or socially valued activities like paid work, education or training; retirement if over state pension age; or looking after a family); (d) political activity (including voting, membership of political parties and of national or local campaigning groups); and (e) social activity (social interaction with family or friends and identification with a cultural group or community). Exclusion from each dimension is assessed separately and the authors point to the absence of a distinct group of 'socially excluded' individuals. Few individuals were found to be excluded on all dimensions in any one year and even fewer were identified as having experienced multiple exclusion for the whole period under study.

Jonsson (1999) explores the implications of the 'social exclusion' concept for gender. The author argues that if state benefits are linked to the labour market (as in Germany or France) or linked to means testing (as in the US or UK) rather than being linked to citizenship (as in Scandinavian countries), then women by virtue of the gendered divisions of labour (being more involved in unpaid work at home, more part time work, etc.) would be more likely to be socially excluded.

As the above studies indicate, in industrial countries, patterns of social integration are institutionalised and fairly clearly defined and 'social exclusion' applies to those outside accepted norms. Exclusion from participation in society is associated, for example, with loss of rights associated with work and the welfare state, long-term unemployment, breakdown of social ties and disaffiliation (Gore and Figueiredo 1997). The excluded are a minor proportion of the population.

4.4 Application to developing countries

The concept of 'social exclusion' has gradually diffused from the North to the South mainly through the efforts of United Nations agencies like the ILO, UNDP, UNESCO, UNRISD, WHO and UNHCS (Clert 1999). Most active was the International Institute of Labour Studies (attached to the ILO), which carried out considerable conceptual and empirical background work on the concept in relation to developing countries, in preparation for the World Social Summit held in Copenhagen in 1995.

In many developing countries, however, due to structural heterogeneity, defining what is 'normal' may not be that simple. It is questionable whether the concept of 'social exclusion' as developed originally in industrial countries can be applied in developing countries. Besides, in developed countries social exclusion is often seen as a phenomenon affecting people who previously had a good standard of living. In contrast, in developing countries in many instances, many people have never had an acceptable standard of living. The discussion here therefore may have to begin right from the point of defining a basic standard of living (Câmara et al. 2004). Possible ways of operationalising the concept in developing countries are discussed below.

4.4.1 Exclusion from the welfare state

There are many differences in the political histories, magnitude of insecurity, administrative resources, and budget constraints in developing countries, compared to industrial countries. Given these differences, very few social security measures exist comparable to those in developed countries. Consider for instance the provision of income support of the kind given through the social security system in developed countries.

If attempted in developing countries, such support is likely to have to be given to over half the population in many countries as compared to about 10–15 per cent of the population in industrial countries. This would require 'an incomparably higher level of fiscal commitment in relation to resources' (Osmani 1991: 305). Further, in situations where poor food and hygiene predispose people to frequent illness, sickness insurance schemes may well 'turn out to be an actuarial disaster' (Osmani 1991: 305).

Of the social security schemes that exist, despite enabling legislation coverage is very low: state support for the infirm and disabled is negligible; education support is limited and does not usually extend beyond primary school; state pensions cover a minority; and health care which, although subsidised, is spread very thinly and haphazardly (Burgess and Stern 1991). People identified in developing countries as being 'socially excluded' on the basis of exclusion from social security measures would thus include the majority of the population. Given the lack of a well-formed welfare state, applying the concept of 'social exclusion' in terms of lack of access to the welfare state, as it was developed originally, would mean defining the majority as socially excluded, rather than a minority, which does not make much sense.

4.4.2 Exclusion from promotive social security

Given the lack of a well-developed welfare state, a second option is to explore 'social exclusion' in the context of social security schemes as they have emerged in developing countries in response to the specific circumstances and particular problems that exist there.

In developed countries, social security is generally seen in terms of specific programmes (Burgess and Stern 1991; Atkinson and Hills 1991). These involve social assistance (designed to relieve poverty), social insurance (concerned with providing security and spreading income over the life-cycle), and categorical transfers (directed to redistribution). Social security relies on two key assumptions, viz. 'a legitimated state and a pervasive labour market as the basis for most people's livelihoods' (Wood 2001: 1). Supporting assumptions are the existence of sophisticated and regulated financial markets which enable strong links to be established between the state and the market to support sectors and institutions concerned with savings, pensions and insurance (Wood 2001). Drèze and Sen (1991) suggest that social security in developing countries, in contrast, is not just a matter of state activity but includes activism of the public, non-governmental organisations, and social, political and humanitarian institutions. They distinguish between protective and promotive security. The former is taken to include measures concerned with the protection of living standards from serious decline (for instance by prevention of famines). The latter includes measures concerned with the promotion and enhancing of normal living conditions. These deal, for example, with regular and persistent deprivation like endemic hunger or rampant morbidity. Promotive social security could thus be seen as being in spirit similar to social security schemes that exist in industrial countries. Given this broad definition of social security, it would be quite difficult to identify individuals who do or do not benefit. Drèze and Sen (1991) thus suggest judging the efficacy of social security in terms of the effect such schemes have on the lives that people are able to lead. They propose assessing this effect by looking at the fulfilment of 'capabilities' of people (for details on the capabilities approach see Chapter 3 in this book). Similarly, Burgess and Stern (1991) argue that in developing countries, a definition of social security based on state programmes would be too narrow and should also include contributions of the household and community. They thus suggest the desirability of a broader approach to looking at social security centred on objectives rather than just government means. They define the objective of social security as being 'the prevention, by social means, of very low standards of living irrespective of whether these are the results of chronic deprivation or temporary adversity' (1991: 43). While they do not suggest that means are unimportant, they propose placing emphasis on outcomes instead.

Under such a broad interpretation of social security, individuals who do not achieve certain minimal standards of functionings related to health, nutrition and education (as suggested by Drèze and Sen 1991 and Burgess and Stern 1991), could thus be considered 'socially excluded'. This approach then becomes very similar to the capability approach to poverty (see Chapter 3). Such studies assessing indicators of health, nutrition and education have in fact been carried out in developing countries, though not under the rubric of 'social exclusion' (e.g. Drèze and Sen's monograph on India, 1995).

4.4.3   Exclusion as defined in relation to employment

Another possibility is to define 'exclusion' in relation to employment status. This would be similar to the methodology of many of the studies of developed countries where it has been recognised that employment is not just about income, but also about social networks and a sense of self-worth, both of which atrophy with long-term unemployment.

Using employment status to classify individuals as 'socially excluded' in developing countries is fraught with problems, however, as the percentage of the population engaged in the organised sector is a minority.

In India for example, according to the National Sample Survey data for 1987–8, of all those classified as employed, only 14 per cent were regular employees with a regular salary and various perks and privileges. Others were either casual labourers or self-employed, with all the 'attendant uncertainties it would entail on their livelihoods' (Nayak 1994). Citing more recent data for India, Sinha et al. (2004) mention that around 88 per cent of the working population in India is comprised of informal workers. Using the developed country criterion of employment would thus result in the majority of the population being classified as unemployed and 'socially excluded'.

More fundamentally in rural economies, seasonally determined irregular employment as well as casual employment may well be considered the norm. It is not clear that such individuals classified by developed country standards as unemployed or underemployed could, by virtue of that fact alone, be considered as being excluded from the usual activities of the society they live in and therefore, as being 'socially excluded'.

4.4.4 Concepts paralleling 'social exclusion'

Because of the absence of both the welfare state and pervasive formalised labour markets, attempts to apply SE using European criteria are problematic. Therefore attempts to implement 'social exclusion' in developing countries have modified criteria for application of the concept in a variety of ways.

These can be broadly divided into two categories: first, using a predetermined set of criteria (e.g. political rights or basic welfare) to identify those who are excluded and secondly, classifying a group a priori as being socially excluded (e.g. scheduled castes in India) followed by an investigation of the possible dimensions of exclusion that they may face. Some studies belonging to each of these two groups are noted below.

(a) Use of a predetermined set of exclusion criteria

Appasamy et al. (1996), in an ILO study on India, define social exclusion in terms of exclusion from basic welfare rights. They concentrate on the dimensions of health, education, housing, water supply, sanitation and social security. Attempts are made to identify percentages of individuals with no access/inadequate access to each of these rights. The analysis is disaggregated by state, location (urban and rural), gender, age, income level, asset-base, religion and caste. The conclusion of the authors is that a large proportion of the Indian population is excluded from the minimum welfare services defined in the paper. This makes exclusion the norm rather than the exception. Exclusion can assume various forms: there may be overt denial of access (e.g. to certain caste groups) or provision of low quality facilities. Access may be restricted to those who are formally employed or there may be some minimum income requirement to gain access to services. Assessing exclusion in Brazil, Câmara et al. (2004) view exclusion through the lens of a basic standard of living. They develop a social inclusion/exclusion index which comprises four dimensions: autonomy, life quality, human development and equality. Each dimension has a range of minus one (total exclusion) to plus one (total inclusion). A set of variables obtained through censuses and surveys (extending from 1987 to 1999) in São Paolo, in Brazil, are used to capture each dimension. Rather than concentrating on individual deprivations, however, the authors identify particular geographical areas of social exclusion within São Paolo, using spatial analysis techniques.

Nayak (1994) focuses in India on (i) exclusion from basic goods due to (monetary) poverty; (ii) exclusion from employment – including a discussion of the difficulties in conceptualising employment as in the developed countries; (iii) exclusion from rights – particularly the right to a secure childhood in the context of child labour; and (iv) exclusion on the basis of caste which the author recognises as an exclusionary dimension of central importance in India. Having documented these four types of exclusion, Nayak concludes by stressing the value of the social exclusion approach in capturing processes by which individuals/groups are not only excluded from a basic standard of living but also from political and economic decision-making, and from social security. The author believes this justifies policies to promote their inclusion even if such policies may exclude those who are relatively better off.

In the ILO study based in Venezuela, Cartaya et al. (1997) map out the main social and political rights and the institutional framework from which these rights have developed. Based on this map, they attempt to identify individuals and groups most likely to be excluded from these rights and describe the processes through which the exclusion occurs. The authors point out that a reconfiguration of the institutional structure wrought by the reforms of the 1990s was generating two opposing tendencies: further deterioration in material conditions but at the same time the re-emergence of autonomous political organisation that might counteract growing exclusion. They did not think it possible at that stage to predict what the net impact of these opposing tendencies would be.

In another ILO study, Figueroa et al. (1996) explore economic, political and cultural exclusion in Peru – identifying groups that suffer exclusion and the process of exclusion. Economic exclusion is explored in terms of exclusion from markets like labour, credit and insurance, which are fundamental for livelihood. Political exclusion includes exclusion from rights like property rights, social protection rights, and basic public services (health, education and justice). Cultural exclusion has mainly to do with membership of social networks. Exclusion in all three aspects is found to be most severe for indigenous Indian populations living in the Andean and Amazonian areas. They also find that similar exclusion is being experienced by some urban populations – especially recent migrants and those displaced by political violence.

The ILO study for Tunisia, by Bedoui and Gouia (1995) used the perceptions of certain groups of people (unemployed people, housewives and working women) to define who they considered socially excluded. They concluded that a range of indicators were required to identify exclusion. Further, exclusion appeared to be defined differently by different people depending on their social status and living conditions. While housewives considered employment the basic factor for integration, working women considered 'social exclusion' as incorporating aspects like literacy, illness and disability. Most unemployed individuals defined exclusion as a lack of income and unemployment, although a significant proportion did not consider being unemployed as being excluded. The responses led the authors to conclude that both employment and a guaranteed income source were important indicators of integration.

(b) A priori classification of a group as being socially excluded

Here, the group that is known to be in danger of 'social exclusion' is identified a priori, on the basis of some known features of the groups. The focus of these studies is on a description of the a priori defined groups, an investigation of the extent to which these groups are actually experiencing multiple deprivations, and an analysis into the processes involved in such deprivations. Examples of such a priori identified groups in the different studies include: (i) rural residents, salaried middle strata (i.e. the mass intellectuals) 'who were in a state of latent unemployment' and long-term unemployed in Russia (Tchernina 1995); (ii) six urban and three rural groups in Tanzania (the former include beggars, stone-crushers, peddlers and street traders, open-air food vendors, casual labourers, and fresh fish dressers, while the latter comprise the landless, near-landless, and those without access to fertilizer) (Tibaijuka and Kaijage 1995); (iii) day labourers, a group called the *Akhadam* (who have physical features resembling the Africans but languages and religious practices the same as the rest of Yemeni society), the returned emigrants of the Gulf war, and inhabitants of remote rural villages in Yemen (Hashem 1995); (iv) groups based on ethnicity in Cameroon (Inack et al. 1995); and (v) women and ethnic minorities as well as hill people, poorly educated farmers, workers in the informal sector, and homeless people living under bridges in Bangkok in the study based in Thailand (Phongpaichit et al. 1995). (vi) A recent report by the World Bank investigates exclusion faced in Colombia, by indigenous peoples and Afro-Colombians (World Bank 2005). Statistical evidence indicated that these groups showed limited participation in education, limited access to public infrastructure and services, high levels of unemployment and employment in low level jobs.

Most of the research in both categories discussed above, although classified under the 'social exclusion' label, is quite similar to earlier multidimensional poverty studies. Poverty research that earlier looked at 'landlessness' now looks at 'exclusion from land'; those that looked at gender, caste or race-based 'discrimination' now look at 'exclusion' on the basis of gender, caste or race; those that looked at 'access' to health, nutrition or education now look at 'exclusion' from basic rights or basic capabilities; studies on 'child labour' are recast as looking at 'exclusion from a secure childhood'; earlier studies on 'income or monetary poverty' are recast as 'exclusion due to poverty'. Thus the concept of 'social exclusion', as it originated in Western Europe although not directly applicable, seems to have played a role in the reopening of old debates and discussions in developing countries under new terminology. It also helps shift the emphasis from assessing outcomes to looking at processes.

Some common ground does of course exist in discussions of social exclusion across developed and developing countries. The debate on social exclusion in China, for example, shows similarities to the concept as understood in Western countries in the context of the welfare state as well as that in developing countries where a majority (rather than a minority) are vulnerable and powerless. Li (2004) identifies four categories of 'social exclusion' in the pre-reform period (1949–78): people who did not benefit from government job and welfare allocations; people who relocated or fell out of structurally recognised categories; exclusion of politically 'bad' people from social rights; and the exclusion of rural residents from urban society. In the post-reform period (post-1978), Li (2004) discusses social exclusion (in terms of lack of protection by the system) faced by people who lost previously held benefits granted by the government. Another category facing exclusion is that of 'rural workers'. These rural to urban migrants are distinguished from other permanent urban residents by registration under the *Hukou* system. Addressing the problems of this underclass would require broader policies supporting active integration, rather than just banning ID checks or removal of the *Hukou* system (Li 2004).

Interesting common ground analysed in developed as well as developing countries in the context of social exclusion and poverty is that of social capital. Exploring anti-poverty policies in the North and South, Mosley and Dowler (2003) discuss the increasing emphasis placed on social capital in research in both hemispheres over the previous decade. Similarly, in an overview of research on social exclusion in developing countries, particularly in Latin America, Bhalla and Lapeyre (2004) also focus on the impact of social capital. The importance of social networks is discussed in the context of 'marginality' which can be compared with the 'underclass' in the United States. With regard to the methodology followed in our empirical work, we used two approaches, both based on methods tried by the ILO. First, as with the ILO study on Tunisia in the first category above, we tried to get community members in Peru to decide on what they considered as socially excluded groups. Second, we followed the ILO procedure of analysing characteristics of groups identified a priori as being in danger of 'social exclusion'. Based on a number of studies on data for India, the scheduled castes and tribes are accepted as being among the main groups in India most deprived and vulnerable to poverty in multiple dimensions. For India, we therefore decided to explore the issue of deprivation in multiple areas for this group of scheduled castes and tribes. For Peru similarly we decided to focus our attention on the indigenous population, who have been identified in a study by Figueroa et al. (1996) as being particularly prone to being 'socially excluded'. We explore the implementation of the social exclusion approach in India and Peru further in Chapters 6 and 7.

4.5 Conclusion

In conclusion, it is apparent from the discussion in the previous sections that poverty analyses in industrial and developing countries have progressed beyond monetary poverty. Given the economic and social differences, however, approaches to poverty have progressed in directions specific to developed countries on the one hand and developing ones on the other. Thus, while in industrial countries the concept of 'social exclusion' related to the welfare state and formal employment has developed, in developing countries concepts related to 'capabilities', basic needs, risk aversion, vulnerability, and sustainable livelihoods have emerged. Attempts have been made to apply the 'social exclusion' concept to developing countries. In the context of the welfare state and formal employment, attempts to modify and apply it have largely resulted in a repetition and relabelling of poverty studies (broader in scope than monetary poverty) that have already been carried out in developing countries. It appears therefore that rather than trying to transplant the concept, it might be worth concentrating on incorporating the advantages of 'social exclusion', like its emphasis on process, into existing frameworks in developing countries.

Notes

1. In the US the term 'underclass' in essence refers to a group of people with similar problems to those referred to by the term 'social exclusion'. In this chapter we restrict ourselves to exploring the approach as implemented in Western Europe and subsequently developing countries. Further, only the use of the concept in academic research is explored. For details on the use of the terms amongst development agencies and non-governmental organisations see Clert (1999).
2. In recent years monetary poverty analysis has progressed beyond absolute measurements with relative monetary poverty lines being regularly used in Europe. Further, it could be argued that, even in its conceptualisation, the monetary approach does incorporate a relative element. See Ruggeri Laderchi (Chapter 2).

5
Participatory Methods in the Analysis of Poverty: a Critical Review

Caterina Ruggeri Laderchi

5.1 Introduction

This chapter reviews and analyses the use of participatory methods in poverty analysis. In contrast to the previous chapters, this chapter will not present one way of conceptualising poverty and then measuring it (what we have labelled an 'approach'), but rather it describes and analyses a set of methods which has entered into the standard toolkit for poverty analysis. We will focus on what these methods can contribute to our understanding of poverty, how the insights they offer differ from those obtained with other methods and how these insights can be integrated into poverty analysis more generally. These methods, in fact, have the potential to contribute unique insights – and have already contributed to a richer understanding of the multidimensional facets of poverty, and especially to the legitimisation of that view. The inclusion of participatory methods in the standard toolkit for poverty analysis, however, cannot escape serious questioning concerning the value of adopting these methods outside the tradition and beyond the purpose for which they were devised. This becomes apparent when analysing their epistemological roots and the way their use has responded to different analytical needs over time. As these methods have been developed with action rather than analysis in mind, their adoption in mainstream poverty analysis has raised concerns among practitioners that this adoption plays only lip-service to true participation and exploits the potential for quick and extractive collection of information. Similarly, concerns have been raised by non-practitioners on the scientific value of the findings offered by these methods.

We will start this brief review of participatory methods in poverty analysis by discussing the concept of participation, its contested meanings and the broad lines which characterise its evolution. These methods have not emerged in a vacuum: their development arises from, and feeds into, the way 'participation' opposed, as well as became part of, mainstream development discourses. And in the process of adoption and mainstreaming, they have largely lost their role in reversing power relations in the analysis of reality and their potential for mutual learning for action. We will then turn to a more focused discussion of participatory methods, highlighting how they have been adopted in poverty analysis, which tools have been used and the insights they provide, as well as the results of recent comparative research. Participatory methods have not been immune to criticisms and we will review the main ones, some of which can be addressed by combining elements of standard survey techniques with participatory methods. The final section will identify key trends and challenges in the use of participatory methods for poverty analysis on the basis of the previous discussion.

Before proceeding, a short warning is needed. Some might object to 'participatory methods in poverty analysis' as a useful analytical category, as the methods are just methods and what is of interest is the framework in which they are used and the methodology which underlies them. In other words, we might be accused of having chosen an angle at once too specific and too heterogeneous. We found, however, that this label was useful to delimit the area we wanted to explore, without undertaking an in-depth exploration of all the other uses and contexts in which participatory methods have been adopted.

5.2   Meanings revisited: the concept of participation[1]

Three big shifts seem to have characterised the debate on participation. In the 1970s 'popular participation' was seen as an important component of rural development and basic needs strategies, and as such figured in the programmatical statements of many international agencies. In the 1980s it became associated with discourses of grassroots self-reliance and self-help, with NGOs often having to fill the void left by a retreating state as a consequence of neo-liberal reforms. The 1990s saw participation being advocated on a larger scale, being moved beyond the boundaries of project or grassroots interventions to other spheres of social, economic and political life. Participation came then to be seen as a tool for important policy objectives such as 'empowerment' and 'good governance', while maintaining, at least in theory, a role as an end in itself.

A comprehensive review of the concept of participation (Cornwall 2000), however, highlights how this reading in terms of 'shifts' hides a number of conflicting views which shaped the way participation was redefined over time, as well as elements of continuity. Three main 'tributaries' to the conceptualisation of participation are identified, and their influence traced throughout its evolution: discourses of participation based on self-determination, those based on efficiency, and those emphasising mutual learning. These three ways of thinking respectively reflect views on participation as a process *by* the people at whom development projects and programmes are aimed, *for* the people (with a development agency taking the initiative and often limiting participation to consultation) or *with* the people.[2]

These different tributaries of participation coexisted, and as participation was translated from the programmatic declarations of the 1970s to practice in the 1980s, the different views were clearly reflected in the *modus operandi* of different agents in their projects. Mainstream development agents like the World Bank designed projects where participation was translated into identifying beneficiaries whose consensus had to be sought by sharing information, and whose resources could be tapped to make the project more efficient. At the same time, many self-development organisations, especially in the South, took up the challenge of developing people's self-awareness and agency through a variety of tools, ranging from visuals to theatre. Interestingly, neo-liberal reforms and the rolling back of the state, together with donor efforts to support NGOs' activities in filling the void in the provision of goods and services, had as byproducts the partial convergence of different actors' ways of operating, as well as the positioning of participation more firmly into mainstream development rhetoric.

This process of mainstreaming did not cover all elements of participation, however. The political emphasis on power relations at the heart of the concept of 'empowerment' was lost in the transposition from the periphery to the centre, and participation became compatible with the overarching market-oriented economic paradigm. At the same time, as some concept of participation (though not necessarily one in which there was a shared understanding) became central, new ways of fostering participation and of engaging in participatory processes were sought. Developments in the techniques used by grassroots organisations as rapid assessment devices in the communities they were working with seemed to provide the answer, as their data gathering nature appeared also able to initiate processes of engagement of community members.

Participatory methods developed in the context of Participatory Rural Appraisal (PRA) therefore became the central tool used by development agencies to embrace participation. While we will look into the methods more carefully in the next section, it is worth concluding this one by pointing out that a difference in understandings of participation and different agendas by different actors continued, and even the adoption of similar methods could not bridge these gaps.[3]

5.3   Ideas and tools: from PRA to participatory poverty analysis

Participatory Rural Appraisal has been defined as 'a growing family of approaches and methods to enable local people to share, enhance and analyze their knowledge of life and conditions, to plan and to act' (Chambers 1994a: 953). It emerged in the early 1990s building on the insights and methodological innovations arising from a variety of sources, including: 'activist participatory research' with its use of 'dialogue and participatory research to enhance people's awareness and confidence' (Chambers 1994a: 954); agroecosystem analysis contributing a series of tools such as diagramming, mapping, scoring and ranking of different actions; the insights provided by the work of applied and development anthropologists; and those of field research in farming systems, emphasising farmers' capabilities of conducting their own analysis; and most notably the developments of Rapid Rural Appraisal (RRA).

RRA had already taken in insights and methods from these other sources, and provided a quick way of gathering information on local realities building from local people's insights. RRA questioned the urban biases implicit in outsiders' role as development consultants (so-called 'development tourism') by giving a more significant role to local knowledge, but nonetheless still elicited for analysis by outsiders. Further, RRA challenged the way knowledge was generated, and responded to the challenges of 'hard science' (McGee 1997) by stressing the two key principles of ' "optimum ignorance" (find out as much as you need to know now) and "appropriate imprecision" (there is no need to know everything exactly)' (Cornwall 2000: para. 4.1). RRA also opened the door to methodological experimentation, appearing in different forms, among which Participatory RRA emerged (ibid.) later developing into PRA.

The core difference between RRA and PRA lies not only in the extent to which local people are included in the research, but also in their ultimate purpose. 'A PRA is intended to enable local people to conduct their own analysis, and often to plan and take action' (Chambers 1994a: 958). By becoming a way in which participation was enacted, the qualitative and often visual tools used in PRA acquired a new and distinctive character. In practice, however, the extent to which these tools effectively brought about participation in all the phases of the project cycle has been questioned, leading to many criticisms from those who sought a radical change in the way development efforts were conducted.

Without dwelling here on the pros and cons of PRA and the way it was implemented, it is important to stress that the flexibility of the methods meant that it was possible to use them within alternative methodologies. Often in practice, therefore, it was their cost effectiveness and the timeliness with which they produced results, rather than their empowering effects, which underpinned the support they were given.[4]

If the widespread adoption of participatory techniques challenged the extent to which their distinguishing features were maintained in practice, further challenges have been posed by the 'scaling up' and the 'scaling out' of PRA from project planning to becoming an input into policy-making. The most evident form of scaling up has been the Participatory Poverty Assessments (PPA) introduced by the World Bank to complement the quantitative analysis of Poverty Assessments, in the face of criticisms of their exclusive money-metric focus. These PPAs have spread rapidly. Interestingly, the use of participatory analysis was seen as only one of the ways in which poverty analysis could become more participatory. In parallel, efforts were made to involve a variety of actors within and outside government in the overall Poverty Assessment process, and in the identification of a policy agenda that the World Bank would then reflect in its lending programme. Such efforts were not always successful, but the case of Peru was seen as one worth emulating as the Poverty Assessment provided supporting analysis for the elaboration of a government strategy which was then fully integrated into the World Bank lending programme (World Bank 1996). Arguably these were only the beginnings of a shift towards a model of working in partnership with the government and local actors that for the World Bank is now epitomised by the Poverty Reduction Strategy Papers (see World Bank 2003 for an overview and an evaluation of the first generation PRSPs).

The process of relying on participatory tools for setting policy priorities has been pushed even further by 'scaling out' participatory analysis with cross-country studies. A major example is the extensive study called *Voices of the Poor* (Narayan et al. 2000), commissioned as background work for the *World Development Report 2000/2001*. From a methodological point of view, introducing a cross-country dimension involves facing new issues of standardisation of the methodology as well as grappling with the need to translate local and contextual findings into broad and encompassing categories.

These new developments have proved controversial. They have been described as ways in which the participatory research agenda has been co-opted for instrumental ends by new converts such as the World Bank (McGee 1997), while the extent to which the consultations ('rapid consultative exercises that deploy a range of qualitative methods to gather people's view', Cornwall 2000: 29) have been participatory and have truly addressed issues of power, allowing local people to take greater control of their realities, has been questioned. Further, trade-offs have been identified between the scale of research and the ability to capture key elements of the local context – which anyway might be hard to respond to for national policy-makers (White and Pettit 2004).

The challenges implicit in this type of scaling up had already been foreseen by those advocating PPAs. In the words of a document which proved very influential in setting PPAs in the World Bank research agenda, 'the scope for, and nature of, participation changes in character when applied in circumstances beyond that of an individual project . . . The challenge in developing methods for participatory poverty analysis involves the adaptation of these "listening devices" to enable local level experiences, perceptions and analyses to speak to the national debate on poverty and social policy' (Norton and Francis 1992: 9).

By delinking participatory techniques from direct involvement with community projects and planning, the road was open for more extractive uses of the PPAs. And indeed the emphasis was initially in providing information which could stimulate better policies. A new generation of PPAs, however, seems now to have taken up the challenge of influencing the policy process (Cornwall 2000). 'A wider spectrum of actors have been drawn into these processes, which place as much emphasis on the impact of their learning on their agency within the policy processes as on the information that is produced' (Cornwall 2000: para. 5.2.2).

In this last decade of rapid expansion in the reach of the language and the tools of participation we therefore also find the conflicts which characterised earlier decades. The dichotomy between an efficiency- and a rights-based argument for participation still remains, as does the debate on how deep is the commitment shown to participation as a legitimate end by those who proclaim it. Further, the above discussion of how the World Bank tried to make its poverty assessments more participatory illustrates how difficult it is to escape the multiple though interlinked meanings of participation. In that case participation was simultaneously seen to mean, on the one hand, PPA and participatory research on poverty, focusing on local communities and their analysis of poverty elicited by outside researchers, and, on the other hand, participatory processes with national institutions and actors (mostly in government) aimed at empowering them to set a common agenda to be supported by an 'outsider' international financial institution. While in what follows we will turn more specifically to the methods adopted by participatory poverty analysis, it is worth underscoring that their application is often in contexts characterised by multiple meanings and conflictual interpretations of participation.

5.4   The methodology of participatory poverty analysis

From a methodological point of view, participatory poverty analysis can be characterised as using contextual methods of analysis (Booth et al. 1998), i.e. data collection methods which (taking a poverty-related definition) 'attempt to understand poverty dimensions within the social, cultural, economic and political environment of a locality' or of a group of people (Booth et al. 1998: 52), by privileging local people's perceptions. Though different research methods can be contextual to different degrees, this categorisation juxtaposes participatory methods with methods which aim to standardise data collection and analysis: for example, large household surveys. This way of classifying approaches offers the advantage of breaking away from the quantitative–qualitative dichotomy which is generally seen as characterising the comparison of survey and participatory data, but which does not consider the potential of obtaining quantitative information from participatory poverty analysis (through rankings for example; other ways of quantifying information are discussed below).

Participatory approaches, however, are not only contextual, they also emphasise poor people's creativity and ability to investigate and analyse their own reality (Chambers 1994a). Therefore, they try not only to understand reality at the local level, but they do so through local people's own analysis. For a researcher this involves not only adopting a set of different tools, but also completely different behaviours and attitudes (Gujit and Braden 1999). By recognising their role as outsiders, researchers need to redefine themselves as facilitators who have to share in local knowledge and be willing to review their own values and perceptions critically. These behavioural elements are central to the success and truthfulness of the exercise, though they are also among the most difficult to standardise and to verify *ex post*, when looking at existing research.

One important challenge to participatory poverty analysis is that the non-extractive nature of the exercise and the effort not to raise expectations that cannot be met is not easy to reconcile with the policy focus of the poverty analysis, when those policies are remote from the local level.

5.4.1   The tools

A variety of tools are used in PRA. A classification into visualised analysis, interviewing and sampling, and group and team dynamic methods has been suggested (Cornwall et al. 1993, quoted in Estrella and Gaventa 1998). Examples include: participatory mapping and modelling (people are asked for example to make maps or three-dimensional representations of their social, demographic and health environment); time lines and trend and change analysis (describing changes in land use, changes in cropping patterns, chronologies of events relevant to local life); seasonal calendars (describing seasonal variations in activities, diet, labour, expenditure, debts); wealth and well-being grouping and rankings (by categorising households or individuals the poorest are identified by locally perceived well-being indicators, and often as a byproduct a wealth of information on livelihood strategies, assets, access to factors of production is gathered). As the tools of participatory poverty analysis are often adopted in a sequence, the assessment can be tailored appropriately so as to fit the context and the issues to be analysed. Further, different tools are used in order to triangulate (i.e. validating through cross-checking) the results, which might allow different insights to emerge.

The variety of these methods, their focus on well-being indicators which do not need to be brought back to a monetary metric, and their flexibility distinguish them from other methods which elicit self-perception data, either through structured questionnaires (as for example in identifying the minimum level of income necessary for the poverty line, for instance in Pradhan and Ravallion 1998) or through focus groups (e.g. the work done by the New Zealand Poverty Measurement Project, see Stephens et al. 1996).

In performing a PPA, care is needed to choose tools and sequences which are well suited to capture the core elements of deprivation in the specific context and the specific aspects of interest in the assessment. This might imply, for example, adopting different sequences for urban and rural contexts.

As an example of the variety of issues which might be investigated in a PPA, in Table 5.1 we present a description of the issues and methods considered in the World Bank's Zambian PPA in rural areas.

Table 5.1: Issues and methods in the PPA in Zambia (rural areas)

Issues	*Methods*
Perceptions and indicators of wealth, well-being, poverty. Vulnerability, powerlessness, local terminologies and their correspondence with such ideas. Differences in perceptions by gender	Wealth/well-being grouping, for criteria and indicators Social mapping Semi-structured mapping
Perceptions of change over time in welfare, indicators, terms of trade	Timeline (for migration, rural terms of trade, environment, etc.) Income and expenditure patterns trend analysis
Access to services (and usage of services) such as health, education and credit. Preferences – especially where choice between options is possible. Perceptions of services, including views (or awareness) of recent change. Again, different perceptions and values for men and women	Institutional diagramming Semi-structured interviews Trend analysis of services – e.g. health, education, agricultural extension, marketing
Seasonal stress: food security, health, general livelihoods	Seasonal calendar (health, food security, food intake, access to fuel, water, etc.). Comparative seasonal calendars (good years, bad years, average years)
Assets of rural communities (access to services, common property resources, other natural resources)	Resource mapping Focus group discussion Institutional diagramming (Venn/Chapati diagram)
Assets of rural households	Wealth ranking/grouping Livelihood analysis
Coping strategies in times of crisis	Livelihood analysis Semi-structured interviews Ranking exercises
Perceptions of consumption levels in terms of food, clothing, and relation to well-being	Well-being grouping/rankings on expenditure outlets, social mapping Semi-structured interviews
Community-based support mechanisms for the rural poor (community 'safety nets')	Institutional mapping Semi-structured interviews
Long-term environmental trends (for example, declining soil fertility, declining rainfall)	Historical transects Community time lines Resource mapping at different points in time Trend analysis
Role of community institutions in service/infrastructure provision	Institutional mapping Semi-structured interviews

Source: de Graft Agyarko (1997) in IDS (1998).

Looking through the table, two main features stand out: one is the variety of issues discussed and the other is the number of methods suggested for treating every issue. The detailed breakdown shows that different issues can be dealt with jointly or sequentially, which reinforces the importance of careful planning of the sequences to be adopted, not least to avoid repetition which would be time wasting as well as boring for the participants. It is also clear that, though a PPA is meant to inform policies, not all types of poverty-related research would be equally concerned with discussing policy options, especially if the research is unlikely to have a direct bearing on the options available. It could therefore raise expectations which cannot be fulfilled.

5.4.2   The analysis

The final phase of a participatory poverty analysis is the analysis of the outputs – an essential element of the process and a very sensitive one. A well-structured analytical process requires understanding, consensus and action, and it also requires lengthy engagement of the researcher and the community (Gujit and Braden 1999). A subset of individuals might be involved in this stage and this will then also require cross-validation with others and feeding back the results to the community as well as to other final users (in the case of poverty analysis, users involved in poverty reduction policies and strategies).

Analysis entails making sense of all the outputs produced by different groups on different media to arrive at an assessment. Ideally it should be local people themselves who synthesise the results, but this is not necessarily the case. And experience shows that the capacity, or the self-confidence, to perform such an analysis also needs to be built, as the romantic myth of the 'village analyst' might not stand a reality check (Gujit and Braden 1999). It is common that field reports are given back to the community and scrutinised by them. As already discussed, new generations of PPAs are trying to make this 'final phase' the beginning of a process of change in the community and in the way people participate in the policy process, going well beyond the production of one snapshot of poverty at a given point in time.

Understanding how the results are arrived at should be helped by the fact that participatory approaches include the documentation of all the stages of the process. In fact, the documentation of the process might help in understanding features like the interpretation given to quantitative outputs (ordinal or cardinal), or the role played by different groups (whether all have been given the same exercise, whether different people have been asked to synthesise outputs produced by others, etc.).

Furthermore, the practice of participatory methods encourages self-reflective criticism (e.g. McGee 2002), and understanding the interaction between the researchers and the community might help put results in context.

Arguably, documenting the process is rather ineffective as a mechanism to ensure quality – scrupulous and committed researchers will perform and document a process characterised by attentive questioning of their own assumptions, while others will perform all these tasks as steps in a recipe, without the critical awareness which characterises good processes. Further, not unlike the case of long methodological annexes in monetary poverty analysis, it is unlikely that the readers will have much time or expertise to delve into the procedural details, so that the key findings as highlighted by the researchers are the ones which are going to have an impact.

Important challenges to how truly participatory the process is arise in this final phase – the conversion of local reality as analysed by poor people into final reports. And the problems which arise seem to be hard to deal with even when following best practices. Inevitably, every assessment is done for some purpose, and that purpose is likely to be reflected in the elements which are highlighted. And even the more committed and soul-searching of the researchers adopts some criteria to understand the reality she is faced with in order to make sense of its complexity.

A recent analysis of the findings of the first wave of PPA in Africa found these contained certain themes that had not been highlighted in the main overviews of PPA results. However, what is perhaps more striking is what is missing even from this expanded list. There is a range of other issues for poverty analysis that seem important a priori but that are notably absent in the majority of cases. 'There are several possible ways of explaining the particular pattern of emphases and absences in the first round PPAs' (Booth et al. 1998: 67). They cite 'obvious' selectivity at various levels due for example to 'pressures on writers of country synthesis reports to highlight findings that have immediacy for policy makers' (ibid.: 67) or the indirect influence of the strategic policy framework adopted by the World Bank on the way themes were organised.

It is hard to see how PPAs can get away from those kind of constraints, which represent both a natural need of the researchers to refer to some known context and a logical consequence of doing analysis for a particular purpose. Before concluding this section, it is worth noting, as an aside, that the passage quoted above raises an important foundational point: can a truly participatory approach deal with a priori held beliefs? Should it, and if so how much? To give a practical example, should a researcher prompt local people to discuss an issue which they have not mentioned on the basis of some prior held belief that the issue is of importance?

5.5 Insights from participatory poverty analysis

Even if the participatory analysis of poverty does not posit a definition of poverty, its findings often describe a pattern which seems to go beyond the specific context in which they have been undertaken. These include the findings that assessments of well-being are multidimensional, that individuals have complex coping strategies and that their priorities reflect values, preferences and time horizons which are highly context-specific and strongly influenced by social institutions.

Despite the high degree of contextualisation of the findings, general patterns emerge from participatory assessments. A report for the study *Voices of the Poor* summarised the findings from the poverty analysis from 23 countries describing people's perceptions of well-being and ill-being in terms of six dimensions (Narayan et al. 2000: 21): *material well-being*, 'often expressed as having enough'; *bodily well-being*, 'which includes being strong, well and looking good'; *social well-being*, 'including caring for and settling children'; *self-respect, peace and good relations in the family and the community*; *security*, 'including civil peace, a safe and secure environment, personal physical security and confidence in the future'; *freedom of choice and action*, 'including being able to help other people in the community'.

The identification of these dimensions is of interest because it shows that it is possible to extrapolate some general patterns across national studies of poverty. At the same time, other frameworks could have been adopted to summarise the findings, thereby giving a different emphasis to the findings. This indeed raises the issue, discussed in the previous section, of how much this convenient and convincing framework for presenting results truly 'emerges' from the analysis – which is not meant to be a criticism of this specific study, but rather of the whole idea that any interpretation of reality might emerge spontaneously. Having focused attention on the processes by which knowledge is produced, participatory techniques (or at least a certain use of participatory techniques in which local people themselves are not involved in framing the results) cannot now eschew the same scrutiny which they advocate for other sources of knowledge.

It should also be noted that others have tried to build on the insights of participatory poverty analysis to create analytical frameworks.

One such example is the asset framework (Booth et al. 1998), built on a conceptual reorganisation of the findings of the first PPAs on Africa, as well as of other contextually derived evidence. This framework is based on 'the key proposition . . . that the notion of capital is a powerful entry point for causal explanations of poverty. Capital is understood in a broad sense as any "stock" which is capable of being stored, accumulated, exchanged or depleted, and which can be put to work to generate a "flow" of income or other benefits' (Booth et al. 1998: 68). An extremely interesting feature of such an approach is that it can potentially be applied to integrate insights from both contextual and non-contextual methods.

5.6 Comparing poverty analysis

The spread of PPAs and the challenges which they pose to other methods, especially monetary poverty analysis, has meant that quite a lot of attention has been drawn to exploring the differences between methods. Clearly, adopting a broader point of view than the one adopted in monetary assessments leads to a more complex view of poverty. Discrepancies between different types of assessments are often noted – there is a 'trade-off among some poor groups between income and other sources of self-respect' (Shaffer 1996: 33). For example, in a participatory assessment conducted in Armenia, single pensioners were consistently ranked as the poorest in their communities, though their levels of income were not such as to justify it. What the participatory assessment highlighted was rather their sense of isolation within the community itself (Robb 1999).

Even more telling is the comparison of the apparent divergence between the Ugandan PPA (UPPAP) and the findings from household surveys (UNHS) (McGee 2004). The first highlighted poor people's perception of a deterioration in their well-being, while the latter shows a trend of rising consumption per capita over four subsequent years. Apart from the wider set of concerns which are captured by the PPA, and the different time spans to which data refer (with participatory methods recovering information on past decades and household surveys providing a series of snapshots in the 1990s), other important points emerge from the comparison. Rising expectations which characterise poor people's perceptions, as well as the increasing market dependence (often accompanied by liquidation of assets), are found to play an important role in the apparent divergence. This comparison, by pointing out that the data are not intrinsically comparable, helps to provide a more complete picture of deprivation in Uganda with different methods contributing different insights. At the same time, the comparison stresses the importance of some methodological features (for instance the PPA's disaggregation by gender, region, etc. vs. the household level analysis of the household survey; the country-wide representative sample of the household survey vs. the hand-picked choice of districts in the UPPAP to cover a plurality of situations) which have a bearing on the results of the two assessments, and which are a challenge for any comparative study.

Various studies have tried to overcome some of the methodological barriers to comparability and to scrutinise the claim that 'PRA techniques produce very similar quantitative data results to that of standard questionnaires' and that 'they do this in a way that is (i) more cost-effective to funding agencies; (ii) less time-intensive for recipient communities; (iii) more enjoyable for recipient communities (e.g. IIED 1997)' (Davies, et al. 1999: 6). We will take up these claims in turn.

The effective possibility of obtaining quantitative information from participatory assessments affects the extent to which participatory techniques can replace other more mainstream ones. In this respect distinctions are made between different forms of quantitative outputs. Wealth rankings, for example, are often found to result in similar rankings to monetary ones (Scoones 1995). At the same time it is noted that 'A comparison of the different rankings demonstrates the need to carry out several different rankings in order to explore the diversity of local perceptions' (Davies et al. 1999: 77), as 'women rankings' are found to differ the most from those of survey data, pointing to gender as an important axis of difference in that context (with ecological zone, age and ethnicity being suggested as others, possibly more important in other contexts).[5] Further, it is noted that though correlations of rankings might be rather high, the adoption of a single indicator from survey data might not proxy local people's rankings correctly, even when that indicator is one to which local people attach importance. Wealth or well-being evaluation takes into account, in fact, several indicators, with an implicit evaluation of the trade-offs between achievements in one or the other. At the same time, discrepancies might be found between what is assumed by local people and what is happening, as local knowledge of certain issues might be imperfect (discussed further below). In the case in question it was found, for example, that the difference in the rankings of two households depended on an overestimation of the level of remittances they were believed to be receiving.

An interesting feature of wealth rankings is that, since they arrive at some form of ordinal information, their numerical nature is not much disputed.[6] Other quantitative outputs based on attempts to present the information gathered with participatory techniques in a cardinal form have been much more criticised (see more below). In the Zimbabwean study mentioned above, it was found, for example, that 'while some fairly similar results were obtained for some variables, there were some major differences and that for the more quantitative data the PRA information seemed less reliable than the survey and key informant data' (Davies et al. 1999: 24). Interestingly the authors also point to confusion in the standard survey as different types of baskets people produced had been aggregated into one question, while there was a clear gender differentiation in production of different types of baskets. This gender division of labour and the tendency to interview men as household heads resulted in biases in the estimation of income.[7]

As far as cost-effectiveness is concerned, participatory assessments allow the researchers to gather a great deal of information in a relatively short time. Further, participatory methods can be applied to the analysis of issues for which monetary assessments would require a great amount of data. Kozel and Parker (1999), for example, relate that in a large exercise comparing participatory with survey-based assessments the description of better-off households was very similar across the two types of analysis. Participatory analysis, however, also allowed a discussion of dynamic issues, which would have required the availability of panel data in a monetary assessment. These exercises showed that the determinants of improvements in welfare were different from the causes of existing wealth. While landowning people were considered better off, acquisition of land was difficult and it was not seen therefore as a way of improving one's lot.

At the same time, the Zimbabwean study we referred to above also discussed cost-effectiveness, and arrived at the conclusion that 'the community time spent in PRA exercises was very roughly five times greater than that spent in the household survey' (Davies et al. 1999: 27). The authors also recognise, however, that other objectives need to be considered in the selection of methods. If the assessment is part of the preparatory work for a project, for example, participatory techniques, even if more time-intensive, might be chosen as they enhance the degree of community involvement. Further, that study chose to operate groups of rather large size with a consequent increase in the estimated opportunity cost of time spent doing the participatory exercises.

A different issue, also related to time, is that participatory assessments, though more rapid than anthropological techniques, require the researcher to spend some time with a community and to let the views of poor people themselves shape the understanding of poverty. A study comparing targeting criteria based on a traditional survey and participatory assessments of well-being found that survey information was highly deficient. In rural areas, in fact, the income module of the questionnaire proved very deceptive as it only recorded labour income. Participatory assessments, in contrast, were able to identify a variety of livelihood sources (McGee 1999). Such a narrow characterisation of income sources from the traditional survey, however, seems more an example of bad practice – though one which the people responsible for the survey did not seem very keen to address claiming it would further complicate the administration of the questionnaires – than a necessary characteristic of the monetary approach. A general argument on the inflexibility of questionnaires as research tools when compared to participatory techniques, however, seems well founded, and points to the need to base questionnaires on substantial previous knowledge of the environment in which the surveys are to be run.

5.7 Criticisms

In this section we will briefly review the major criticisms which have been raised about participatory techniques in poverty analysis, although we will not deal specifically with some concerns which have been raised by practitioners doing PRA about PPAs, such as the danger of 'scaling up' (both in terms of participatory exercises undertaken and in terms of moving from local assessments to national ones) and the move away from a non-extractive methodology which PPAs might entail.

A first fundamental criticism has already been noted. This refers to the relation between poor people's perceptions and the final output of participatory assessments. The literature on participation refers to 'self-critical epistemological awareness' (Chambers 1997) on the part of the researcher as the crucial element which ensures that the former are translated into the latter. This should ensure that results are questioned and confirmed by triangulation, so that individual perceptions are contextualised. It seems nevertheless that there are elements of inescapable arbitrariness in the process, even when following best practice. Making sense of a complex reality, as revealed by multiple outputs, means that some effort of synthesising and structuring information has to be performed, and these efforts are not value free. It seems therefore that being aware of one's valuational load does not make an assessment value free, only more honest.[8] Rew et al. (2005) document an unsuccessful attempt at informing a large poverty reduction programme in Northern Orissa on the basis of PRA and household survey data. They find that the researchers' implicit assumptions, as well as the donors' agenda, ended up in research outputs which mirrored what the villagers thought the programme could plausibly deliver, as well as in a depiction of reality which fitted with these presumptions. Interestingly they note that even the visual tools adopted reflected the implicit agenda of the researchers (in this case, based on land issues) and contributed to this process of confirming expectations.

Critics of participation have also raised some fundamental concerns about the idea of participation as a decision-making mechanism in general. There are different aspects to this argument. One is that 'Questions about participation cannot avoid the issue of political power, local power, populism and representation. They cannot avoid issues of moral pluralism . . . or cultural diversity' (da Cunha and Junho Pena 1997: 20). Similar concerns with 'the myth of the community' have also been voiced by commentators on participatory techniques. Examples of sources of heterogeneity within the community include age, gender, ethnicity and poverty itself. Improved methods, and ethnographic analysis of every stage of the research process have been suggested as possible solutions (McGee 1997), and indeed proved successful in redesigning the knowledge base at the basis of the project in the Northern Orissa case mentioned above (Rew et al. 2005). Also in India, a review of participatory processes remarked that power relations in the community reinforce social and economic disparities so 'webbed with the social roles that the excluded sections are not even aware that they are being exploited' (Narayanan 2003). Far from offering a learning platform for discussion and negotiation, 'because participation is a social act that springs from a preexisting set of social relations it is more readily applied in situations that condone and reinforce the set of social relations' (da Cunha and Junho Pena 1997: 1). And as the process of constructing 'social knowledge' (Razavi 1998) relies on public and formal events it might be difficult to disentangle the voices of poor people from the influence of existing power structures. From the point of view of research and assessment rather than participatory governance, the issue can be addressed, if not necessarily solved, by appropriate methodological steps – for instance careful selection of group facilitators ensuring that they are aware of local structures while not expressing their own views, group composition and triangulation, by working with other groups and by using different instruments to calibrate the informative value of any given assessment, or to identify whose reality is being counted, in a fashion not dissimilar to what would happen if one was using key informants. Further, important decisions on how to present the research and its aims need to be taken, aiming to prevent participants from seeing the assessment as responding to some special interests (for example those of the people or organisations who have been instrumental in organising a meeting, especially NGOs, donors, etc.). It seems inescapable, however, that if something more than a description of different views is to be arrived at, some interpretation of how the views can be reconciled needs to be performed.

Another kind of criticism is represented by the example of women collectives in Chiapas investing large amounts of money in unproductive investments on the basis of incorrect local knowledge (da Cunha and Junho Pena 1997). What if local people don't have the appropriate local knowledge? Such an example goes right against the fundamental principles of participatory approaches, i.e. that poor people are best able to analyse their own reality. The approach might not reach the 'appropriate' conclusions in rapidly changing conditions (for instance in marginal land subject to population increases and rapid environmental degradation) or in the context of increasingly complex markets. As far as PPAs are concerned, however, it seems hard to see what kind of 'misinformation' could prevent people from identifying their own criteria of well-being or their own descriptions of the dynamics which affect it.

On more technical grounds, participatory techniques do not escape some of the important problems faced by welfare economics in general such as how to make interpersonal comparisons of well-being. 'Determining whether the decision represents the group's best interest is difficult because it requires comparing interpersonal well-being, whether by aggregating preferences or establishing a hierarchy of preferences' (da Cunha and Junho Pena 1997). While this is quite a damning criticism from an economist's point of view, it might be worth remarking that economists themselves adopt concepts (such as social welfare functions or household preferences) which presuppose that those same issues have been resolved, without having specified how. This does not mean, however, that disregard for the difficulties of making interpersonal comparisons should be limitless. For example, attaching a cardinal value to different types of rankings in order to deduce the intensity of the superiority of one option over the other, or the importance of one criterion over the other in determining someone's well-being, seems to be very arbitrary.

Serious concerns can also be raised about the elements that participatory assessments miss structurally. For example, both anthropological studies and participatory ones find that often poor people identify *other* groups as even poorer than themselves. Remarkably, these poorer groups are described in very unfavourable terms, almost as belonging to a subhuman category, and they are 'regarded with mixtures of pity, fear, disgust and hatred' (Narayan et al. 2000: para. 32). At the same time they appear to be excluded from the poverty analysis – possibly because they are cut off from social relations with the rest of society and have fallen out of the reciprocity networks for too long. Nothing, however, is made of this finding,[9] and no explanation is given of why they are not reached by the assessments – while knowledge about them is crucial for designing policies to alleviate the worst forms of poverty.

Further, the narrow contextualisation of participatory assessments may impose limitations, preventing them from capturing a more general picture from which differentiation might emerge. For example, when analysing different kinds of communities, one might not be able to capture the perception of the differences between them, which could be an important component of deprivation when the different communities interact. A case in point is again the unsuccessful research done in Northern Orissa which conflated different tribal groups with very different livelihoods and needs and with a strong social differentiation between them into a single 'Scheduled Caste and Tribes' category.

In conclusion, basing an assessment on participation and consensus, however well any dissent is documented, is effectively built on the idea of finding a shared interpretation of reality. And the way in which consensus is reached and its ability to represent all the views (rather than internalised constraints and lack of real empowerment) can be challenged even when best practice is followed, as there might not be as pervasive a homogeneity as initially assumed. The impossibility of solving some fundamental conflicts, and doubts on whose voices are really heard (especially when there is a risk of overlooking important axes of difference within the community) therefore represent serious challenges to this approach. This, of course, might affect different uses of participatory methods in different ways, depending on the context and the issues considered.

5.8 New frontiers: combined methods

From the debate on PRA new insights have been gained. This has led to questioning the original characterisation of participatory approaches as antithetical to the collection of household survey data. It has also led to attempts to use participatory and non-participatory techniques interactively, exploiting their respective strengths – an agenda now vigorously championed by the Q-squared network, which explores and disseminates research that integrates the two aspects of qualitative and quantitative methods (see Kanbur 2002). Carvalho and White (1997) synthesised the possibilities for such an approach in functional terms as: first, integrating quantitative and qualitative methodologies (for instance using one type of method to identify key categories to be studied with the other, or using insights from one method to inform the sample design to be used with the other method); secondly, examining, explaining, confirming, refuting and/or enriching information from one approach with that from the other; and thirdly, merging the findings from the two approaches into a set of policy recommendations. A three-fold methodological classification has been suggested by Rao and Woolcock (2003): first, *integration in parallel*, in which the quantitative analysis focuses on providing orders of magnitude, providing the 'big picture', and extrapolates to a wider context, while the qualitative analysis illuminates processes, identifies unobservable factors that might plague the quantitative analysis and illustrates details by allowing a closer look at discordant patterns; secondly, *integration in series* with qualitative analysis providing the grounding and contextualisation of the data collection, and with an analysis which is both qualitative and quantitative; and thirdly, *iterative integration* in which 'varying degrees of dialogue between the qualitative and quantitative traditions' are sought.

A Poverty Assessment in Guatemala (Tesliuc and Lindert 2004) provides an example built on the parallel analysis of an integrated household survey to which a risk and vulnerability module had been added and a participatory study of ten villages. While the household survey provided a broad view, particularly of differences between regions and by ethnic group, the participatory study probed into perceptions of exclusion, access to services and household responses to shocks. An example of in series integration is provided by Kozel and Parker (2003) where participatory activities in 30 villages in Uttar Pradesh and north and central Bihar informed and sharpened the design of an integrated household survey in 120 villages (including the 30 on which the participatory activities were undertaken). Findings that emerged from this study included documenting the heterogeneity of the poor with three main categories emerging: the destitute poor who had suffered major negative shocks, the structurally poor whose social identity (especially in terms of caste) prevented them from accessing economic resources, and those that were termed the 'mobile poor' who have more resources than the two other groups and have the potential to escape their poverty. The differences between perceptions of mobility held by the poor and survey findings were also highlighted. Another example of integration in series, which could be labelled as integration in series *ex post* as the two methods did not have to be conceived as part of a whole, is provided by Carter and May (1999), whose identification of households in a large survey was based on a livelihood classification scheme derived from a participatory assessment. Similarly, Scoones (1995: 86) suggested using 'wealth ranking . . . as cost-effective research tool for examining issues of wealth and poverty in rural context, perhaps setting the agenda for subsequent, more detailed and focused studies into particular aspects'.

The development of Q-squared types of methods has also been criticised. First, even its proponents admit that it can be time consuming and costly, as well as suffering from the lack of a natural constituency in one discipline. Secondly, from a methodological point of view, a number of differences including in the well-being measure and the concept of well-being ultimately adopted, as well as in the type of generalisations possible in each method, create obstacles to the integration of the insights emerging from different methods (Shaffer 2002). Finally, and more strictly from the perspective of participatory research, Q-squared methods could be criticised as bringing participatory techniques into the mainstream poverty analysis toolkit, thereby changing their non-extractive nature, making them respond to outsiders' priorities as well as bringing about the danger of a routinisation of the process (Chambers 1994b). This seems, indeed, to have been the case in the Northern Orissa case discussed by Rew et al. (2005). It is undeniable, however, that any method, when adopted as an off-the-shelf solution, without contextualising the analysis and delving deeper into possible incongruences, poses these dangers.

5.9 Conclusions

From the initial programmatic endorsements of participation in the 1970s to the widespread adoption of participatory processes today, intended to initiate a new dynamics of change and empowerment, the language and methods of participation seem to have entered the centre of development thinking and practice. In this chapter, however, we have tried to show that participation is a portmanteau term which covers a number of different things. We discussed this issue both by looking at the concept of participation and the tensions in the way it is conceptualised by different agents, and by discussing the way participatory methods have been used in the analysis of poverty.

The central challenge faced in using participatory methods for poverty analysis is implicit in moving participatory techniques from the project level to policy processes. While in fact there have been examples of Participatory Poverty Analysis which have greatly contributed to the policy debate at the national level, many examples of cosmetic participatory research, performed for extractive purposes and without a commitment to empowering local people to have a greater say in policy processes, can also be found. We also discussed criticisms of a different kind, challenging the idea of participatory methods as accurate and appropriate research tools for poverty analysis. In this context, it is important to consider instances of comparative research adopting different methods of analysis, both participatory and non-participatory, highlighting their relative strengths and weaknesses. In the light of these debates, a move to new and integrated frameworks for the analysis of poverty seems almost inevitable. Such a research agenda has now entered the mainstream of development practice, though close scrutiny of whose voices are being recorded and what it means to be listening are issues which remain central to any future development of these methods.

Notes

1. This section draws greatly and, hopefully not too grossly, on Cornwall (2000), simplifying some of the arguments as they make a necessary backdrop to our subsequent discussion. It is to the original comprehensive and authoritative source that the interested reader is referred for a more in-depth discussion of the concept of participation.

2. More formal analyses of difference within different models of participation have been put forward in various typologies of participation, each pointing to different 'axes' of difference characterising alternative models of participation. Arnstein (1971) considers a 'ladder of participation' graduated by the extent to which citizens have control over decision-making. Pretty (1995) considers instead the different uses for which a development agency can initiate participatory processes. White (1996) considers a more complex set of criteria to categorise participation, including what it means to different agents and what is it for.

3. Arguably, however, the adoption of participatory methods set in motion other processes, creating new spaces for dialogue and participation and transforming behaviours and attitudes of various kinds of actors in unexpected ways. Cornwall (2000) provides a range of examples in this respect.

4. It is worth noting, however, that this view might err somewhat in its optimism on the spread of acceptance of PRA as a 'serious' source of hard evidence on poverty (McGee 1997). The alternative, i.e. the widespread adoption of PRA as an expensive window dressing exercise, cannot be entirely ruled out at least in some instances.

5. Scoones (1995), however, raises some doubts on whether different focus groups for men and women are sufficient to capture the extent of intra-household difference, and more generally on the significance of rankings at the household level whether based on surveys or local people's perceptions.

6. Though of course it can be disputed on ethical grounds whether it is acceptable to ask members of the community to arrive at such ordinal information.

7. On similar lines, in another study on a sample of Zimbabwean households (Scoones 1995) one of the reasons responsible for differences in the wealth rankings between male and female groups was found in women's greater awareness of (and importance given to) cash income sources generated by women.
8. It could also be argued that often not enough emphasis is put on self-critical epistemological awareness to be displayed when letting patterns 'emerge' from all kinds of different results.
9. Thanks to Howard White for drawing our attention to this point.

6
Poverty in India: a Comparison of Different Approaches

Ruhi Saith with contributions from Abhilasha Sharma

6.1 Introduction

In Chapter 1, we compared the theoretical backgrounds to four different approaches to poverty. We saw that the different approaches are based on differing underlying understandings of the space that poverty is to be measured in. Further, they suggest different remedies for poverty alleviation.

In the current chapter and in Chapter 7 this comparison is extended to an empirical analysis, in which individuals identified as being in poverty by the four different approaches are compared. The analysis methodology and results for India are presented in this chapter. Chapter 7 pertains to the empirical analysis for Peru.

Empirical analysis for India was carried out on secondary data (NCAER/UNDP 1994 database) as well as a smaller set of primary data. Section 6.2 contains details of the data used and the methodology of analysis including a discussion of the indicators and thresholds used to define poverty by the different approaches and techniques used for comparison of the groups identified as being 'poor'. In Section 6.3, we present results of analysis of secondary data. Section 6.4 contains details on the collection of the primary data and results of its analysis. The overall findings are summarised in Section 6.5.

6.2 Data and analysis methodology

We first provide details of the data used, followed by a description of the analysis methodology.

6.2.1 Data

As mentioned in Section 6.1, we used secondary data (NCAER/UNDP 1994 data) as well as collecting primary data. The latter were collected from rural and urban locations, conducting a household survey as well as using participatory methods. We were able to use the secondary data to perform country-level comparisons for three of the four approaches (monetary, capabilities and social exclusion). The primary data provided us with information to carry out a comparison across all four approaches, including the participatory one, though on a smaller sample.

Secondary data: Although dated, we used the NCAER/UNDP 1994 multipurpose survey data. This is because our primary research interest is in comparing approaches to poverty analysis across the same data, rather than obtaining snap-shot information on the current poverty status. The information contained in the NCAER/UNDP 1994 database is extensive and pertains to monetary poverty as well as capability (e.g. education and health) and social exclusion (e.g. data on employment status, social welfare schemes, caste) approaches.

The survey was administered to 33 000 rural households, from over 1765 villages and 195 districts in 15 states and the north-eastern region in India (Shariff 1999), between January and June 1994. Most of the information collected pertains to the year before the survey (1993–4). A stratified sample was used for selecting districts from within states and sample households within selected villages (details of stratification in Shariff 1999). We have included weights when analysing this data, so that the sample might be considered nationally representative.[1]

New data: Since the secondary data does not contain information related to the participatory approach, we collected new data so as to have information related to all four approaches on the same sample. The fieldwork to collect this data included household surveys as well as participatory techniques. Field locations were selected from regions in the northern state of Uttar Pradesh, known to have high levels of poverty. The rural location was Sandoli, a village in Baarabanki district, 25 km from Lucknow, and the urban location was a slum, Hatha Sitara Begum, in Lucknow.

It is important to note that the data collected in the fieldwork covers a small population in a single village and a small slum. Thus the comparisons between the four approaches undertaken on these data are less well founded than the findings from the large data sets. Nonetheless, it represents an important component of the research as a whole, as it enables us to contrast findings from participatory data with the other approaches, for the same sample.

6.2.2   Analysis methodology

Our intention is to compare the degree of overlap in poverty identification between the different approaches as commonly implemented.

Table 6.1: Four different approaches to poverty analysis: indicators and thresholds

Approach	Indicator	Threshold
Monetary	• For NCAER/UNDP data: per capita income • For field data: per capita consumption expenditure	Poverty line: The official poverty line for India (adjusted for the year and place), which is linked to the purchase of minimal calorie levels and other essential expenditure, is used
Capabilities: education	• Age >= 7 & <= 14 (child): currently enrolled/literate	Child: 'Poor': If neither currently enrolled in school nor literate 'Non-poor': If either currently enrolled in school or is literate
	• Age >= 15 (adult): literate	Adult: 'Poor': If classified as not being literate 'Non-poor': If classified as being literate
health	• Age <= 12 (child): The indicator is a combination of three anthropometric indices – height for age, weight for height and weight for age	Child: 'Poor': If values for any of the three anthropometric indices are < −2 (< −3 for severe) standard deviations from the NCHS median value 'Non-poor': If values for all three anthropometric indices are >= −2 (>= − 3 for severe) standard deviations from the NCHS median value standard
	• Age >12 & <60 (adult)*: self-reported chronic illness	Adult: 'Poor': If suffering from self-reported chronic illness 'Non-poor': If not suffering from self-reported chronic illness

117

combined	• Age >= 7 & < 60: Indicator obtained by combining the appropriate education and health indicators for different age groups	Poor: If 'poor' in either of health/education 'Very poor': If 'poor' in both of health & education 'Non-poor': If 'non-poor' in both health and education
Social exclusion	• For NCAER/UNDP data: caste • For field data: information obtained by focus group discussions	NCAER/UNDP data: Individuals belonging to scheduled castes/tribes classified as socially excluded Field data: A number of aspects related to social expulsion identified by focus group participants
Participatory	• Information obtained using participatory techniques. For comparison with other approaches, well-being ranking used as an indicator	'Poor': Individuals belonging to households ranked to have low well-being 'Non-poor': Individuals belonging to households ranked to have medium or high well-being

* The terms child and adult used here and throughout this chapter do not correspond to any official classification. Rather, they are used to distinguish between the younger and older age groups for which varying indicators have been used.

This has therefore influenced our choice of indicators and thresholds (Table 6.1). In addition, the choice has also been guided by data availability constraints and input from focus group discussions during the field work.

Monetary approach

As discussed in Chapter 2, the *indicators* commonly used for poverty identification in the monetary approach are per capita income and per capita consumption expenditure. Consumption is, however, often argued to approximate welfare more closely than income (as discussed in Chapter 2).

In our comparative analysis, we use both income and consumption indicators. For analysis of the NCAER/UNDP data which does not contain information on consumption expenditure in a systematically accessible format, we use per capita income. For the new data we collected information which allowed us to calculate per capita consumption expenditure.

As mentioned in Chapter 2, White and Masset (2003) are amongst recent authors who demonstrate the importance of considering household size (to account for economies of scale) and composition (to account for differences in calorie and other requirements of individuals of differing ages, by using adult equivalence scales) when assessing monetary poverty. Since the focus of our study is on the comparison of approaches as commonly implemented, however, we restrict our analysis to the per capita indicators, without accounting for household size or composition.

With regard to the *threshold* for poverty, as mentioned in Chapter 2, most industrial countries use a relative poverty threshold. Here we use the official poverty line for India which, as with most developing countries, is intended to be an absolute threshold. Appropriate values were calculated taking into account prices for the local region and the year for which the data had been collected (Shariff 1999).[2] The poverty line calculated thus ranges from Rs 1954/capita/year for Andhra Pradesh to Rs 2922/capita/year for Kerala. The extreme poverty line was calculated as the average of the per capita income levels of those identified as being below the official per capita poverty line.

Capability approach

As discussed in Chapter 3, an ideal implementation of the capabilities approach involves interpersonal comparison between capability sets. This is because the capability set assesses potential, with the choice of how this potential is exercised being left to the individuals themselves.

Given practical difficulties with obtaining such data however, in practice the comparison is usually carried out between 'chosen functioning vectors'. Further, in developing countries given the fact that even 'basic capabilities' may not be possessed by all individuals, empirical work is often restricted to basic functionings. At the level of some 'basic functionings' – in particular, basic health and nutrition – one can reasonably assume that people who show a shortfall did not have any alternative. For example, the number of people who could afford to eat but were fasting (or on a hunger strike) and thus functionally under-nourished is likely to constitute an insignificant minority. Assessing basic functionings does therefore in an indirect manner reflect the capability set.

An overview, in Chapter 3, of previous theoretical attempts and empirical work suggests that in most studies, education, nutrition and health have been included as 'basic functionings'. In empirical work presented here, we too decided to concentrate on these dimensions. The indicators and thresholds for each of the selected basic functionings are as follows:

(a) *Education*: The following indicators were used depending on the age group. (i) For children aged between 7 and 14, we used a combination of current enrolment and literacy, so as to capture the most elementary levels of education. Using literacy alone would exclude children in lower classes who are not yet literate (but being currently enrolled have the potential to be).[3] Using current enrolment by itself as an indicator of education would exclude children who dropped out with increasing age. If they have, however, received a level of education that conferred basic literacy we consider them as education 'non-poor' despite not being currently enrolled. (ii) For individuals aged 15 or above, we use literacy as an indicator of education.[4]

When interpreting results, we need to be aware that the enrolment indicator could result in overestimation. Although children may be currently enrolled, this does not guarantee attendance.

(b) *Nutrition and health*: For assessment of nutrition and health, indicators used again varied depending on the age group. For the age group below 13, the assessment was based on anthropometric measures.[5] Anthropometric indices reflect the outcome of food intake as well as quality of health-related care and infrastructure (sanitation, drinking water). The indices used were the following: (i) ratio of height for age: if low (stunting), this indicates chronic growth retardation; (ii) weight for height: if low (wasting) this indicates recent or 'acute' growth retardation; and (iii) weight for age ratios: this is a measure of overall nutritional status and if low (underweight) indicates both long-term and recent growth retardation. The references against which these were calculated are the National Council of Health Statistics (NCHS), international reference medians obtained for a group of American children. A Z-score cut-off point of < -2 standard deviations is used to classify those with low values for the indices as suffering from moderate undernutrition and a cut-off point of < -3 standard deviations as suffering from severe undernutrition. The use of such a reference median, however, is controversial.[6] Besides, it is not clear whether a low anthropometric score is a necessary and/or sufficient condition to label an individual as undernourished (Svedberg 1991).[7] An additional limitation to be borne in mind when interpreting the results is that data for severely malnourished children who did not survive would be missing from such an analysis.

We have combined the information from the three anthropometric indices to construct two indicators: (i) undernourished and (ii) severely undernourished. A child is considered undernourished or nutrition-poor if he/she is classified as being either stunted or wasted or underweight (i.e. below 2 standard deviations from the median values for any of these indices). The use of such a comprehensive indicator, taking into account all three conventional indices (i.e. stunting, wasting and underweight), is also recommended by Svedberg (2000). Since the proportion of nutrition-poor in India was found to be more than 70 per cent using the 'undernutrition' indicator, we constructed a severe 'undernutrition' indicator by lowering the threshold. According to this a child is considered severely undernourished if severely stunted/wasted/underweight (i.e. values for any of these three indices are 3 standard deviations below the median). In our discussions for this chapter, we focus on the severely undernourished group. For Peru where undernutrition is less prevalent than in India, the focus in the empirical analysis has been on the undernourished group – see Chapter 7.

We were unable to use an anthropometric indicator (e.g. body mass index, BMI) for the age group above 12 years, as such data were not collected in the NCAER/UNDP 1994 survey. Of the information available, we decided to use 'self-reported chronic illness'.[8] The incidence of chronic illness increases sharply in our data from the age of 60 onwards, suggesting that after this age chronic illness is largely age-related. Thus we used chronic illness as an indicator of health for individuals aged above 12 and below 60. It is important, however, to remember that the indicator used, being self-reported, depends on the levels of education, awareness and perceptions of individuals responding to the question. Besides better access to health services (including diagnostic tests) is associated with higher levels of reported incidence of such illnesses. Further a chronic illness indicator does not distinguish between chronic diseases of affluence and those related to poor sanitation, deficient diet and infections. From the capability point of view, however, it can be argued that health poverty as an outcome is important irrespective of the antecedent causes. As with nutrition, adults who have suffered from the most severe chronic illness resulting in death would be missing from our data. Given the limitations of the self-reported chronic illness indicator, it would be worth exploring the use of BMI in future work.

(c) *Combined capability indicator*: We constructed an indicator that includes both health and education. Using this indicator individuals are classi-fied as follows: (i) poor: if classified 'poor' in *either* education *or* health using the indicators described above; (ii) very poor: if classified 'poor' in education *and* health; and (iii) non-poor: if classified non-poor in both education and health.

Having selected indicators to be used for the monetary and capabilities approaches, the comparison of these indicators across approaches can be carried out in two ways. One is to compare the continuous values of the indicators themselves (e.g. a comparison of incomes, with z values for anthropometric measures). The other is to construct a dichotomous indicator from the continuous values by using a pre-determined cut-off value (e.g. the poverty line for income or consumption expenditure or defining 'x' standard deviations below the median, as cut-off as for nutri-tion indices). Each has its advantages and disadvantages. The former has been criticised as not explicitly focusing on those who are below the 'poverty line' or 'cut-off', and also for the excess weight that would be given to outliers. Moreover, for some indicators in the non-monetary dimensions, e.g. chronic ill health, as defined above, and primary school enrolment or literacy, the only option is to use the dichotomous approach as these are inherently discrete variables. Criticisms of the latter (e.g. by Ravallion 1995) include the fact that by creating dichotomous variables a lot of the underlying information on the indicator is not used. Moreover, the cut-off points can be quite arbitrary. Further, if there is a measurement error in the indicator values, then it is likely to create misclassifications. Most analyses of monetary poverty, however, use a dichotomous approach related to a poverty line, and this is what we have followed in our analysis. Individuals have thus been classified as 'poor' or 'non-poor' with regard to monetary, education and health indi-cators using a pre-defined threshold. Overlaps in poverty identification by using this classification are then examined by the construction

of 2X2 contingency tables which are presented in the results section
(Section 6.3).

Social exclusion approach

As discussed in Chapter 4, in industrialised countries (where the concept
originated), the term 'socially excluded' typically refers to people who
are excluded from the receipt of state benefit or those who are unemployed and thus excluded from what are considered societal norms of
work participation. Problems of defining 'normality' are especially great,
however, in applying the concept to multipolar societies, as in developing countries. Attempts have been made, especially by the International
Labour Organisation (ILO), to develop alternative ways of implementing
the social exclusion approach. In our analysis of social exclusion, we use
two such methods that have been most commonly applied in the
context of developing countries. These methods are:

(a) A priori group identification: In this method, groups that are vulnerable to social exclusion, as suggested by previous research and/or
accepted as such in the society concerned, are identified a priori as
the 'socially excluded' group. Different dimensions of poverty of
these groups are then compared with other groups. With regard to
India, there is definitive research evidence suggesting the role
played by caste in differentiating access and the correlation of caste
with poverty in different dimensions. We therefore decided to
explore the issue of social exclusion by identifying a priori the caste
groups considered vulnerable and then exploring the extent of
monetary and capability poverty amongst individuals belonging to
these groups.
(b) As discussed in Chapter 4, given the high degree of heterogeneity in
non-industrial societies, society-specific characteristics of social
exclusion need to be identified. One way of doing this is by collecting
participatory inputs on what may locally be considered characteristics
of exclusion. Thus, as a second method, we decided to conduct
focus group discussions (FGDs) on the issue during fieldwork with
the intention of using insights from these discussions to decide on
criteria for identification of the 'socially excluded'.

Participatory approach

The methodology followed and the information obtained by the participatory approach as well as the results of fieldwork data analysis are
detailed in Section 6.4. The participatory information was collected

using techniques, such as social mapping and well-being ranking complemented by focus group discussions (the tools and techniques used are largely based on those suggested by Praxis – the Institute for Participatory Practices, Patna Bihar).[9] Well-being ranking allowed us to obtain an ordinal classification of households into different categories of well-being: high, medium and low.

6.3 Results: NCAER/UNDP data

Monetary and capability profiles are presented first (including results of a logit analysis) followed by a comparison of poverty identification by different approaches.

6.3.1 Poverty profiles

Poverty profiles are descriptive, providing details of the proportions of people in different socio-economic groups and the levels of monetary and capability (education and health) poverty within these groups (Table 6.2). The groups analysed here are those that have conventionally been investigated in a number of poverty analyses for India (e.g. Harriss-White et al. 1992). Systematic data related to these groups were also available from the NCAER/UNDP data. These socio-economic groups (elaborated in Table 6.2) include religion, caste, gender, the level of education and the gender of the head of the household the individual belongs to, the literacy level of adults in the household, the size of the household, its dependency ratio, the main household occupation, the land holding status, the region of the country the individual belongs to and the development index of the individual's village.

In Table 6.2, the numbers in the row labelled 'overall %' give the overall percentage of individuals in the population estimated as being in monetary and capability poverty using the indicators and thresholds given in Table 6.1. As indicated in Table 6.2, monetary 'poor' individuals (based on per capita income), were estimated to comprise 38 per cent, while the extremely poor comprise 18 per cent. Amongst adults, education 'poor' individuals (based on literary status) comprise 52 per cent of the population. Twenty-six per cent of children are classified education 'poor' (based on the combined enrolment and literacy indicator). Seven per cent of those in the 13 to 59 year age group are classified chronically ill. Amongst children aged below 13, 70 per cent are classified as being undernourished and 44 per cent as being severely undernourished.

Column 1 in Table 6.2 gives an estimate of the percentage of individuals belonging to the different socio-economic subgroups. With regard to

Table 6.2: Poverty profile

Socio-economic group			Monetary poverty %		Education poverty %		Health poverty %		
			Poor	Extreme poor	Adults	Children	Children Under nutr	Severe	Adults
Overall %			38	18	52	26	70	44	7
Group	Sub-group	Sub-group %							
		(1)	(2)	(3)	(4)	(5)	(6)	(7)	(8)
Religion	Hindu	85	37	17	52	25	70	44	7
	Muslim	10	45	20	55	35	72	47	8
	Christian	2	26	13	22	5	67	44	7
	Other minorities	3	39	20	53	21	63	39	10
Caste	ST	10	47	23	66	37	72	49	7
	SC	20	50	25	65	33	71	46	7
	Non SC/ST	69	33	15	46	22	69	43	7
HH Head Gender	Male	96	38	18	52	26	70	44	7
	Female	4	37	19	51	23	69	43	7
Gender	Male	53	37	17	38	19	71	45	7
	Female	47	39	18	67	33	68	43	7
HH Head Education	Illiterate	48	46	22	78	40	71	46	7
	Primary	25	36	17	32	15	70	43	7
	Middle	23	26	11	25	9	69	43	7
	University	3	12	7	16	4	68	42	6

HH literacy	Both	39	27	12	20	5	68	41	7
	Male	33	39	18	59	25	70	46	7
	Female	3	42	21	58	11	68	41	8
	None	25	52	26	100	53	71	47	8
HH size	Up to 4	19	26	10	56	21	71	46	9
	5 to 7	49	39	18	51	26	70	44	7
	8 and above	32	43	21	50	26	70	45	5
Dependency ratio[1]	0	7	17	6	44	–	–	–	9
	>0 to 0.5	25	29	12	47	21	70	47	7
	>0.5 to 1	33	36	16	52	23	70	44	7
	>1 to 2	28	48	24	59	27	70	44	7
	>2	7	54	31	71	35	69	43	6
HH Occupation[2]	Agr	46	31	15	52	24	70	44	7
	Sal/Prof	14	16	6	31	11	67	42	6
	Wage	24	62	33	69	37	71	46	8
	Other	16	38	14	46	24	71	45	8
Land holding[3]	Marginal	31	45	21	52	26	69	44	7
	Small	19	26	10	50	23	70	44	7
	Medium	11	16	7	47	22	69	44	6
	Large	7	10	5	44	19	67	40	5
	Landless wage	17	66	36	71	37	71	46	8
	Landless other	16	35	14	42	21	72	46	7

Continued

Table 6.2: Continued

Socio-economic group			Monetary poverty %		Education poverty %		Health poverty %		
			Poor	Extreme poor	Adults	Children	Children Under nutr	Severe	Adults
Group	Sub-group	Sub-group %							
Overall %			38	18	52	26	70	44	7
		(1)	(2)	(3)	(4)	(5)	(6)	(7)	(8)
Region[4]	North	5	29	14	47	14	64	38	10
	Central (U)	30	42	20	60	35	73	47	6
	Central (L)	18	42	20	60	33	67	44	8
	East	12	47	22	41	25	73	49	10
	West	12	32	15	48	15	68	38	6
	South	22	28	13	45	14	67	40	6
Village development Index[5]	Low	30	43	21	63	37	70	46	7
	Medium	40	38	18	53	23	70	45	7
	High	30	32	14	41	16	69	42	7

(1) Dependency ratio: (nos. of male children + nos. of female children + nos. of old males + nos. of old females)/(nos. of adult males + nos. of adult females). Children refers to age <15, old refers to age >59, and adult to age 15–59.

(2) HH occupation: Household occupation – this categorisation is based on the main source of income of the household.

(3) Land holding: This refers to the land holding status. The *India Human Development Report* (Shariff 1999) does not give the actual land sizes used for the classification but mentions that the conventional sizes are used – possibly those used by the NSSO which are as follows: Marginal – Less than 1 hectare; Small – 1.01–2.00 hectare; Semi-medium – 2.01–4.00 hectare; Medium – 4.01–10.00 hectare; Large – 10 + hectare.

(4) Region: This classification from the NCAER/UNDP data is based on geographical regions within the country. States included in each region are as follows: (a) North: Himachal Pradesh, Punjab and Haryana, (b) Upper central: Uttar Pradesh and Bihar, (c) Lower central: Rajasthan, Madhya Pradesh and Orissa, (d) East: West Bengal and the North-eastern states, (e) West: Gujarat and Maharshtra and (f) South: Karnataka, Andhra Pradesh, Kerala and Tamil Nadu.

(5) Village development index: This is an index constructed for reporting in the *India Human Development Report* by collating information related to infrastructure and amenities in the village (like accessibility, media and communication, basic needs like safe drinking water and electricity); education-related factors (like accessibility of educational institutions, female–male student ratio in primary schools, schemes like midday meals, scholarships); health-related factors (like accessibility to health facilities) and other development-related variables (like proportion of irrigated area to cropped area, number of government/NGO schemes in the village). Based on a score, villages are classified as having low, medium or high levels of development.

religion, for example, 85 per cent of the individuals are estimated to be Hindus, 10 per cent to be Muslims, 2 per cent to be Christian and another 3 per cent as belonging to other minority religions (like Sikhism, Jainism and Buddhism). Column 2 gives the percentages of individuals within different socio-economic subgroups who are estimated as being in monetary poverty and column 3 in extreme monetary poverty. Similarly columns 4 to 8 give estimates of levels of education and health poverty within these subgroups. The percentage of the population estimated to be in monetary or capability poverty in each subgroup (columns 2 to 8) is compared with the overall percentage of the particular poverty (overall % row).

We also carried out a logit analysis (see results in Table 6.3). The analysis is repeated for the same groups as those considered for constructing the poverty profiles, but controlling in each case for other factors. The subgroup that constitutes the highest proportion of the population for that particular socio-economic group is taken as the base group in the logit analysis. Thus for instance, the base group with regard to religion was taken to be Hindus (which at 85 per cent constitute the highest percentage of any religious subgroup) and so on. Logit result coefficients for these base groups are given in Table 6.3 as '0', against which the values and sign of coefficients for other subgroups are to be compared.

Monetary poverty profiles

As shown in Table 6.2, the overall level of monetary poverty in India in 1994 is estimated to be 38 per cent, with 18 per cent being extremely poor (extreme poverty line is as defined in Table 6.1). The rates of monetary poverty vary across different socio-economic groups (see column 2 in Table 6.2). The distribution of extreme poverty (column 3) largely follows a similar pattern.

In the subgroups based on religion, 45 per cent of Muslims are estimated as being in monetary poverty as compared to overall average poverty levels of 38 per cent. At 26 per cent, Christians are estimated to have lower than average levels of monetary poverty. Amongst the subgrouping based on caste, individuals belonging to the scheduled castes and tribes show higher than average levels of poverty at 50 per cent and 47 per cent. Other socio-economic groups associated with poverty levels substantially higher than average levels of poverty are as follows: in the household occupation category, individuals from households whose major source of income is wage labour (62 per cent); and in the land holding category, individuals from landless households (66 per cent). Although there is no significant difference in the levels of poverty of

Table 6.3: Monetary, education and health poverty: logit results (coefficients)

Socio-economic group		%	Monetary poverty		Education poverty[1]		Health poverty[1]	
			Poor [2]c = 0.24	Extreme c = −1.07	Adults c = −0.39	Children c = −3.11	Children c = −0.43	Adults c = −2.52
Religion	Hindu	85[3]	0.00[4]	0.00	0.00	0.00	0.00	0.00
	Muslim	10	−0.02	−0.18*	0.37***	0.47***	0.07	0.14**
	Christian	2	−0.33	−0.14	−1.40***	−0.77***	0.05	−0.01
	Other minorities	3	0.32***	0.38***	0.03	−0.25*	−0.16*	0.22**
Caste	ST	10	0.36***	0.23**	0.76***	0.44***	0.25***	−0.15**
	SC	20	0.15**	0.11	0.61***	0.16**	0.06	−0.05
	Non SC/ST	69	0.00	0.00	0.00	0.00	0.00	0.00
HH Head Gender	Male	96	0.00	0.00	0.00	0.00	0.00	0.00
	Female	4	0.06	0.23**	−0.22***	−0.02	0.01	−0.03
Gender	Male	53	0.00	0.00	0.00	0.00	0.00	0.00
	Female	47	0.05***	0.05***	1.42***	1.04***	−0.07***	0.12***
HH Head Education	Illiterate	48	0.00	0.00	0.00	0.00	0.00	0.00
	Primary	25	0.00	0.06		−0.21***	−0.03	0.12**
	Middle	23	−0.24***	−0.14*		−0.61***	−0.03	−0.01
	University	3	−0.84***	−0.07		−1.20***	−0.04	−0.08
HH Literacy	Both	39	0.00	0.00	0.00	0.00	0.00	0.00
	Male	33	0.05	0.02		1.55***	0.14***	0.00
	Female	3	0.17	0.18		0.69***	0.02	0.18*
	None	25	0.18**	0.15		2.72***	0.15***	0.12*

		N						
HH size	Up to 4	19	−0.70***	−0.66***	0.34***	−0.49***	0.07*	0.22***
	5 to 7	49	0.00	0.00	0.00	0.00	0.00	0.00
	8 and above	32	0.73***	0.66***	−0.07**	0.30***	0.10***	−0.30***
Dependency ratio	0	7	−0.80***	−0.68***	−0.42***	0.12*	0.14***	0.22***
	>0 to 0.5	25	−0.27***	−0.30***	−0.20***	0.00	0.00	−0.03
	>0.5 to 1	33	0.00	0.00	0.00	−0.15**	0.00	0.00
	>1 to 2	28	0.36***	0.35***	0.26***	−0.18**	0.00	0.01
	>2	7	0.56***	0.67***	0.71***		−0.07	−0.10
HH Occupation	Agr	46	0.00	0.00	0.00	0.00	0.00	0.00
	Sal/Prof	14	−1.85***	−2.03***	−1.06***	−0.68***	−0.18***	−0.10*
	Wage	24	0.29***	−0.03	0.42***	0.22*	−0.02	0.11*
	Other	16	−0.88***	−1.27***	−0.45***	−0.34***	−0.12**	0.06
Land Holding	Marginal	31	0.00	0.00	0.00	0.00	0.00	0.00
	Small	19	−1.25***	−1.20***	−0.10**	−0.13*	0.03	−0.02
	Medium	11	−2.07***	−1.82***	−0.26***	−0.09	0.06	−0.16**
	Large	7	−2.79***	−2.3***	−0.43***	−0.16	−0.07	−0.18**
	Landless wage	17	0.64***	0.71***	0.38***	0.17*	0.10*	−0.07
	Landless other	16	0.57***	0.70***	0.19***	0.40***	0.21***	−0.04
Region	North	5	−0.81***	−0.57***	−0.24**	−0.73***	−0.13**	0.14**
	Central (U)	30	−0.31***	−0.26***	0.05	0.24***	0.18***	−0.22***
	Central (L)	18	0.00	0.00	0.00	0.00	0.00	0.00
	East	12	0.19*	0.18	−0.71***	0.08	0.26***	0.22**
	West	12	−0.61***	−0.45***	−0.43*	−0.83***	−0.20***	−0.43***
	South	22	−1.03***	−0.70***	−0.52**	−0.93***	−0.11	−0.49***

Continued

Table 6.3: Continued

Socio-economic group		%	Monetary poverty		Education poverty[1]		Health poverty[1]	
			Poor [2]$c = 0.24$	Extreme $c = -1.07$	Adults $c = -0.39$	Children $c = -3.11$	Children $c = -0.43$	Adults $c = -2.52$
Village development index	Low	30	0.22***	0.26***	0.31***	0.36***	-0.01	0.03
	Medium	40	0.00	0.00	0.00	0.00	0.00	0.00
	High	30	-0.10*	-0.17**	-0.40***	-0.11*	-0.01	0.09*
		F =	96.1	64.07	282	97.09	7.38	12.27

(1) The age group for assessment of adult education is $>= 15$yrs, for child education $>= 7$ & $<= 14$, adult health is >12 & <60 and child health $<= 12$yrs. The entire sample is however included with regard to monetary assessment as the proportions of monetary poverty within the subgroups were largely similar for both age groups.

(2) c = constant for the logit equation.

(3) Gives the proportion of the entire sample that comprises the subgroups.

(4) The base group against which groups are assessed was taken to be the subgroups that constitute the highest proportion of the population. Thus the base group consists of Hindu, Non-scheduled caste/scheduled tribe, Male household head, Male gender, illiterate head of household, household education group with both at least one male and one female adult literate, medium size household, dependant group with equal number of dependants and working age members, main source of income being the occupation agriculture, Marginal land ownership, individuals from Lower Central region and villages with a Medium village development index. Logit result coefficients for these subgroups are given in the table as '0' against which the values and sign of coefficients for other sub groups are to be compared.

* Indicates significance at 10% level; ** Indicates significance at 5% level; *** Indicates significance at 1% level.

individuals belonging to male or female-headed households, women (39 per cent) show only marginally higher levels of poverty than men (37 per cent). This is not surprising given that intra-household distribution has not been taken into account (see details on methodology of selection of indicators for the monetary approach).

Individuals from villages with a 'low' development index show higher than average levels of monetary poverty (43 per cent) while individuals from villages with 'high' levels of development show lower levels (32 per cent) than average. Monetary poverty progressively decreases with the increase in the level of education of the head of the household (from 46 per cent for an illiterate head to 12 per cent for a university educated household head) as well as with increase in numbers of literate adults in the household (from 52 per cent for households with no adult literate members to 27 per cent for households with at least one adult male and one adult female literate member). The rate of poverty increases with household size (from 26 per cent for households with less than four members to 43 per cent for large households with eight or more members). We do not, however, account for economies of scale with regard to consumption, and this may well be responsible for the higher rates we see amongst larger households. Poverty also increases with the dependency ratio. Individuals from households with more than twice the number of dependants (individuals age < 15 or > 59) than individuals in the working age group (age 15 to 59), show 54 per cent in monetary poverty as compared to 17 per cent amongst individuals from households with no dependants. Monetary poverty varies to some extent depending on the region of residence. The highest levels of poverty (47 per cent) are found amongst individuals from the eastern region of the country and lowest levels amongst individuals from the northern (29 per cent) and southern (28 per cent) regions of the country (see Table 6.2 for details on the states that comprise these regions).

As seen from Table 6.2, the pattern of extreme poverty largely follows that seen with poverty. Socio-economic subgroups showing higher than average levels of extreme monetary poverty are largely the same as those discussed above.

With regard to the logit analysis (see Table 6.3), the relationships between the different subgroups and levels of poverty identified in the profiles mainly hold, even when other factors are held constant. The few significant differences that emerge are as follows. The association between the subgroups based on religion and poverty (i.e. Muslims having higher than average and Christians lower than average levels of monetary poverty), does not persist except for the subgroup 'other' minorities (i.e. minorities other than Christian and Muslim). The positive association between individuals belonging to the scheduled tribe or scheduled caste group and monetary poverty persists, but is shown to be highly pronounced only for the scheduled tribes. Further unlike the profiles, a significant and positive relationship is identified between being a female individual and monetary poverty. Since intra-household allocation of resources has not been taken into account, the only reasonable explanation for females showing higher levels of monetary poverty could be that households that are monetarily poorer have a higher number of female members. This relationship persists with regard to extreme poverty. Further in the logit analysis, although gender of the head of the household is not found to show an association with monetary poverty, a positive relationship is identified with female headship with regard to extreme poverty. This supports findings of some other studies which indicate that a larger number of female headed households are likely to be in extreme monetary poverty compared to male headed households.

Education poverty profile

It was estimated from the NCAER/UNDP data that 52 per cent of Indian adults and 26 per cent of children were education 'poor' (Table 6.2). Overall, education poverty follows a similar pattern to monetary poverty with groups with higher likelihood of being monetary poor, also having a higher likelihood of being education poor. Unlike monetary poverty, however, where the difference between males and females is minimal, there is a large gender difference in the levels of education poverty. Females have substantially higher levels of education poverty (67 per cent amongst adults and 33 per cent amongst children) compared to males (38 per cent amongst adults and 19 per cent amongst children). Interestingly, while for adults education poverty is largely similar depending on whether there is at least one adult literate male or at least one adult literate female member, for children education poverty is much lower in households with at least one adult literate female member (11 per cent) compared to households with at least one adult literate male member (25 per cent). This confirms the now established fact of the role played by educated female members in promoting education amongst children in the household. Similar to the pattern for monetary poverty, education poverty amongst children is higher in larger size households. This could be due to the larger number of dependants and an inability to provide education to all children in the household. In the case of adults, however, education poverty is higher in smaller households. This may well be indicative of the recent attempts by the state to improve education levels. These would be reflected in larger households with more younger members. Individuals from the eastern region, although showing the highest levels of monetary poverty (47 per cent), show the lowest levels of education poverty amongst adults (41 per cent). This reflects historically higher levels of education that existed in this region, probably associated with the role of missionary activity. Education poverty in other regions mainly follows the same trend as monetary poverty, with adults from the upper and lower central regions showing higher levels of education poverty followed by individuals from the western and northern regions with the southern region showing low levels of monetary as well as education poverty.

Significant findings from the logit analysis (Table 6.3) which add to the information from the profiles is as follows: other factors remaining constant, amongst adults, Muslims persist in showing higher levels of education poverty and Christians lower levels than the base group. Individuals belonging to scheduled tribes show higher levels of education poverty compared to those belonging to the scheduled castes, who in turn show higher levels than the base group. Whilst the profile analysis did not reveal a relationship with the gender of the household head, in the logit analysis adults from households with a female head are found to show lower levels of education poverty. This finding again confirms the role that educated female members have been found to play in promoting education of children in the household. As with the cross-tabulation results, female adults continue to show higher levels of education poverty and poverty levels are higher amongst larger households. With regard to children, other factors remaining constant, the positive relationship between education poverty and belonging to the scheduled tribes is much more pronounced than for the scheduled castes. No significant relationship was identified between gender of the head of the household and education poverty of the children. With an increase in education levels of the head of the household, however, there is a progressive decrease in the education poverty of children. Education poverty is lower amongst households with at least one adult literate female as compared to households with a adult literate male or no literate adults. Unlike with adults (but as with monetary poverty), smaller size households are associated with less education poverty and larger households with higher levels. In contrast to monetary poverty as well as education poverty amongst adults, households with a higher dependency ratio show lower levels of education poverty. A significant relationship between land ownership and education of children is not obvious except for the group that are landless (but are not wage labourers) who show significantly higher levels of poverty.

Health poverty profile

Amongst children aged less than 13 years, levels of undernutrition (two standard deviations below the median) are very high. Ten per cent are classified as wasted, 63 per cent as stunted and 29 per cent underweight. This is very high compared with the 2.3 per cent for each of the indices, which is the expected base line prevalence in the reference population (i.e. if the Z score cut-off of < -2 standard deviations is used, this would be the percentage of the reference population which would be expected with a normal distribution, to be classified undernourished even if they are 'healthy' individuals). Assessing levels of severe undernutrition (three standard deviations below the median), 3 per cent are classified as severely wasted, 41 per cent as severely stunted and 9 per cent as severely underweight (in a normal distribution the expected percentage would be 0.1 per cent). The proportion classified as undernourished (in any one of the three anthropometric indices) is 70 per cent, and 44 per cent are classified severely undernourished (see columns 6 and 7 in Table 6.2). With regard to health, 7 per cent of the individuals between ages 13 and 59 are considered to be health poor because they suffer from chronic illness (column 8 in Table 6.2).

Profiles reveal that levels of undernutrition and severe undernutrition as well as chronic illness remain largely similar amongst the different socio-economic groups, with the greatest variability being due to the region the individual belongs to. The upper central and eastern regions show higher levels of nutrition poverty and northern and eastern regions show appreciably higher levels of chronic illness than other regions.

Unlike the profiles where no strong relationship between chronic illness or undernutrition and belonging to a particular socio-economic group is identified, some interesting relationships are identified in the logit analysis (Table 6.3). Logit analysis for children has been carried out only with regard to the severe undernutrition indicator. Children belonging to the scheduled tribes show significantly higher levels of undernutrition. Female children are found to show lower levels of nutrition poverty. Although education of the household head has no relationship with undernutrition, the literacy levels of adults in the household show a relationship. The presence of at least two literate adults is associated with lesser undernutrition than just one literate adult or no literate adults. Larger size households are associated with higher undernutrition. As with monetary and education poverty, individuals belonging to households whose main source of income is from salaried jobs or professional services, are associated with lower levels of undernutrition. As with childhood education, individuals belonging to landless households (but not involved in wage labour) are associated with levels of undernutrition which are higher than even those of landless wage labourers. Levels of child undernutrition are significantly lower in the western and northern regions but higher in the east and upper central compared to the lower central. There is no significant relationship with the Village Development Index.

Individuals belonging to the scheduled tribes show (other factors remaining constant) lower levels of chronic illness. However, the chronic illness indicator depends on individuals' own assessments of their state of health and it appears that this depends on their assessment of what is normal and the availability of health care, and does not necessarily reflect any 'objective' state of health. This view is supported by the fact that with undernutrition in contrast, higher levels (although only marginally higher) were identified amongst scheduled tribes (49 per cent) as being undernourished compared to others (43 per cent) – see Table 6.2. Females show higher levels of chronic illness, while larger sized households are associated with lower levels of chronic illness than smaller sized ones. Households with no dependants show higher levels of chronic illness (probably older people living alone – this seems to fit in with the earlier finding of smaller households showing higher levels of chronic illness – we do, however, in our analysis try to minimise such distortions by restricting the analysis using a chronic illness indicator to individuals aged below 60). Increase in landownership is associated with lower levels of chronic illness. Although individuals living in the northern region show lower levels of monetary and education poverty, they show higher levels of chronic illness (other factors remaining constant). Individuals living in the western region show lower levels of chronic illness which reduce even further for individuals living in southern states. There is no significant relationship with the Village Development Index.

Taken together, then, the above comparison of the poverty profiles for monetary, health and education dimensions reveals that some socio-economic groups with higher levels of monetary poverty are also groups showing higher levels of education poverty: for example, individuals belonging to Muslim or SC/ST households, people in households with poorly educated heads and high dependency ratios, small or no landholding, and those from villages with lower values for their Village

Development Index. There are, however, some groups with high levels of monetary poverty but low levels of education poverty – for example adults in the eastern region and vice versa (adults in small sized households). Health and nutrition poverty does not, however, show much association with different socio-economic groups or correlation with levels of monetary poverty.

6.3.2   Poverty overlaps

Profile comparisons suggest that there may be considerable overlap especially between monetary and education poverty, given that the socio-economic characteristics of individuals identified as being in poverty in these dimensions are similar for quite a few groups. But this depends on whether, within these groups, it is the same individuals who are in both monetary and education poverty. The construction of contingency tables allows us to explore the extent of overlap between the different dimensions of poverty, at an individual level.

Individuals are classified in contingency tables using the monetary poverty line, as 'poor' or 'non-poor' (see columns in Figure 6.1). The same individuals are also classified using a capability indicator as 'poor' or 'non-poor' (see rows in Figure 6.1). MpCp gives the percentage of individuals classified as 'poor' by the monetary as well as capability approaches. MnCp gives the percentage of individuals classified 'non-poor' by the monetary, but 'poor' by the capability approach. MpCn gives the percentage of individuals classified 'poor' by the monetary, but

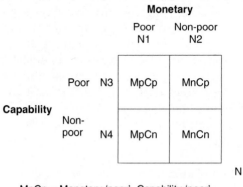

MpCp = Monetary 'poor', Capability 'poor'
MnCp = Monetary 'non-poor', Capability 'poor'
MpCn = Monetary 'poor', Capability 'non-poor'
MnCn = Monetary 'non-poor', Capability 'non-poor'

Figure 6.1: 2 × 2 table

'non-poor' by the capability approach. MnCn gives the percentage of individuals classified as 'non-poor' by the monetary as well as capability approaches. N1 is the percentage of cases that are classified by the monetary approach as 'Poor' and N2 the percentage classified as 'Non-poor'. N3 is the percentage of cases that are classified by the capability approach as 'Poor' and N4 the percentage classified as 'Non-poor'.[10] N gives the total number of cases.

A chi-squared test is carried out to determine the independence of the monetary and capabilities categorical distributions. The degree of association is indicated by Cramer's V.[11]

The chi2 tests for Table 6.4 reject the null hypothesis of independence for monetary and non-monetary dimensions. This therefore indicates the presence of a correlation between monetary and capability poverty. The correlation is, however, very low as assessed by the Cramer's V (values < 0.2 for both education indicators and < 0.05 for both health indicators). This holds true for extreme monetary poverty as well.

Given the low correlation, we explore Table 6.4 further to investigate the extent of overlap and lack of overlap in the dimensions of poverty. Restricting our discussion below to the comparison of monetary (rather than extreme monetary poverty) and capability poverty, our findings are as follows.

As shown in Table 6.4 (a–j), the proportion of individuals identified as being monetary 'poor' and 'non-poor' varies depending on the age group being considered, but is approximately around 40 per cent and 60 per cent respectively.[12] The 'poor' and 'non-poor' proportions with regard to education for adults are 52 per cent and 48 per cent and for children 26 per cent and 74 per cent respectively. With regard to health, the proportions of adults classified health 'poor' and 'non-poor' are 7 per cent and 93 per cent and of children are 44 per cent and 56 per cent respectively.

The proportion of individuals who are consistently classified, i.e. classified as being 'poor' by both monetary and capability indicators (MpCp) and non-poor by both (MnpCnp), ranges from 52 per cent for monetary vs. health for children to 64 per cent for monetary vs. health poverty for adults (figures not shown in tables). It is noteworthy, however, that a large number of individuals comprise the MnCp and MpCn groups, being poor in one and non-poor in the other dimension. Such inconsistent classifications range from 36 per cent for monetary vs. health poverty for adults to 48 per cent for monetary vs. health poverty for children. Exploring these inconsistencies further, if the monetary approach is used to classify poverty, as seen from row % in Table 6.4 (a–j), 59 per cent of education poor adults and 43 per cent of education

Table 6.4: Overlap between monetary and capability poverty: contingency tables

(a) Total Monetary vs Education (adults)

		Monetary Poor	Monetary Non-poor	Total
Cap. Poor	col %*	62	47	52
	row %	41	59	100
Cap. Non-poor	col %	38	53	48
	row %	27	73	100
Total		34	66	100

Cramer's V: 0.15
Total Cases N: 121 836

(b) Extreme Monetary vs Education (adults)

		Monetary Poor	Monetary Non-poor	Total
Cap. Poor	col %	64	50	52
	row %	19	81	100
Cap. Non-poor	col %	36	50	48
	row %	12	88	100
Total		15	85	100

Cramer's V: 0.10
Total Cases N: 121 836

(c) Total Monetary vs Education (children)

		Monetary Poor	Monetary Non-poor	Total
Cap. Poor	col %	34	19	26
	row %	57	43	100
Cap. Non-poor	col %	66	81	74
	row %	38	62	100
Total		43	57	100

Cramer's V: 0.17
Total Cases N: 36 643

(d) Extreme Monetary vs Education (children)

		Monetary Poor	Monetary Non-poor	Total
Cap. Poor	col %	36	23	26
	row %	29	71	100
Cap. Non-poor	col %	64	77	74
	row %	18	82	100
Total		21	79	100

Cramer's V: 0.12
Total Cases N: 36 643

(e) Total Monetary vs Health (adults)

		Monetary Poor	Monetary Non-poor	Total
Cap. Poor	col %	7	7	7
	row %	37	63	100
Cap. Non-poor	col %	93	93	93
	row %	35	65	100
Total		35	65	100
		100	100	100

Cramer's V: 0.01
Total Cases N: 116 939

(f) Extreme Monetary vs Health (adults)

		Monetary Poor	Monetary Non-poor	Total
Cap. Poor	col %	8	7	7
	row %	17	83	100
Cap. Non-poor	col %	92	93	93
	row %	16	84	100
Total		16	84	100
		100	100	100

Cramer's V: 0.01
Total Cases N: 116 939

(g) Total Monetary vs Health (children)

		Monetary Poor	Monetary Non-poor	Total
Cap. Poor	col %	47	43	44
	row %	46	54	100
Cap. Non-poor	col %	53	57	56
	row %	44	56	100
Total		45	55	100
		100	100	100

Cramer's V: 0.13
Total Cases N: 57 836

(h) Extreme Monetary vs Health (children)

		Monetary Poor	Monetary Non-poor	Total
Cap. Poor	col %	46	44	44
	row %	23	77	100
Cap. Non-poor	col %	54	56	56
	row %	21	79	100
Total		22	78	100
		100	100	100

Cramer's V: 0.02
Total Cases N: 57 836

140

Table 6.4: Continued

(i) Total Monetary vs Capability

	Monetary Poor	Monetary Non-poor	Total
Cap. Poor			
col %	59	45	50
row %	43	57	100
Cap. Non-poor			
col %	41	55	50
row %	30	70	100
Total			
col %	100	100	100
row %	36	64	100

Cramer's V: 0.14
Total Cases N: 143 249

(j) Extreme Monetary vs Capability

	Monetary Poor	Monetary Non-poor	Total
Cap. Poor			
col %	61	48	50
row %	20	80	100
Cap. Non-poor			
col %	39	52	50
row %	13	87	100
Total			
col %	100	100	100
row %	17	83	100

Cramer's V: 0.10
Total Cases N: 143 249

* The values in these tables have been rounded to the nearest per cent.

poor children who are classified as being monetary non-poor would be excluded. Similarly for health, 63 per cent of health poor adults and 53 per cent of nutrition poor children would be excluded. If the extreme monetary poverty line is used the proportion of capability poor individuals who are excluded increases further. The exclusion ranges from 71 per cent for education poor children to 83 per cent for health poor adults.

Similarly if, using the capabilities approach, indicators related to one or combined dimensions are used to classify poverty, monetary poor individuals in the MpCn cell who are classified as non-poor by capabilities indicators would be excluded. As seen from column % in Table 6.4 (a–j), anywhere between 38 per cent of Mp (if adult education is used) to 93 per cent of Mp (if chronic illness is used) will be excluded as they are not in capability poverty but are in monetary poverty.

Thus, if individuals classified as poor by one approach are targeted for special sector help on the assumption that they would also be poor in other dimensions, our results show that considerable proportions of people classified as 'poor' according to the dimensions related to other approaches would be left out.[13]

It might be argued that the proportion of cases identified as showing an overlap in monetary and non-monetary poverty depends on the particular indicators and the thresholds used. If different indicators or different poverty lines were used it is possible that a substantially higher proportion of individuals would be classified as overlapping in poverty in the different approaches. With regard to indicators, data limitations impose certain restrictions on the choice of indicators. For example, we did not have BMI values although this could possibly have been a more appropriate indicator of adult health and would be worth exploring in future work. To the extent possible, however, we have tried to use the most appropriate indicators as well as ensuring that these are also used commonly for policy purposes. We explore below the impact of altering the thresholds used.

Altering the thresholds

In order to explore the dependence of overlap on the thresholds used, we investigate the impact of altering the threshold at which the poverty line is drawn for monetary indicators. Figure 6.2 shows levels of poverty amongst different monetary decile groups (from group one comprising 10 per cent of the population with lowest levels of income to group ten with the 10 per cent of the population that has the highest levels of income).

142

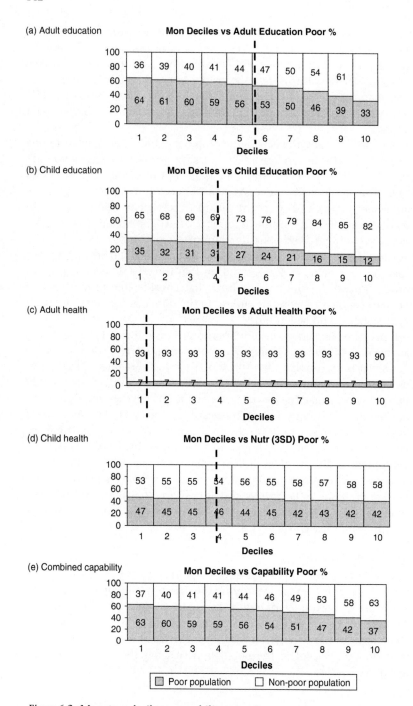

(a) Adult education

Mon Deciles vs Adult Education Poor %

(b) Child education

Mon Deciles vs Child Education Poor %

(c) Adult health

Mon Deciles vs Adult Health Poor %

(d) Child health

Mon Deciles vs Nutr (3SD) Poor %

(e) Combined capability

Mon Deciles vs Capability Poor %

☐ Poor population   ☐ Non-poor population

Figure 6.2: Monetary deciles vs capability poverty

For adults, decile groups from 1 to 10 show progressively lower levels of education poverty (as indicated by the shaded area in the graphs in Figure 6.2a) with the lowest monetary decile (1) showing 64 per cent of individuals belonging to it as being education 'poor' and the highest monetary decile showing 33 per cent of individuals as being education 'poor'. Although this suggests that being monetarily richer steadily reduces the chances of education poverty in adults, the findings also show that even at higher monetary deciles, high levels of education poverty still persist, with 50 per cent of the individuals belonging to as high as the seventh monetary decile being education 'poor'.

We also explore here the effect of using a single threshold such that the same percentage of individuals are identified as 'poor' for the different dimensions. (Glewwe and van der Gaag 1990, for example, a priori set a threshold such that 30 per cent are identified by different indicators as 'poor' for data from Côte d'Ivoire.) We use a monetary poverty line drawn so as to classify as 'poor' the same percentage of adults that have been classified by the education indicator as 'poor' (i.e. 52 per cent – see Figure 6.2a). Even in this case, we find that a considerable proportion of individuals (an average of around 44 per cent) are still found to be education 'poor' amongst the remaining 48 per cent of (monetary non-poor) individuals.

Similarly for children (Figure 6.2b), levels of education poverty progressively reduce in the higher monetary deciles. Even in the highest monetary decile the level of education poverty at 12 per cent is about one-third of that in the poorest monetary decile (at 35 per cent). Again if we look at overlaps with the monetary poverty line drawn so as to classify as 'poor' the same percentage as is classified as education 'poor', i.e. 36 per cent, a considerable percentage of children (around 20 per cent) are classified education 'poor'. For adults as well as children there does not appear to be a well-defined monetary threshold above which education poverty levels fall sharply. Just raising the monetary poverty line, therefore, does not significantly eliminate the lack of overlap with those who are education 'poor'.

Similarly with nutrition (see Figure 6.2d), there is some small reduction in the proportion of those that are nutritionally 'poor' from the first decile through to the tenth (47 per cent to 42 per cent). As above, we draw a monetary poverty line such that the same percentage (44 per cent) of children that are nutrition 'poor' are classified as monetary 'poor'. We find that in the remaining 66 per cent of monetary non-poor individuals an average of 43 per cent children (almost the same as the overall level) are classified as being nutrition 'poor'. With chronic illness

(Figure 6.2c), however, the proportion of those identified as being 'poor' remains the same from decile 1 through to decile 10. So it is not the case that altering the poverty line threshold would allow for a higher overlap with those that are poor in health, as classified by the chronic illness indicator, than the overlaps captured by the current official line.

As with education and health, exploring the proportion that is classified poor using the combined capability indicator (Figure 6.2e) in the different monetary decile, reveals that even as high as the seventh monetary decile more than 50 per cent are 'poor' in either education or health.

6.3.3   Social exclusion

A comparison of the social exclusion approach with capabilities and monetary approaches is addressed separately in this section, given the special issues that this approach raises. As discussed in Chapter 4, in industrialised countries, patterns of social integration are institutionalised and fairly clearly defined and 'social exclusion' applies to those outside accepted norms. The excluded are minorities. In many developing countries, however, due to structural heterogeneity of their societies, defining what is 'normal' may be more difficult. It is questionable whether the concept of 'social exclusion' as developed originally in industrialised countries can be applied in developing countries (for a detailed discussion see Chapter 4). For example, an analysis of the UNDP/NCAER data revealed that about 64 per cent of the working population is involved in insecure informal employment (see Table 6.5)

In fact, as discussed in Chapter 4, in rural economies seasonally determined irregular employment and casual employment may well be considered the 'norm' and it would be meaningless to consider two-thirds of the working population as 'socially excluded', based on industrialised country criteria of employment status.

Given the difficulties in transplanting the concept of 'social exclusion' from industrialised to developing countries as indicated above, attempts have been made to modify it to suit particular contexts. One of the ways in which it has been operationalised by the ILO has been to identify, based on previous research, groups know to be discriminated against and/or vulnerable to poverty in various dimensions. Levels of poverty and processes that lead into it are then investigated. In the context of India, extensive research has demonstrated that caste is a factor of central importance forming the basis of much social discrimination. Following this approach here, we explore the extent to which identification of individuals as 'socially excluded' based on their caste/tribe, overlaps

Table 6.5: Distribution of individuals by employment (NCAER/UNDP data)

Employment category	%
Formal employment	6
Stable agricultural employment	25
Insecure informal employment	64
Unemployed/unwilling to work	5
Total	100

with identification of individuals as 'poor' by monetary or capabilities approaches.[14]

The NCAER/UNDP data show that the scheduled castes (SC) and scheduled tribes (ST) are estimated to constitute almost one-third of the population (see Table 6.2). Individuals belonging to SC/ST are estimated as having a higher likelihood of being monetary 'poor' (around 50 per cent compared to 33 per cent for non-SC/ST) or 'extreme poor' (around 25 per cent compared to 15 per cent for the non-SC/ST group). Adults, as well as children belonging to SC/ST households, are more likely to suffer from education 'poverty' compared to individuals belonging to the non-SC/ST groups. In adults around 65 per cent are education 'poor' compared to 46 per cent for non-SC/ST. In children, around 35 per cent are education 'poor' compared to 22 per cent for non-SC/ST. Malnutrition amongst children, however, seems to be only very marginally higher for SC/ST (being 49 per cent for ST, 46 per cent for SC and 43 per cent for non SC/ST). The state has a limited system of positive discrimination and implements some welfare measures directed specifically towards people classified as belonging to scheduled castes/tribes. Using the social exclusion approach (as operationalised here with regard to poverty identification) to motivate the development of positive discrimination policies that help integrate such groups and reduce poverty in different dimensions can be beneficial. It is important, however, to be aware as indicated in Table 6.6, that if developmental benefits were directed on the basis of caste/tribal status, there would be a significant percentage of individuals who, despite being left out on the basis of not belonging to the scheduled castes/tribes, may in fact be in monetary poverty (60 per cent of the monetary poor); or capability poverty (ranging from 58 per cent of the educationally poor for children to 69 per cent of the chronically ill adults).

Table 6.6: Percentage of capability OR monetary poor
classified as SC/ST and non-SC/ST

	Caste status	
	% SC/ST	*% Non-SC/ST*
Monetary poor	40	60
Extreme monetary poor	42	58
Adult education poor	38	62
Child education poor	42	58
Adult health poor	31	69
Child health poor	35	65

6.4   Methodology and results: field data

As mentioned earlier, given the lack of information on people's own
experiences and perceptions of poverty in the NCAER/UNDP data, fieldwork was carried out to collect data that would allow a comparison of all
four approaches, including the participatory approach.

First we present in brief the methodology followed in the field for
collection of data (Section 6.4.1). Results of analysis of fieldwork data are
presented in Section 6.4.2. In the first subsection, we present
contingency tables constructed, as with the NCAER/UNDP data, for a
comparison of the groups identified as being in poverty by the different approaches. The insights obtained into social exclusion by the
participatory technique of focus group discussions (FGDs) are discussed
in the second subsection.

6.4.1   Methodology of field data collection

The fieldwork consisted of the use of a standard door-to-door questionnaire survey as well as participatory methods. Households in the village
Sandoli and in a part of the Hatha Sithara Begum slum, that had an
adult member available in the house to answer questions were included
in the survey. Information was collected in September 2001 and the survey related to the previous agricultural year – i.e. from July 2000 to June
2001. We were able to survey 198 rural and 105 urban households and
collect information related to monetary and capability poverty. The
participatory approach used techniques such as social mapping and
well-being ranking complemented by focus group discussions (the tools
and techniques used followed those suggested by Praxis – Institute for
Participatory Practices, Patna Bihar). Well-being ranking allowed us to
obtain an ordinal classification of households into different categories

of well-being, as assessed by individuals from the community, based on the criteria they themselves consider important. This permitted a comparison of the classification of these households in terms of monetary and capability poverty with the ranking obtained by participatory techniques. The focus group discussions were aimed at discovering what the individuals living in the study areas understood by poverty. The discussions were also intended to inform us about people's perceptions of capabilities. Further, our theoretical review highlighted problems associated with applying the social exclusion approach as developed in industrialised countries to the context of developing countries. So we decided to use the participatory FGDs to obtain some information on local perceptions of social exclusion.

Participatory well-being ranking

The process followed to obtain well-being ranking of households was as follows. The ranking exercise was carried out by three different groups in each of the rural and urban settings. In both settings, there were two male groups and one female group with an average of eight people per group. Within each group, every effort was made to ensure that there were individuals from different parts of the village as well as from different castes, religious groups and levels of education. We tried to ensure this by requesting people from different parts of the village/slum to participate and succeeded to some extent. We also explained to the community head the subjects we intended discussing and our need to include people representative of different socio-economic groups. Individuals in each group were asked to categorise the households in the village or slum (using small rectangular cards – with one card representing one household), into three groups – low, medium and high in terms of overall well-being. We wanted the group to take into account factors that they themselves considered important for the assessment of 'well-being', so we were very careful not to give any leading suggestions on any particular indicator/indicators to be used for the classification.[15] People in the group discussed amongst themselves various aspects of overall well-being, such as the ownership of assets, the regularity of income, the ability to educate children etc. and on this basis, each group reached a consensus on the category of overall well-being each household was to be allotted to. At the end we asked each group to list the criteria on the basis of which they had allotted the households to the various categories (see Table 6.7). Comparing the categories that each household had been placed in by each of the three groups, we allotted each household to a single final category. The household was allotted to the category it was placed in by at least two

Table 6.7: Well-being ranking – characteristics of individuals belonging to different ranks

Characteristics	Well-being rank		
	High	Medium	Low
Main occupation			
(**Rural**)	Agriculture or regular salaried job particularly government job	Wage labourers; allied agricultural activities like livestock, milk	*
(**Urban**)	Government jobs or prosperous business (e.g. chikan** or dhobi***) or regular salaried job, particularly government job	Wage labourers; some businessmen (but in debt)	Wage labourers/rickshaw drivers/domestic jobs (e.g. maids) or no regular job
Land possessed			
(**Rural**)	Large amount****	Marginal amount but not cultivated (e.g. one handicapped person)	Landless or small amount of land
Assets			
(**Rural**)	Tractor	*	*
Level of dependency			
(**Rural**)	Low*****	*	High
(**Urban**)	Low	Sons supplement income	High
Food availability			
(**Rural**)	Enough to eat and left overs	Just adequate (none left over)	Inadequate (unable to fill their bellies)

	Adequate and left overs	Just adequate (none left over)	Inadequate
(Urban)	High amongst adults		
Education			
(Rural)	Minimum	*	*
(Urban)	Children enrolled in schools	Have resources to enrol children in school but cannot sustain expenses – usually drop out	Don't even have enough resources to enrol children in school

* The classification into ranks and the subsequent attribution of particular characteristics to different levels of ranking was done by the persons who took part in the wealth ranking exercise. If there are any blanks, it is because the group involved in the exercise did not explicitly voice this as a factor considered in allotting a household to a particular ranking (e.g. occupation considered by rural groups in allotting households to high or medium ranks, was not explicitly voiced as a factor for classifying households in low rank. It may well have been used implicitly).

** Chikan refers to a traditional local art of thread work on cloth.

*** Dhobi refers to a person engaged in washing and ironing clothes. The requirement to wash and iron the chikan cloth before sending it off to be sold results in the dhobis benefiting from the local chikan business.

**** The exact size of land was not specified as this was a rough relative assessment.

***** The level of dependency was expressed by discussants in general terms, e.g. as having many (or few) children or elderly members or having many (or few) working members. Numbers were not specified.

of the three groups. In cases of households which were allotted to different categories by each of the three groups, we intended ranking these households using a fourth group. It was not possible, however, to arrange a fourth ranking session as by then people were reluctant to give more time. We therefore decided to exclude these households from the analysis (15 households in the rural area and 18 in the urban slum).

The characteristics used by groups to classify households in the three categories of well-being – high, medium and low – were as shown in Table 6.7 for urban and rural areas. As shown in Table 6.7, the definition of well-being used by people in the village and the slum is similar. Income-related or monetary criteria (for example, regular jobs) are considered important by both. The perception of well-being includes a combination of monetary and non-monetary factors. In rural areas, for example, the possession of assets like tractors and amount of land are important criteria for well-being. The presence of sons in the household was also a commonly accepted social indicator of well-being. People in urban areas considered the ability of the household to educate children an important criterion. Households with minimal education were classified in the low or medium category and households with high level of education and children going to school were classified in the high category. Another non-monetary factor is social status. A widow in the urban area was ranked in the low category due to her social status in the community although in monetary poverty terms she belonged to the high category.

6.4.2   Results: field data

Participatory vs monetary and capabilities approaches

Using field data, we compared those identified as being in poverty by participatory well-being ranking (low rank) with those identified as being in monetary or capability poverty. We first present results of a comparison of the participatory well-being ranking with the monetary classification. For the monetary classification, the poverty line calculated for urban Uttar Pradesh by the U.P. state Planning Commission for 1999–2000 was updated using the Consumer Price Index for Industrial Workers for 2000–1. This updated poverty line of Rs 5054 per capita per year was used to classify individuals as 'poor' or 'non-poor' (Table 6.8).[16]

As shown in Table 6.8, a similar proportion appear to have been classified by participatory ranking as 'low' (36 per cent) as those classified as being below the monetary poverty line (35 per cent). Careful examination of those groups that do not overlap (i.e. MpWn and MnWp) reveals

Table 6.8: Well-being ranking versus monetary approach (field data for an urban slum in U.P.)

	Monetary poor	Monetary non-poor	Total
Well-being ranking poor			
col %*	54	26	36
row %	53	47	100
Well-being ranking non-poor			
col %	46	74	64
row %	25	75	100
Total	100	100	100
	35	65	100

Total cases N: 574

the following (see Table 6.8). If the monetary indicator is used to identify poverty, as seen from the row % almost half (47 per cent) of the well-being poor would be excluded as they are in monetary non-poverty, although ranked in terms of well-being as low. Similarly, as seen from the column %, if well-being ranking is used to identify poverty, almost half (46 per cent) of the monetary poor people would be excluded as they are monetary poor but ranked as having medium or high well-being (i.e. non-poor).

As a proportion of the total (Figure 6.3a) we find that the overlap between those classified as being of a medium and high well-being, with those being monetary non-poor (MnWn), is much higher (at almost half the population – 48 per cent), compared to the overlap between those classified as having low well-being and classified as being below the monetary poverty line – WpMp (at only 19 per cent). Thus it appears that people take monetary factors into account when classifying individuals as having a medium or high well-being to a greater extent than they do when classifying individuals as having low well-being. In the latter case, non-monetary considerations appear to play a larger role.

If we look at the distribution of individuals ranked as having low well-being (shaded part), according to monetary deciles (Figure 6.3b), we find that while low deciles do show a higher proportion as being ranked low, even the highest deciles (8 to 10) show almost one-fifth to one-third of the population ranked as having low well-being. This is further confirmation that monetary status is not the only criterion taken into consideration when defining low well-being. Given that the monetary

(a) Overlap

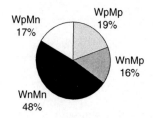

Monetary vs Well-being Ranking

(b) Monetary deciles vs well-being ranking

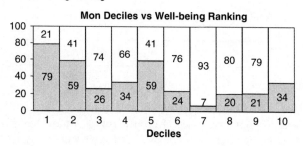

Figure 6.3: Monetary vs participatory well-being ranking

and participatory approaches rest on 'different epistemological and ethical underpinnings' (Shaffer 1996: 32 and see Chapters 2 and 5), it is not surprising that groups identified by the two approaches vary significantly.

Results of a comparison of findings of the monetary, capabilities and participatory approaches are presented in Table 6.9. Irrespective of whether the monetary classification or well-being ranking is used, quite a high proportion of capability poor individuals are classified as non-poor with regard to well-being and monetary poverty. As shown in Table 6.9a, if the monetary classification is used, the percentage of capability poor individuals classified as monetary non-poor ranges from 43 per cent (for health poverty for children) to 75 per cent (for health poverty for adults). Similarly if well-being ranking is used, a high proportion of capability poor individuals ranging from 43 per cent (for health for children) to 65 per cent (for health for adults) would be classified as well-being non-poor. Thus if resources were targeted based on either monetary criteria or well-being ranking on the assumption that people would be lifted out of other types of poverty, the results indicate that a

Table 6.9a: Percentage of capability poor classified as
monetary poor and non-poor

	Monetary	
	Poor %	Non-poor %
Education poor (Adults)	40	60
Education poor (Children)	56	44
Health poor (Adults)	25	75
Health poor (Children)	57	43

Table 6.9b: Percentage of capability poor classified as
well-being ranking poor and non-poor

	Well-being ranking	
	Poor %	Non-poor %
Education poor (Adults)	45	55
Education poor (Children)	56	44
Health poor (Adults)	35	65
Health poor (Children)	57	43

considerable proportion of individuals who are actually poor in terms of
education and health would be excluded.

Results: Social exclusion

One of the possible ways of operationalising the social exclusion concept
is to use participatory focus group discussions to define social exclusion.
In this exercise we should note that the groups that participated in the
FGDs were different from those which ranked households in terms of
well-being.

In the rural area one of the FGDs comprised female scheduled caste
members. The other two comprised a mixed caste female (there were
only Hindu women in this group) and a mixed caste and mixed religion
(including men belonging to Hindu and Muslim religions) male group.
In the urban area two FGDs were conducted – one mixed caste and
mixed religion male and one female group. The female group was predominantly Muslim (although belonging to different groups – Sheikh,
Sayed and Pathan) except for one woman belonging to a scheduled
caste. None of the participants in any of the FGDs saw themselves as
being socially excluded. Even those belonging to the lower castes, while

mentioning the existence of boundaries with upper castes (e.g. with regard to sharing food, or the site of residence), did not consider themselves socially excluded. The study consequently did not generate a useful definition of social exclusion.

Rather than an idea of exclusion of people from day-to-day life, people used a concept of *social expulsion*. This applies only to very specific cases under very specific circumstances. The *expulsion* takes the form of not being invited to any events in the community. Further, other people from the community would not participate either in a happy occasion in such a socially expelled household (e.g. weddings, the birth of a child, etc.) or a sad event (e.g. funeral). The female rural scheduled class group and the two urban groups mentioned that individuals who had married without parental consent, or couples involved in inter-caste or inter-religious marriages were subject to social expulsion. Such people may be forced to relocate to the edge of the communities' territory. Rural women mentioned that they would exclude anybody suffering from leprosy (this is supported by Harriss-White's findings – detailed in Chapter 8 – in a village of lepers isolated from the rest of society). The male rural group considered individuals who indulged in alcoholism (drunkards) and/or smoking as potential candidates for social expulsion, certainly by their own household. Similarly the female urban group considered anti-social behaviour like stealing or drinking as grounds for such expulsion. Yet, even when asked specifically about the role of caste, the rural female scheduled class group as well as the mixed female group were quite insistent that although there was a distinction between the upper and lower castes, especially with regard to eating food together and their areas of residence, there was no exclusion of lower castes from other activities in the community. Female members belonging to the scheduled caste did not consider themselves as being socially excluded.

It is important to note here that this failure to identify categories of social exclusion may partly reflect the way the concept was interpreted in group discussions. The focus was on identifying individuals who were not excluded from daily normal activities – like socialising, attending celebrations, eating, working, living etc. Although members belonging to the lower castes did not live in the same areas as or eat with upper castes, they only considered it social exclusion when members within their own caste were not allowed to eat with them or live amongst them – e.g. individuals with some diseases or couples married without parental consent. This differs from one way the concept has been interpreted in the developing country context, i.e. applying it to people who are significantly disadvantaged with respect to employment and political participation in the economy as a whole.

6.5 Summary

We have presented an empirical analysis of data for India comparing groups of people identified as 'poor' by different approaches. For the nationally representative NCAER/UNDP data, we explored monetary, capabilities and social exclusion approaches. Results reveal that, while the identification of poverty by monetary and capabilities approaches shows some correlation, it is quite low. A substantial proportion of individuals identified by one approach as poor may be classified as non-poor by another. Poverty profiles as well as logit analysis reveal the socio-economic characteristics of groups that are most likely to be in monetary and/or capability poverty or non-poverty as the case may be. The results indicate that the socio-economic characteristics of individuals being classified in different types of poverty, do vary. These results provide support to the finding that overlaps in classification by different approaches are low.

With regard to the social exclusion approach, the investigation of a group a priori classified as excluded, namely individuals belonging to SC and ST households, reveals that individuals belonging to these groups have a higher probability of suffering from monetary as well as capability poverty than individuals belonging to non-SC/ST households. A significant number of those classified by this approach as being socially excluded do not, however, classify as 'poor' by other approaches.

For new data collected by fieldwork a comparison was made between monetary, capabilities and participatory approaches. The findings are similar to those of the NCAER/UNDP data in that it is not necessarily the case that individuals identified as being monetarily 'poor' are also identified as being education or health 'poor' or even poor by participatory well-being ranking. The correlation between approaches is low and some individuals identified as poor by one approach are identified as non-poor by another. In fieldwork, we tried to used focus group discussions to define criteria for social exclusion. But the criteria identified related more to a concept of social expulsion, rather than exclusion.

Empirical work thus indicates that those who count as being poor are likely to differ according to the approach. This is not surprising given the differences underlying the conceptualisations of the approaches and the differences in socio-economic characteristics of individuals in different types of poverty. The substantial lack of empirical overlaps between monetary poverty and other types means that development policies which are targeted according to one type of poverty will involve serious targeting errors in relation to other types. Thus if monetary poverty is used as the sole criterion for targeting of benefits, it will have to be supplemented by other kinds of social transfers according to appropriate criteria if these errors are not to be very large.

Notes

1. Using a simple random sample from the population would generate a similarly distributed sample, but may not generate adequate numbers for certain subgroups of interest, e.g. women in the reproductive age group, to permit reliable inferences to be drawn for such groups. The procedure of stratification and variable sampling fractions addresses this problem, while retaining the randomness of selection. First the population is divided or stratified (as has been done with NCAER/UNDP data collection) into different groups (or strata). Within each of these strata, a random sample is then taken, using a sampling fraction suitable to that particular stratum so as to allow the collection of information related to a sufficient number of cases, to allow an analysis of the stratum separately. The use of such variable sampling, however, means that the profile of the collected sample does not match that of the population it is obtained from. In order to eliminate this distortion and obtain unbiased estimates about the population that the sample intends to represent, the sample needs to be adjusted. This is ensured by attaching differential sampling weights to the sampled unit's probability of selection into the sample. The weights are the reverse of that unit's probability of selection into the sample. Applying the weights restores the profile of the sample to that of the population (Forth and Kirby 2000).

2. The poverty line for India, as determined by the task force of the Planning Commission (1979), is partly normative and partly behavioural. The normative part comes from the fact that the poverty line is defined in terms of the per capita expenditure level at which the average per capita, per day calorie intake is 2400 calories in rural areas and 2100 calories per capita per day in urban areas. By the use of inverse linear interpolation being applied to the data (28th round NSS data for 1973–4) on average per capita monthly expenditure and the associated calorie content of food items, the level of expenditure associated with obtaining the requisite calories, per capita per day, was obtained. The behavioural part relates to the fact that the observed consumption expenditure levels that were associated with the appropriate calorie intake allowed for some margin for non-food consumption needs (as determined from the data rather than normatively). The procedure for updating the poverty line taking into account state-specific prices is outlined by the Planning Commission (1993).

The calorie levels mentioned earlier were estimated as average rural or urban per capita requirements calculated using the age-sex-activity specific calorie allowances recommended by the Nutrition Expert Group in 1969 and using the age-sex-occupational structure of the population (rural and urban separately).

3. If we accept the view that going to school has wider benefits than just that of becoming literate – in terms of allowing socialisation, increasing self-confidence and self-esteem – we would want to take into account children who are enrolled in school, irrespective of their literacy status.

4. During the fieldwork, both in urban and rural areas, discussants in the FGDs were of the view that at the very least children should have completed secondary education for it to be useful, especially in terms of gaining employment. Having any level of education below that was according to them neither here nor there. Given the low levels of literacy and primary school education itself, however, we felt that an analysis using a lower threshold was necessary before using secondary level completion as the education poverty threshold. For the empirical analysis for Peru, however (Chapter 7), such a higher threshold has been investigated. In the NCAER/UNDP data, literacy is defined as ability to read and write. In the fieldwork, however, we enquire about the ability to read, write and understand.

5. Anthropometric indices for the age group below 13 were available to us in the NCAER/UNDP data and we used this data for our analysis. Strictly, however, it is preferable to restrict the analysis to a younger age group. WHO recommends that for weight/height measurements, maximum age to be used for males is 11.49 and for females is 9.99 (Sullivan and Gorstein 1999).

   Preliminary analysis, however, revealed that although analysing data related to a higher age group, our results are robust. The findings with regard to overlap in poverty identification by the monetary approach, when using a $<= 12$ year age group were largely similar to those obtained using indices for the $<= 5$ year age group, in the NCAER/UNDP data.

6. These standards suffer from the major shortcoming that they were obtained from measurements of infants primarily fed infant formula food and in whom complementary feeding was initiated before 4 months. There is thus concern that the NCHS curves are inappropriate for breastfed infants and exaggerate the estimation of undernutrition (de Onis et al. 1997). Based on recommendations by the 1993 WHO Expert Committee, a study was undertaken to develop a truly international reference standard based on breastfed infants from multiple countries, living in healthy environments which would not limit their genetic growth potential (de Onis et al. 1997). The study has recently been completed and the WHO recommends the use of the new standards for any future studies in this domain.

7. If a child reacts to nutritional stress first by reducing physical activity below a critical level, the child could be undernourished although anthropometric indicators remain normal. On the other hand, if food intake is lowered, the body could adapt in a number of ways (physiologically, behaviourally and metabolically) with costless adjustments to body size. While it is accepted that such adjustments cannot proceed indefinitely, there is no agreement about the crucial cut-off point below which such adaptation impairs health (Svedberg 1991).

8. We did not use acute illness as an indicator of health poverty (although data were available). Though such information is useful to make general statements, e.g. about the incidence of acute illness at any given time, it would be inappropriate to classify individuals as health 'poor' or 'non-poor' on the basis of the one possibly very short-lived episode. Further, the focus group discussants in the fieldwork rejected acute illness as an indicator, arguing that most people suffered from such illnesses on and off and they considered this a normal way of life. Rather it was chronic illness and illnesses serious enough to need hospitalisation that were said to be indicators of ill-health.
9. *PRA Methods Pack: Tools and Techniques*, Praxis, Patna, India. Details available on PRAXIS web site (http://www.praxisindia.org).
10. We assume here that all individuals classified by the monetary approach as being 'poor' or 'non-poor' are classified correctly as also those classified by the capability approach. Depending on the limitations of indicators used, however, there may be some errors associated with these classifications.
11. Since the numbers in the analysis are very large, however, it would be expected that chi2 values would tend to be large and therefore quite likely to reject the null hypothesis of independence. We therefore decided to calculate in addition a statistic assessing the strength of correlation which would eliminate the effect of sample size. We use the Cramer's V statistic which measures the strength of association, with higher values indicating higher strength. Values range from 0.0 (no correlation) to 1.0 (perfect correlation). Cramer's V compares the observed table with the one expected under no relationship and standardises this comparison eliminating the effect of sample size (N) and the size and shape of the table.

$$V = \sqrt{\frac{\chi^2}{N \cdot min[(r-1)(c-1)]}}$$

Where χ^2 = chi2; N = total number of cases in the table. Min $[(r-1)(c-1)]$ = number of rows-1 or number of columns-1 whichever is smaller. It is because of its ability to eliminate the effect of sample size that it is sometimes used together with chi2 in the case of large size samples.
12. Figures for monetary 'poor' and 'non-poor' differ from the figures for Table 6.2 as the sample included in each table here is restricted to the age group for which the education/health/combined capability indicator has been obtained.
13. It is possible that within certain socio-economic groups, overlap between monetary and capabilities may be considerably higher than average and in certain others lower. In this chapter, we have not looked at overlaps within specific subgroups.
14. As described in Chapter 4, the social exclusion approach involves looking at the processes leading to poverty. The focus of this study, however, is on investigating the extent of overlap of identification of poverty, between different approaches.
15. We did not mention words like 'Garibi' which would suggest a stress on monetary aspects. Rather we used words like 'Sukhi' to indicate an overall good life.

16. During fieldwork in the rural area, data were collected for consumption expenditure and imputed values were obtained for home grown produce. Data on the proportion of the home grown produce that was sold and the proportion that was used at home were, however, not collected. It was thus not possible to impute values for the home grown produce that contributed to the consumption expenditure. Due to this shortcoming, we were unable to classify rural households based on their consumption expenditure and were thus unable to carry out this analysis on rural data. Results presented in this section are thus restricted to the urban data.

7
Poverty in Peru: a Comparison
of Different Approaches

Susana Franco

7.1 Introduction

In the first chapters of this book, we have looked at four different approaches to the definition of poverty: monetary, capabilities, social exclusion and participatory. These approaches arise from different conceptual bases, which have implications for the indicators that should be used to measure poverty. However, the different definitions that result would be of little importance in many respects if the same people were considered to be poor independently of the definition chosen. Chapter 6 has addressed this question, using empirical evidence from India and concluding that definitions do in fact matter. In this chapter we are going to explore whether the conclusions from Chapter 6 are specific to India or whether they hold when a country with different socio-economic conditions is considered. We therefore use evidence from Peru to explore the question of whether the same individuals are identified according to the different definitions; and also the characteristics of the individuals that are identified as poor by the various definitions.

Section 7.2 describes the data used in the study and the indicators chosen to measure each of the approaches to poverty. Section 7.3 presents the poverty profiles according to these different indicators using a data set that is representative nation-wide. A set of socio-economic characteristics of individuals and households for which data were available has been chosen in order to explore the prevalence of poverty in each group. Through this mechanism we identify the groups that show higher rates of poverty and we explore the congruence of the different approaches. Section 7.4 continues the analysis using a logit regression to investigate the characteristics that are likely to increase the probability of being poor according to each of the approaches, taking into account the possibility that some of those characteristics are correlated.

In Section 7.5 we look at the overlap between monetary and capability poverty, to investigate whether those two approaches identify the same set of individuals. The question of whether any lack of overlap is due to the threshold chosen is explored in Section 7.6.

Section 7.7 presents the results from two case studies, first using the definition of poverty that emanated from focus group discussions (FGDs) and then the results with regard to overlap or lack of overlap between the individuals identified as being poor according to the different definitions of poverty. Conclusions and policy implications are presented in Section 7.8.

7.2 Data and indicators

This empirical exploration of different measures of poverty in Peru has been carried out at two different levels:

(a) using a data set that is representative of the whole country. We work with the Encuesta Nacional de Niveles de Hogares sobre Medicion de Niveles de Vida (ENNIV), which follows the Living Standards Measurement Surveys methodology developed by the World Bank. The survey was carried out in May and June 2000 and covers 18 754 individuals in 3977 households. This part of the analysis is developed in sections 7.3 to 7.6.

(b) conducting two case studies, one in an urban area and the other in a rural one. We combined quantitative and qualitative techniques, using participatory techniques to explore people's perceptions of poverty and carrying out a survey that provided additional information.

The indicators and thresholds chosen for our analysis of poverty are presented in Table 7.1. These choices were based on the arguments presented in Chapters 2–4, but were constrained by the availability of data in the ENNIV.

Following the discussion in Chapter 2, the indicator chosen to measure monetary poverty was based on household expenditure as a measure of per capita consumption. Despite its shortcomings, this is preferred over the indicators based on income data both from a theoretical point of view and in terms of accurate measurement. Equivalence scales have not been adopted to take into account the differences in demographic structures within the households. There were two main reasons for this

Table 7.1: Indicators and thresholds used for the different approaches

Approach	Name of indicator	Definition	Threshold
Monetary	– Per capita expenditure		(a) Total poverty line, by area, based on Basic Consumption Basket (b) Extreme poverty line, by area, based on Basic Food Basket
Capabilities: Education	• Adult (age >= 18): – Literacy – Primary – Secondary	– Self-reported ability to read and write – Completion of primary education – Completion of secondary education	Yes/No Yes/No Yes/No
	• Child (age >= 6 & < 18): – Enrolment	– Currently enrolled in education	Yes/No
Capabilities: Health	• Adult (age >= 15 & < 60): – Chronic – Ill	– Suffering from any chronic illness – Suffering from an illness in the previous four weeks	Yes/No Yes/No
	– Bedridden	– Having to stay in bed or stop working due to illness during the previous four weeks	Yes/No
	• Child (age < 5): – Stunting	– Height for age ratio	– 2 Standard Deviations from NCHS median
	– Wasting	– Weight for height ratio	– 2 Standard Deviations from NCHS

Indicator	Description	Value
– Underweight	– Weight for age ratio	median – 2 Standard Deviations from NCHS median
– Undernourished	– If undernourished according to any of the above	Yes/No
Social Exclusion:		
– Employment[1]	– Unemployed, employed in precarious conditions or self-employed in the informal sector	Yes/No
– Insurance[1]	– Having medical insurance	Yes/No
– Pension[1]	– Affiliated to a pension system	Yes/No
– Credit	– Access to any type of credit in the household	Yes/No
– Savings	– Access to any type of savings in the household	Yes/No
– Social Programmes	– Any member of the household benefiting from a social programme	Yes/No
– Land Ownership[2]	– Ownership of at least 50% of the land they work	Yes/No

Note: NCHS stands for National Council of Health Statistics, the organ that calculated the reference values that are used for international comparisons. (1) Only computed for the individuals in the work force. It excludes those working in agricultural activities. (2) Only computed for those working in agricultural activities.

decision. Firstly because there is still some debate about the use of equivalence scales, particularly in developing countries, and secondly because we decided to use the same definition of monetary poverty that is widely used when analysing this data set in Peru and is the basis for policy debate in the country. Thus, we can use this measure of poverty as a benchmark to compare poverty as measured through the other approaches. This was also the reason to use the same poverty lines that the Instituto Cuanto (2000) defines. The extreme poverty line is set at a level that covers the cost of a basic food basket (BFB) that meets the minimum nutrition values, following the Food Energy Intake method that has been discussed in Chapter 2. The total poverty line is set at a level that covers the cost a basic consumption basket (BCB). This is equal to the BFB plus the cost of other goods and services. It is calculated multiplying the value of the inverse of the coefficient that measures the proportion spent on food with respect to total consumption for the decile that has a level of expenditure on food similar to that of the BFB.

Although ideally the implementation of the capability approach should have been based on the comparison of capability sets, data constraints have reduced our analysis to comparisons between 'chosen functioning vectors' (for an in-depth discussion of the differences between those concepts see Chapter 3). The same constraints provided the reason for reducing the analysis to two sets of basic capabilities of functionings: health (including nutrition) and education. Given that our aim is identifying the particular individuals who are poor, we have avoided indicators that have been used to measure capability poverty at the level of the population, such as life expectancy at birth or infant mortality per thousand deaths, but which cannot be used to assess whether a particular individual is poor or not. Thus, 'education poverty' has been measured using enrolment as an indicator in the case of children. For adults, several indicators, which correspond to different thresholds in the level of education, have been explored when preparing poverty profiles. Those indicators are literacy, completion of primary education and completion of secondary education. The second of those indicators (completion of primary education) seemed the most appropriate to measure this dimension of capability poverty in Peru and was therefore used for the rest of the analysis. The levels of 'health poverty' have also been explored through several indicators. In the case of children, different measurements of undernutrition were used: stunting, wasting and underweight, as well as a combination of all of them, considering a child to be undernourished if they were under 2 standard deviations of the median reference value for any of the other three indicators. Our choice of indicators was severely restricted by the availability of data in the case of adults and we were therefore limited to the use of three crude indicators: whether the individual had been affected by an illness during the previous four weeks, whether the illness had been so severe that it had forced them to stay in bed or stop working, and whether they suffered from any chronic illness. Among these, the combined indicator of undernourishment and the indicator for chronic illness were chosen for the further analysis of the health dimension.

As discussed in Chapter 4, social exclusion emerged in the developed world in relation to the welfare state and unemployment status of the individuals. The translation of the concept to developing countries is not straightforward. It needs to be tailored to represent the particular society addressed. In Peru there have been some studies that have measured social exclusion (e.g. Aramburú and Figueroa 2001). The methodology they use provides an aggregate estimate of social exclusion, but does not allow the identification of particular individuals as being excluded. Other studies have developed the concept of social exclusion in the country at a theoretical level. In their seminal paper exploring social exclusion in Peru, Figueroa et al. (1996: 1) state that 'a social group is considered "excluded" if it is not allowed to participate in some social relations of the social process which are desirable by the group'. The same study defines social exclusion in three spheres (economic, political and cultural):

- *Economic* exclusion occurs when the individuals cannot actively participate in the productive economic systems. This translates into exclusion from the labour, credit and insurance markets.
- *Political* exclusion occurs when a legitimate authority does not guarantee the rights of the person. The rights can be civil (fundamental personal freedoms such as freedom of residence, expression of belief, right to property ownership), political (the right to elect and be elected), social and economic (basic education and health, housing, employment, social security) and cultural.
- *Cultural* exclusion is defined in two areas: the marginalisation of certain groups that do not adhere to the basic requirements of interaction within the community (including language, the ability to read and write, ethical values) and discrimination against individuals considered to be inferior. This translates into exclusion from social

networks. This type of exclusion particularly affects the indigenous population.

Although the different spheres are usually interlinked, an individual might be excluded from some of the areas, but not from others. As with capability, we can explore several indicators that would measure exclusion on the different areas, given the availability of data. Some of the above spheres are more difficult to measure than others. Figueroa et al. (1996) estimate exclusion from some of the indicators using data from different sources. The indicators for which data was available in the ENNIV are presented in Table 7.1. Economic exclusion is measured by the type of employment, access to insurance, credit and savings. The question in the survey with regard to land ownership does not ascertain whether the landholder possesses a property title. In that sense, this indicator measures economic exclusion rather than providing an indication of political exclusion through a legitimated right of property. The right to basic education and health (or rather the access to it) has been explored under the capability approach. Cultural exclusion, measured as the inability to read and write, has also been explored under the capability approach. Indigenous individuals are not specifically identified in the survey, but we have information about the mother tongue of the individuals. This variable can be used as a proxy, identifying indigenous with native speakers.

7.3   Poverty profiles

The level of poverty according to each indicator was computed and poverty profiles were constructed for each indicator to explore different socio-economic characteristics. These characteristics were selected following those in previous studies (World Bank 1999; Escobal et al. 1999) and others given that they were thought to have had an impact on the poverty levels. These characteristics are:

- Race: *White, Mixed* or *Other* race (Chinese/Japanese or black).[1]
- Mother tongue: *Spanish* or *Native*.
- Household head gender: *Male* or *Female*.
- Area: *Lima*, other *Urban* or *Rural* areas.
- Migration: *Migrant* or *Not migrant*. This variable was defined based on whether the household head had moved from the place where they had been born when they were 15 years or older.

- Household size: *Small* (one to four members), *Medium* (five to seven members) or *Large* (eight or more members).
- Gender of the individual: *Male* or *Female.*
- Household head education: *None, Primary, Secondary* or *Higher* completed.
- Dependency ratio: The dependency ratio is defined as the ratio between the number of dependants (people aged less than 15 or older than 60) and the number of people of working age (between 15 and 60). Five subgroups have been defined: *0, (0, 0.5), (0.5 to 1), (1 to 2), higher than 2.*
- Employment of household head:
  - *Employed in the formal sector:* Employed with a contract that is either indefinite or fixed-term.
  - *Employed in precarious conditions:* Employed without a contract or with apprenticeship or similar contract.
  - *Self-employed in the formal sector:* Self-employed legally registered.
  - *Self-employed in the informal sector:* Self-employed not legally registered.
  - *Not-working:* Unemployed or not in the workforce (student, pensioner, etc.).

The results for monetary poverty and education poverty are presented in Table 7.2. The first numerical column of Table 7.2 presents the proportion of the total population in each of the sub-categories (e.g. 95 per cent of the individuals are of mixed race and 29 per cent of the people live in Lima). The rest of the columns provide the percentages of the population that are identified as poor according to each indicator. The first row provides the proportion of the whole of the population or the relevant age group (e.g. those aged 18 and above for adult education) who are poor.

7.3.1 Monetary poverty

According to the official poverty line, the rate of monetary poverty in Peru is 54 per cent, with 15 per cent of the total number of individuals being extremely poor. As shown in Table 7.2, these population averages map unevenly onto the socio-economic characteristics of individuals and households. The values for extreme poverty are obviously smaller than those of total poverty, but they both follow the same pattern identifying groups in which poverty is higher.

168

Table 7.2: Poverty profiles

		Population (*)	Monetary		Education				Health						
					Adults			Children	Adults			Children			
			Poor	Extreme poor	Second	Primary	Literacy	Enrolment	Ill	Chronic	Bed-ridden	Stunting	Under-weight	Wasting	Under-nutrition
TOTAL			**54**	**15**	**49**	**20**	**8**	**7**	**21**	**10**	**6**	**26**	**11**	**3**	**29**
Race	Other	1	30	5	41	21	6	8	25	15	10	45	0	0	45
	White	5	24	5	25	8	2	5	27	21	7	9	6	5	13
	Mixed	95	56	15	51	21	8	7	21	9	6	27	11	3	30
Mother tongue	Spanish	85	51	12	43	16	5	7	20	10	6	22	10	3	25
	Native	15	70	31	80	43	21	7	29	10	7	48	18	1	51
Household head gender	Male	85	55	15	50	20	8	7	21	10	6	27	11	3	31
	Female	15	47	11	46	19	9	7	22	11	6	17	8	2	18
Area	Lima	29	45	5	33	8	2	6	17	12	6	8	4	3	10
	Urban	36	50	8	42	16	5	6	22	11	6	21	9	3	25
	Rural	35	66	30	76	39	17	8	24	8	7	40	16	2	43
Migration	Not migrant	68	57	17	51	21	9	6	22	10	6	30	12	3	32
	Migrant	32	49	10	46	18	7	8	20	10	6	15	9	3	19
Household size	1 to 4	29	32	5	50	22	9	7	24	13	7	24	10	3	28
	5 to 7	50	57	15	49	19	7	6	21	9	6	27	11	2	29
	8 or more	21	78	27	50	20	8	8	18	8	5	26	12	3	30
Gender	Male	49	55	15	46	15	4	7	19	10	6	27	10	3	30
	Female	51	54	14	53	25	12	7	23	10	6	25	12	2	27
Household head education	Less than prim.	7	70	28	81	60	44	11	26	9	8	30	10	2	31
	Primary	40	65	21	71	33	9	9	22	10	6	33	15	3	36
	Secondary	36	54	12	41	7	3	5	21	10	6	23	9	3	26
	Higher	17	22	1	9	2	1	4	21	12	6	12	6	2	14
Dependency ratio	0	7	28	2	36	12	5	24	23	15	6	–	–	–	–
	0 to 0.5	30	47	7	41	14	6	11	19	11	5	15	8	4	19
	0.5 to 1	32	55	14	50	19	7	7	22	10	7	21	9	3	24
	1 to 2	23	67	24	63	30	11	4	23	8	6	35	14	2	37
	Higher 2	8	63	31	79	45	21	3	24	8	5	37	16	2	40
Household head employment	employ-formal	17	37	4	29	8	3	4	21	11	6	12	7	3	15
	employ-precat.	16	66	20	55	21	8	7	22	10	7	27	10	2	30
	self-formal	10	33	7	35	11	4	6	23	11	6	20	8	6	25
	self-informal	41	66	22	63	29	11	8	22	9	6	33	13	2	37
	not-working	17	42	8	44	18	7	9	18	11	5	18	13	3	20

Note: (*) This column shows the proportion of the distribution of the population in the sample in each of the subgroups.

Some important characteristics of those in monetary poverty are as follows:

- The rate of monetary poverty is higher among individuals of a mixed race than for either whites or those of other races.
- It is also higher among those whose mother tongue is a native language rather than Spanish. Native language speakers live mainly in rural areas and are of mixed race.
- Surprisingly, it is higher in male headed households than female headed households.
- The proportion of poor individuals is higher in other urban areas than it is in Lima and even higher in rural areas. Less than half of the individuals in Lima are poor while two-thirds of the individuals living in rural areas are. The difference is even higher when extreme poverty is considered: only 5 per cent of the individuals in Lima are extremely poor, but this figure rises to 30 per cent in rural areas.
- Poverty is slightly greater among non-migrants than among migrants.
- The rate of poverty increases with the household size. This might be the result of not adjusting the poverty line to take into account economies of scale.[2]
- The rate of poverty is lower the higher the level of education of the household head. For instance, 70 per cent of the individuals living in households where the head has not even finished primary education are poor, compared to 22 per cent who are poor in households where the household head has completed higher education. The corresponding figures are 28 per cent and 1 per cent for extreme poverty.
- The rate of monetary poverty also rises with the dependency ratio in the household. In households where the number of dependants is more than double the number of people of working age, the rate of poverty is 63 per cent compared with 28 per cent in households with no dependants. Those figures are 31 and 2 per cent in the case of extreme poverty.
- The type of employment of the household head is also relevant. Monetary poverty is higher among those individuals living in households whose head is either self-employed in the informal sector, or working as an employee in precarious conditions.

7.3.2 Education

As shown in Table 7.1, several indicators have been considered in order to measure the education dimension of capability poverty (education-poverty) in the context of capability poverty. For adults those variables are literacy, the completion of primary and secondary education. The rate of education-poverty is 8, 20 and 49 per cent respectively.

The three indicators of adult education-poverty follow the same pattern:

- In many cases, the groups identified as having greater rates of monetary poverty also show higher levels of education-poverty. This holds for individuals of mixed race, native language speakers and those living in rural areas.
- It also holds for the type of employment of the household head: adults living in households whose head is self-employed in the informal sector or employed in precarious conditions tend to be education-poor.
- As with monetary poverty, the rate of education-poverty is also higher the higher the dependency ratio in the household and the lower the level of education of the household head. In the latter case, we face the problem of a kind of 'built-in correlation', because the household heads are also included when counting the individuals that are education-poor.
- The rate of education-poverty seems to be slightly higher among non-migrants than migrants.
- The gender of the household head does not seem to be relevant in marking differences in the rate of education-poverty.
- Household size, which was a distinguishing factor in terms of monetary poverty, is not significant in education-poverty. This might support the hypothesis that the fact that monetary poverty is higher among larger households is not because the individuals in those households are poorer in a monetary sense but rather because we have failed to include economies of scale.
- An aspect that now becomes relevant is the gender of the individual: the level of poverty among females is higher than among males. This holds for the three indicators considered, but the level of association is highest for illiteracy, followed by completion of primary education and becoming rather small for completion of secondary education: 46 per cent of males have not completed secondary education as compared with 53 per cent of females. The percentages are 15 for males and 25 for females for lack of completion of primary education. The level of illiteracy among women is 12 per cent and only 4 per cent among men.[3]

For children aged between 6 and 17, school enrolment is used to measure whether the young person is education-poor or not. The level of education-poverty among them is relatively low, with only 7 per cent not being enrolled in school. Some of the variables considered above do not seem to make a difference with regard to the level of education-poverty of the children, thus indicating that the differences among the different groups found for adults no longer hold when the education of the children is considered. The variables that make a difference are:

- The level of education of the household head. The percentage of children that are not enrolled in school is higher the lower the level of education of the household head.
- The dependency ratio. The relationship between the dependency ratio and the level of education poverty runs in the opposite direction to monetary poverty. In this case, the lower the dependency ratio, the higher the level of education poverty among the children. The reason for this might be that a limited number of children stay at home to help with the household or farm work. Households with a lot of children will not send one or two to school, but will send the others. Children that do not have any siblings will stay at home to help.
- The type of employment of the household head. Children in households whose head is not working, or who is self-employed in the informal sector or employed in precarious conditions show lower levels of school enrolment.

7.3.3 Health

As with education-poverty, the health dimension of the capability approach (health-poverty) has been measured using several indicators. For adults,[4] the level of health-poverty according to each of these indicators is as follows:

(a) individuals suffering from any chronic illness: 10 per cent
(b) individuals affected by an illness during the previous four weeks: 22 per cent
(c) individuals whose illness was so severe that it caused them to stay in bed or stop working: 6 per cent

All of these variables have the drawback of being self-reported. This might lead to bias if people in some of the groups are more likely to report illnesses than in others. The third variable, for instance, does not show a significant association with any of the groups considered above. It is not clear, though, whether this is because health-poverty thus measured is really independent of the group considered or whether some of the groups, even if their health is worse, will continue working because they cannot afford to take days off.

Both chronic and temporary illness are higher among white people than people of other races and the incidence of illness during the last four weeks is higher among native speakers than among Spanish speakers. The rate of chronic illness is higher in Lima than in the other areas, while the incidence of illness during the previous four weeks is highest in the rural areas. In both cases, the smaller the household size the higher the rate of people with self-reported illnesses. Lower dependency ratios seem to be accompanied by higher levels of chronic diseases, but the relationship does not seem to hold for illnesses during the previous four weeks.

For children under the age of 5 three standard measures of malnutrition have been used to measure health poverty. The rate of malnutrition in children below the age of 5 is: 26 per cent for stunting, 11 per cent for underweight, 3 per cent for wasting and 29 per cent for the combined indicator that considers the child to be undernourished if he/she has been found to be undernourished according to any of the three individual indicators.

Wasting is not associated with any of the social characteristics considered. Underweight is highest among native speakers, in rural areas, among the households whose head has a low level of education, and in households with large dependency ratios. It is not associated with race, the gender of the household's head or the gender of the individual, or with migration status or household size.

Stunting and the combined indicator follow the same pattern.[5] Both of them show lower levels of deprivation among whites and Spanish speakers. For instance, the combined indicator is twice as much for native speakers as for Spanish speakers (51 per cent to 25 per cent). It is highest in male headed households, in rural areas and among non-migrants. Household size and the gender of the individual do not seem to be differentiating categories. Once again the level of malnutrition is higher in households where the head has low levels of education, in those with high dependency ratios and for children living in households whose head is either self-employed in the informal sector or employed in precarious conditions.

7.3.4   Social exclusion

The percentage of individuals identified as socially excluded according to the various indicators for social exclusion, which were defined in

Table 7.1, is as follows:

- Employment: 74 per cent
- Insurance: 79 per cent
- Pension: 83 per cent
- Credit: 83 per cent
- Savings: 90 per cent
- Social programmes: 32 per cent
- Land ownership: 15 per cent

The first five indicators identify a large proportion of the population as being socially excluded. This indicates that its adoption would reflect the definition that Figueroa et al. (1996) use in the sense that these are *desirable* standards. However, they are *not the norm* in the Peruvian society. It also confirms the point made in Chapter 4 about the inappropriateness of transferring Western standards of unemployment and underemployment to notions of social exclusion in developing countries. For our purposes, it does not make sense to use an indicator of social exclusion that, as for those five indicators, identifies at least three quarters of the population as excluded. Access to social programmes might seem a more appropriate indicator. However, social programmes are generally targeted to those with low income. Therefore, the households that do not benefit from them might well include two separate groups: those that were not targeted because of their high incomes and those that, although they should have been targeted, failed to receive the benefits. Only the latter should be considered socially excluded, but our data do not allow us to discriminate between them. We are left with the last indicator, land ownership, which would provide at best a very partial measure of social exclusion and only for the third of the population that are engaged in agricultural activities.

Given that our data do not provide us with better indicators we decided to return to our previous results and identify groups that exhibit higher rates of monetary and capability poverty. Figueroa et al. (1996) suggest that indigenous populations are particularly affected by social exclusion. Our empirical results with regard to the other types of poverty corroborate this. We have shown that the proportion of individuals who are monetary poor is certainly higher among native speakers (our proxy for them) than among Spanish speakers. It is also higher for the different indicators of education-poverty for adults and for children's health. The fact that their levels of poverty are higher in several dimensions might therefore be an indication to suggest that indigenous people are in fact socially excluded.

7.4   Logit analysis

The analysis in Section 7.3 has identified the groups that are more likely to be poor in each dimension of poverty. However, it does not take into account the possibility that some of the characteristics that we have considered might be correlated. For instance, native speakers are likely to be of mixed race, large households might be more common in rural areas than in urban areas, and so on. Logit analysis help us to identify the groups that are more likely to be poor *other things being constant.* That is, if two individuals share all but one of the characteristics being considered, is one of them more likely to be poor than the other? Here we take a base case against which the probability of being poor may be evaluated. This base case is a white male that speaks Spanish as his mother tongue and lives in Lima in a male headed household with 1–4 members and a dependency ratio of zero (meaning that every person works). The household head is not a migrant, has achieved a level of education higher than secondary and is self-employed in the formal sector.

7.4.1   Monetary poverty

Individuals identified as being more likely to be poor are those of a mixed race and native speakers. They are not migrants; they live in a large household with a large dependency ratio whose head has a low level of education and works as an employee in precarious conditions or is self-employed in the informal sector. Characteristics that do *not* affect the probability of the individual being poor include gender, the gender of the household head and, quite surprisingly, rural–urban status. That means that if the only factor that differentiates two individuals is the fact that one lives in Lima while the other lives in a rural area, they are equally likely to be poor.

The factors that affect the probability of being extremely poor are slightly different. The dependency ratio, the level of education of the household head and household size are significant variables in determining the probability of being extremely poor. Mother tongue is also significant, with native speakers being more likely to be extremely poor. Race and the migration status, on the other hand, are not significant. In contrast to total poverty, extreme poverty is affected by the area where the household is situated: extreme poverty is more likely to occur in rural areas than in urban areas, if all the other factors are kept constant.

7.4.2 Education

There are several factors that increase the probability of being education-poor among adults. Females, migrants and native speakers are more likely not to have completed primary education, our indicator to measure the education dimension in the capability approach. The gender of the household head is also a relevant factor, with individuals in male headed households being most likely to be education-poor. It also appears that the larger the household size, the smaller the probability that the individuals will be education-poor. With respect to the area where the household is situated, adults living in Lima are least likely to be poor, followed by those living in other urban areas, with those living in rural areas the most likely to be education-poor. The lower the level of education of the household head and the higher the dependency ratio, the higher the probability of being poor. The type of employment of the household head is also relevant. If they are self-employed in the informal sector or employees in precarious conditions, individuals are more likely to be education-poor.

With regard to children's education, the level of poverty seems to be independent of many of the factors considered. Those that do affect it are the level of education of the household head and the dependency ratio. In both cases the lower they are, the higher the probability of being poor. Children living in rural areas are more likely to be education-poor than those living in urban areas. Among the different types of employment undertaken by the household head, the probability of being education-poor is smallest for children living in households where the head works as employee in the formal sector.

7.4.3 Health and undernutrition

The results for the probability of chronic illnesses are quite different, and in many cases the opposite to those for the probability of being monetary poor. The probability of suffering from a chronic illness decreases if you are an individual of mixed race and if you live in a rural area. The larger the household to which you belong and the lower its dependency ratio the less likely you are to be health poor.

The probability of being undernourished among children is higher for native speakers and non-migrants. It increases with the dependency ratio in the household and it is significantly smaller for those children living in households where the head works as an employee in the formal sector.

7.4.4   Comparison

The objective of this analysis was not only to identify which factors are more likely to affect poverty considering each approach separately, but also to compare whether they are the same for monetary poverty as for capability poverty. Table 7.3 thus combines all the information, showing whether the various characteristics move in the same direction for monetary poverty and for each of the different dimensions of capability poverty.

Taking each of the dimensions in turn, we can see that there are several factors that increase the probability of both being poor in terms of adult education and in monetary terms (native speakers, low household head education, high dependency ratio and certain types of employment of the household head). Some of the characteristics have an impact on monetary poverty but not on adult education poverty (e.g. race) while the opposite happens with others (e.g. the gender of the individual, the area where the household is situated and the gender of the household head). There are a couple of factors (migration status and household size) which do indeed move in opposite directions.

For child education, we have already seen that there are not many factors that, other things being equal, would increase the probability of being poor. That is, even if they have an influence on monetary poverty they do not affect children's education. There are two factors that do not have an impact on either one or the other (the gender of the individual and of the household head), one for which the impact runs in the same direction (education status of the household head), one for which it runs in the opposite direction (the dependency ratio) and one for which, even if there were no impact in terms of monetary poverty, there is an impact in terms of enrolment (living in a rural area). This last case, for instance, means that if two children share the rest of the characteristics and only differ in the area where they live, the one that lives in the rural area is not more likely to be monetary poor, but he/she is more likely to be education-poor.

In terms of adult health we find a large disparity. None of the factors move in the same direction as monetary poverty. There are three factors that have conflicting impacts (race, household size and dependency ratio). Although a certain degree of disparity between monetary and health indicators is to be expected, the fact that the disparity is so large

Table 7.3: Monetary, education and health poverty: logit coefficients

		Monetary		Education		Health	
		Poor	Extreme poor	Primary	Enrolment	Chronic	Under-nourished
Race	Other White	−0.28	−0.94	0.39	0.26	−0.32	1.11
	Mixed	0.75***	0.07	0.08	0.25	−0.80***	0.46
Mother tongue	Spanish						
	Native	0.50***	0.58***	0.99***	−0.05	0.17	0.51***
Household head gender	Male						
	Female	−0.15	0.09	−0.63***	−0.15	0.04	−0.48**
Area	Lima						
	Urban	−0.09	0.37	0.51***	0.22	−0.03	0.83***
	Rural	−0.16	1.40***	0.97***	0.54**	−0.32**	1.20***
Migration	Not migrant						
	Migrant	−0.33***	−0.21	0.14**	0.24	−0.02	−0.35**
Household size	1 to 4						
	5 to 7	1.05***	1.15***	−0.32***	0.22	−0.28***	−0.41**
	8 or more	2.01***	1.96***	−0.39***	0.33	−0.43***	−0.23
Gender	Male						
	Female	−0.02	−0.04	0.97***	0.14	0.07	−0.19

Continued

178

Table 7.3: Continued

		Monetary		Education		Health	
		Poor	Extreme poor	Primary	Enrolment	Chronic	Under-nourished
Household head education	Below primary	1.93***	2.47***	3.92***	0.97***	0.06	0.27
	Primary	1.53***	2.23***	2.68***	0.65***	0.12	0.56**
	Secondary	1.13***	1.88***	0.81***	0.03	0.01	0.21
	Higher						
Dependency ratio	0 to 0.5	0.40**	0.80*	0.25**	-1.12***	-0.24*	-
	0.5 to 1	0.70***	1.37***	0.44***	-1.74***	-0.28**	0.28
	1 to 2	0.91***	1.55***	0.97***	-2.46***	-0.43***	0.85***
	Higher than 2	0.87***	2.17***	1.20***	-2.76***	-0.48**	0.85***
Household head employment	Emp-formal	0.49**	-0.28	0.28*	-0.15***	0.09	-0.60**
	Emp-precarious	1.38***	1.00***	0.49***	0.25	0.04	-0.15
	Self-formal						
	Self-informal	1.15***	0.62**	0.39***	0.19	0.00	-0.15
	Not-working	0.22	0.15	0.10	0.31	0.01	-0.37
	Constant	-3.90***	-7.65***	-5.39***	-2.31***	-0.98***	-2.41***
	F	25.50***	17.14***	87.84***	10.33***	4.38***	9.76***

Note: * indicates significance of the individual coefficients at the 10 per cent level;
** indicates significance at the 5 per cent level; *** indicates significance at 1 per cent level.

raises some doubts about the indicator used. It is possible that some groups under-report their illnesses.

In terms of undernutrition we find that there are some factors which make poverty more likely to occur according to both approaches, and none in which the effects on the two types of poverty are contradictory. For some factors, even if the likelihood of monetary poverty increases, the same does not happen with undernutrition. There are two factors that seem to increase the probability of undernutrition, even though they do not affect monetary poverty: living in a rural area and in male headed households.

7.5 Overlap

This section explores the degree of overlap between the different dimensions of poverty. In order to do so we have chosen one indicator to measure the education dimension of capability poverty: failure to complete primary education in the case of adults and not being enrolled in school in the case of children. Another indicator measures the health dimension: chronic illness for adults and the combined undernutrition indicator for children. A combined capability indicator was also constructed according to which an individual is classified as capability very poor if they are both education and health poor, capability poor if they are either education poor or health poor and capability non-poor if they are neither education nor health poor. We have constructed contingency tables that show the distribution in terms of monetary poverty of those individuals who are capability poor compared to those who are capability non-poor. These are shown in Table 7.4, with the numbers in the cell indicating row proportions. The degree of association is indicated by Cramer's V and log-odds ratio.[6]

These tables point to several conclusions. In general, the proportion of monetary poor people is higher among those who are capability poor (in either the individual dimensions or according to the combined indicator) than it is among those who are capability non-poor. Thus for instance, 63 per cent of those who have not completed primary education are monetary poor, while 44 per cent of those who have completed it are still below the monetary poverty line. This relationship holds if we consider extreme monetary poverty rather than total monetary poverty. For a given capability dimension (for instance, completion of primary education), 22 per cent of those who are education poor are also monetary poor compared with only 8 per cent of

Table 7.4: Characteristics associated with monetary and capability poverty: logit results

	Education																		Health																	
	Adults								Children										Adults								Children									
	↑↑		↑↓		↑=		==		↑↑		↑↓		↑↑		↑=		==		↑↑		↑↓		↑↑		==		↑↑		↑↑		↑↑		↑=		==	
	M	C	M	C	M	C	M	C	M	C	M	C	M	C	M	C	M	C	M	C	M	C	M	C	M	C	M	C	M	C	M	C	M	C	M	C
Race: Mixed					X										X						X												X			
Language: Native	X														X						X								X							
Household head gender: Male			X										X								X				X				X							
Area: Rural					X											X					X				X				X				X			
Migration: Not	X												X								X				X											
Household size: Larger	X												X						X								X									
Gender: Female					X						X						X				X				X											
Household head education: Lower	X										X								X												X					
Dependency ratio: Higher	X										X								X						X											
Head employment:	X												X						X						X								X			
Precarious employee or self-informal																																				X

Note: M stands for monetary poverty and C for capability poverty (either education or health). The signs above each of them indicate whether the logit results suggest that the logit analysis has shown that the relevant factor is likely to increase (↑) the probability of being poor, decrease (↓) it, or the factor is irrelevant (=).

the education non-poor. The only counter-intuitive exception to this pattern is chronic illness. The proportion of monetary poor is higher among the chronically non-ill (55 per cent), than among the chronically ill (45 per cent).

The fact that in most cases the proportion of monetary poor is higher among the capability poor than among the capability non-poor seems to indicate that there is a positive relationship between monetary poverty and capability poverty. However, the low values of the Cramer's V and log-odds tests suggest that the level of association is very low, implying that the extent of overlap is quite low.

The contingency tables can help us to assess the extent of the lack of congruence, which is considerable. For instance, 21 per cent of the children that are malnourished and 37 of adults who have not completed primary education are monetary non-poor, that is more than one in five and one in three respectively. In fact, 42 per cent of those who are capability poor as measured by the combined indicator are monetary non-poor. The figures are bigger when extreme monetary poverty rather than total monetary poverty is considered.

The pie charts in Figure 7.1 illustrate – for the socio-economic groups – the proportions of individuals for which:

(a) overlap exists – either because they are poor both in a monetary and capability dimension (areas marked CpMp) or non-poor in either dimension (CnMn) – and

(b) overlap does not exist, being capability poor but monetary non poor (CpMn) or capability non-poor and monetary poor (CnMp).

The area of overlap, indicated by the combined areas CpMp and CnMn, is quite small. When considering total poverty, we notice that the level of overlapping varies from only 41 per cent in the case of education capability (children) (36 per cent CnMn and 5 per cent CpMp) to 57 per cent in the case of the adult education indicator (44 per cent CnMn and 13 per cent CpMp). As the level of capability poverty is lower for all indicators than the level of monetary poverty, the degree of overlap increases when extreme monetary poverty is considered. This is because the area CnMn will increase more than the CpMp will decrease. Thus the degree of overlapping in terms of extreme monetary poverty varies from 69 per cent for child health to 77 per cent for the other three indicators.

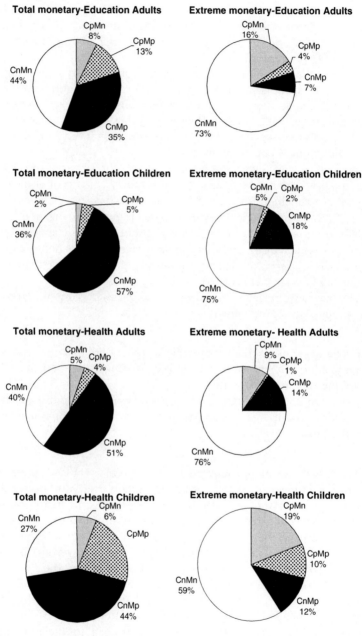

Figure 7.1: Overlap between monetary poverty and capability poverty: pie charts

If we assume that governments want to reach those who are capability poor, but target instead those who are monetary poor, the following consequences will happen in terms of coverage:

- A large proportion of individuals that are *non*-capability poor will be perversely included. This percentage is as high as 57 per cent of school age children when education poverty is considered as an indicator. This is an important factor to consider when resources are scarce.
- Some individuals who are not monetary poor but *are* capability poor will be left out. As much as 9 per cent of the population for which the combined capability indicator has been computed are capability poor (being education and/or health poor) but not monetary poor. For some of the individual indicators the proportion of those left out might seem quite small (2 per cent in the case of child education) but granted that the proportion of children that are education poor and monetary poor is only 5 per cent, this is an error of exclusion of 40 per cent.

7.6 Deciles

One doubt that arises is whether the lack of overlap is large because the monetary poverty line has been drawn too high. This might happen if those people who are capability non-poor but monetary poor are in fact positioned close to the poverty line, albeit below it. Figure 7.2 shows the level of capability poverty prevalent for each monetary decile.

It is evident that in all cases but chronic illness, the level of capability poverty (the shaded area in the figure) decreases as we move from the lowest to the highest monetary deciles. What is also true is that capability poverty is relatively high even in the highest decile. Consider for instance undernutrition: 12 per cent of the children in the highest decile are undernourished. That means that more than one in ten of the richest children are undernourished. If the monetary poverty line had been lowered, the degree of overlap would have been increased, but it would still have remained considerable, as a large proportion of the capability poor would remain above the threshold for monetary poverty.

184

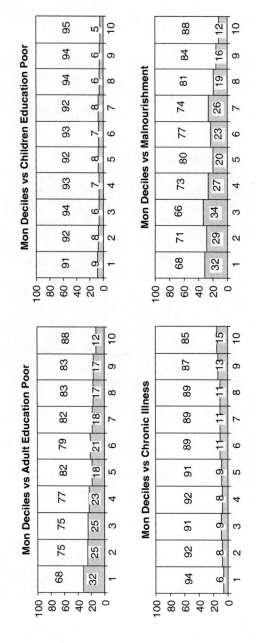

Figure 7.2: Monetary deciles vs capability poverty

Note: The shaded areas represent the proportion of individuals that are capability poor in each monetary decile.

7.7 Case studies

The above results have shed light on the differences between the monetary and capability approaches to poverty. We also undertook two case studies, one rural and one urban, where we used participatory methods, to further explore the analysis of poverty. Through these case studies we have further investigated a definition of social exclusion in Peru and have compared the four approaches, even if at a small scale. In both cases social mapping, wealth ranking and focus group discussions and a household survey were carried out.

The rural study took place in a community called Ninamarca, part of the Paucartambo district in the Andes. The community consists of about 60 households, all dependent on agriculture. Paucartambo, the closest town, is about one hour away by car and two hours on foot.

The urban study took place in two settlements (Virgen de Fatima and Paraiso) in Villa Maria del Triunfo, one of the districts on the outskirts of Lima. The settlements are adjacent to each other and have around 125 households each. They were chosen to generate greater variation than the profile that one of the settlements alone would give. The preliminary visits seemed to indicate, from external household characteristics, that each settlement alone might have been too homogeneous.

7.7.1 Focus group discussions

The social mapping exercise got people talking about aspects of their communities they enjoyed and appreciated, as well as their needs. This constituted the starting point for their definition of poverty.

While discussing what characterises poverty in an urban setting, distinguishing which of those characteristics are causes and which are consequences of poverty, a very rich description of poverty emerged.[7] The main points are summarised here and in Figure 7.3.

- *Precarious livelihoods and assets*. All the groups identified employment as a central need of poor families. In addition to the lack of employment, they mentioned its instability, its low wages and the difficulties of access to jobs for people over 40 years old. They also mentioned the difficulties of saving or obtaining credit from the banks. The Bank of Materials (Banco de Materiales) provided loans to improve their houses in Paraiso, where they had the property titles, but repayment is increasingly difficult because of the economic crisis.
- *Physical insecurity*. The poor are victims of delinquency and robberies, but poverty also induces people to break the law and to join gangs.

Alcohol abuse was also mentioned, in particular problems caused by drunken husbands.

- *Social relations.* Urban people felt that there was a lack of unity among the inhabitants of the settlements. This incapacity to act collectively undermined their ability to overcome routine problems.
- *Institutions.* The need for more support, financial and otherwise, from the institutions (by which they meant government and international aid donors) was mentioned.
- *Material needs.* Lack of money was usually identified as one of the intrinsic characteristics of being poor. This lack of money translated into the inability to cover some of their material needs: lack of food that causes malnutrition, deficient housing conditions (both in terms of the precariousness of the materials used in their construction and the lack of basic infrastructural services) or adequate clothing.
- *Capabilities.* Lack of education referred both to the adults' lack of education that prevents them from accessing better paid jobs, as well as the lack of resources to send their children to school. Lack of willpower was also mentioned: the poor do not do enough to overcome their situation of poverty.
- *Powerlessness.* People in the groups felt a large degree of impotence with respect both to institutions (e.g. government, health and education establishments, police) and those richer than them. They suffered from injustices committed both by the institutions and by employers. They felt, for example, that they were mistreated by the police and health professionals. They felt exploited at work (low pay, long working hours, working with no contracts). They also mentioned racial discrimination.
- *Ill-health.* The experience of health includes first the fact that poor people get ill more easily and, when they do, they do not have resources to buy medicines or to access the services. In addition, people suffer mental health problems that are related to poverty, denominated as 'psychological effects' of poverty by a group of men. Under this category issues such as stress and worries related to lack of employment were included, as well as sadness and quarrels between partners or within families, in some cases leading to the abandonment of the family by the men.

In the rural setting, the definition of poverty that was generated was not so comprehensive, focusing to a larger extent on the material side of poverty. The discussions were conducted with men and women

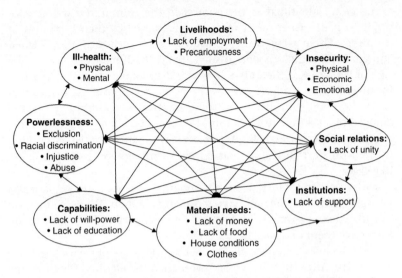

Figure 7.3: Poverty characteristics from a participatory approach (urban case)

separately. The following paragraphs present the picture that was drawn from those discussions.

Women started by affirming that all the peasants are poor, therefore including all members of the community. Then they began to delimit this by saying that the poor are those that do not have enough to buy what they need: their work only provides enough to eat and they do not have enough left to sell. Therefore they do not have resources to buy other things. The cause of this was said to be having little or bad quality land, as well as having few animals. They mentioned that in general there was little land in the ayllu.[8] In some Andean rural areas all the land is communal property, but in the case of Ninamarca the property of the land is passed from parents to children.[9] The land each family has access to depends therefore on what they received from their parents.

Sometimes poverty increased after a bad harvest or due to physical factors such as rain or frost. In these cases the poorest were most affected because they lack coping mechanisms.

Escaping poverty themselves was considered almost impossible, and they only had hope for the next generation. Women placed a lot of emphasis on their children's education which, they believed, would provide them with access to work of higher quality and better wages than their own.

The group identified as the poorest in the community was that of single women, either never married, abandoned by their husbands or widowed. There were cases of widows who, although they owned enough land, could not work it since their sons did not help them. The case of widows was the only one where the women identified changes in poverty status, as widowed women became poorer. As mentioned above, women consider that their poverty is conditional on the amount of land they receive from their parents. There is no way to get out of poverty through land, not even through marriage. According to the women, rich people marry their own kind and poor people do likewise.

With regard to fertility, women found no difference between poor and non-poor families: they all have too many children. While women do not like having so many children because they cannot support them, men force them to have children.

With the male group we also started by asking about their experience of poverty. After that we worked with them to identify which of the characteristics that had been mentioned were considered causes and which were consequences of poverty.

As a cause of poverty they mentioned the 'lack of luck': arguing that sometimes people are unlucky, falling victim to catastrophe and plunging them into poverty without escape.

Men also mentioned having many children as a cause of poverty, since they cannot support them. Nevertheless when they did the wealth rank of the families, they reached the conclusion that you could not really distinguish between them according to the number of children for they were similar in the different strata.

The poor were identified as those having little money, the cause being in many cases that they did not want to work. This was linked to the impact of alcohol consumption.

External shocks were again mentioned as a cause of poverty, the weather in particular, because it can cause bad harvests. The lack of tools to work in the farm was also mentioned as a cause of poverty, as well as having little land. Nevertheless, men said that the fact of having little land could be overcome, because it was possible to rent land. Rents can be paid with cash, in kind or in exchange for work.

Another cause of poverty, for the men, was having to borrow food because own production is not enough to feed the family. The women had nevertheless declared that in their community they all had enough to eat, even if it was just potatoes. It is worth mentioning here that when asked about the organisations operating in the area, the women had mentioned an NGO that provides some food (rice, oil, lentils, beans . . .) which was not mentioned by the men.

The factors considered to be consequences of poverty were: not having enough food, having little stored, with food intake limited to the subsistence products (swede, barley, potatoes . . .) uncomplemented by other products. Another 'consequence' is that they cannot buy consumer goods such as electrical devices, clothes or notepads.

The only characteristic considered to be both a cause and a consequence of poverty was the fact of not having animals: the poor men cannot afford to have animals and as they do not have income from animals, they continue being poor.

In contrast to women, men thought it was possible to escape poverty, through work and with capital. However, after some discussion, they reached the conclusion that access to capital was limited to only a few people, depending to a great extent, once again, on the land that they had received from their parents. Access to credit was mentioned as a way to obtain capital. The Agrarian Bank had provided credit in the past, but it no longer does. Such institutions have replaced the provision of credit by inputs on a rotating basis, tools and training.

We can extract some conclusions with regard to social exclusion, based on the discussions from both case studies. In both cases, the groups denied any form of general exclusion within their small communities: if particular individuals were excluded it was because of personal differences, rather than any general characteristic, such as race or employment status. Things were different when the society as a whole was considered. In the urban setting, the elements described above, particularly those mentioned under *powerlessness*, suggest that the individuals interviewed felt discriminated against when trying to access publicly provided services. They also felt exploited by other members of the society who were better off than themselves in economic terms. The fact that they were living in a slum and they had lower incomes marked them as different. Therefore, that type of social exclusion was suffered by all the individuals in the two urban settlements under study. However, racial discrimination was particularly mentioned, thus confirming that being from indigenous origin is a source of social discrimination in Peru. In the rural case, it is significant that in one of the groups the discussion started with the sentiment that all the peasants are poor. This also seems to indicate that, somehow, they feel that, as peasants, they do not have access to the same opportunities and living standards as other members of the Peruvian society and therefore are socially excluded. In both cases, these elements indicate the

190

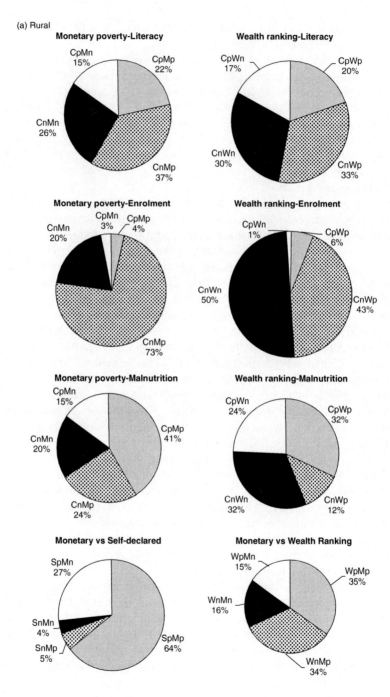

(a) Rural

Monetary poverty-Literacy

CpMn 15%
CpMp 22%
CnMn 26%
CnMp 37%

Wealth ranking-Literacy

CpWn 17%
CpWp 20%
CnWn 30%
CnWp 33%

Monetary poverty-Enrolment

CpMn 3%
CpMp 4%
CnMn 20%
CnMp 73%

Wealth ranking-Enrolment

CpWn 1%
CpWp 6%
CnWn 50%
CnWp 43%

Monetary poverty-Malnutrition

CpMn 15%
CpMp 41%
CnMn 20%
CnMp 24%

Wealth ranking-Malnutrition

CpWn 24%
CpWp 32%
CnWn 32%
CnWp 12%

Monetary vs Self-declared

SpMn 27%
SnMn 4%
SnMp 5%
SpMp 64%

Monetary vs Wealth Ranking

WpMn 15%
WpMp 35%
WnMn 16%
WnMp 34%

Figure 7.4: Overlaps: case studies

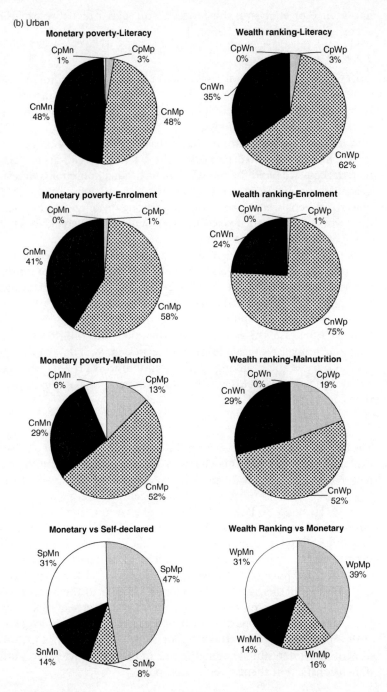

Figure 7.4: Continued

importance of analysing the processes through which the exclusion occurs, a point raised in Chapter 4.

7.7.2   Wealth ranking

Both in the urban and rural cases, a selected number of informants were asked to produce a wealth ranking that would allow comparisons with poverty measured in terms of money and capabilities. Discussion of the discriminants of wealth follows.

In the urban setting, all informants based their ranking on access to work. The ordering also depended on the extent of precariousness of the materials used to build the houses. Female headed households were also identified among the poorest, even if they had jobs. Although the objective criteria seemed to be common among the different informants, there was variation in their perceptions about how the different households ranked according to these criteria.

The number of groups identified according to wealth varied between 5 and 7. When prompted about which of the groups were poor, they generally indicated one or two of the groups, but when asked to evaluate local poverty compared with that of the whole country, only one or two groups were left as *non*-poor.

In the rural case, the women based their decisions on the amount of land and animals that each household possessed. Men did likewise, but they also based their ranking on the ability to work. That is why some female headed households were identified as poor: even if they had land they could not work it.

7.7.3   Overlap

The degree of overlapping between the different definitions of poverty is explored in the series of pie charts in Figure 7.4 and the contingency tables in Table 7.5. As with the national data set, we observe that there is a large proportion of non-overlap between monetary and capability poverty. There is also lack of overlapping between individuals living in poor households, as identified in the wealth ranking, and those that turn out to be poor according to the monetary definition. Wealth ranking and capability poverty also present a significant lack of overlap.

Self-declared poverty, as measured by the answer in the survey to the question of whether the household head considered themselves to be 'very poor', 'poor' or 'non-poor' also shows a high degree of lack of overlap. In general the proportion of people considering themselves to be poor is higher than those who are poor as measured by any of the other dimensions. Interestingly, though, some of those who are poor in other dimensions, report themselves as 'non-poor'.

Table 7.5: Overlap between monetary and capability poverty: contingency tables

(a) Total Monetary vs Education (adults)

	Monetary Poor	Monetary Non-poor	Total
Cap. Poor col %	26.39	14.52	20.23
row %	62.73	37.27	100
Cap. Non-poor col %	73.61	85.48	79.77
row %	44.37	55.63	100
Total	100	100	100
	48.08	51.92	100

Cramer's V: 0.15
Log odds: 0.32

(b) Extreme Monetary vs Education (adults)

	Monetary Poor	Monetary Non-poor	Total
Cap. Poor col %	39.93	17.79	20.23
row %	21.79	78.21	100
Cap. Non-poor col %	60.12	82.21	79.77
row %	8.32	91.68	100
Total	100	100	100
	11.04	88.96	100

Cramer's V: 0.17
Log odds: 0.49

(c) Total Monetary vs Education (children)

	Monetary Poor	Monetary Non-poor	Total
Cap. Poor col %	7.68	5.87	6.98
row %	67.48	32.52	100
Cap. Non-poor col %	92.31	94.15	93.02
row %	60.87	39.13	100
Total	100	100	100
	61.34	38.66	100

Cramer's V: 0.03
Log odds: 0.13

(d) Extreme Monetary vs Education (children)

	Monetary Poor	Monetary Non-poor	Total
Cap. Poor col %	8.81	6.54	6.98
row %	24.37	75.63	100
Cap. Non-poor col %	91.19	93.46	93.02
row %	18.93	81.07	100
Total	100	100	100
	19.31	80.69	100

Cramer's V: 0.04
Log odds: 0.14

Continued

Table 7.5: *Continued*

(e) Total Monetary vs Health (adults)

	Monetary Poor	Monetary Non-poor	Total
Cap. Poor col %	8.21	12.04	9.96
row %	44.88	55.12	100
Cap. Non-poor col %	91.79	87.96	90.04
row %	55.48	44.52	100
Total	54.42	45.58	100
	100	100	100

Cramer's V: 0.06
Log odds: −0.18

(f) Extreme Monetary vs Health (adults)

	Monetary Poor	Monetary Non-poor	Total
Cap. Poor col %	6.26	10.59	9.96
row %	9.19	90.81	100
Cap. Non-poor col %	93.74	89.41	90.04
row %	15.22	84.78	100
Total	14.62	85.38	100
	100	100	100

Cramer's V: 0.05
Log odds: −0.25

(g) Total Monetary vs Health (children)

	Monetary Poor	Monetary Non-poor	Total
Cap. Poor col %	34.18	18.42	28.93
row %	78.78	21.22	100
Cap. Non-poor col %	65.82	81.58	71.07
row %	61.74	38.26	100
Total	66.67	33.33	100
	100	100	100

Cramer's V: 0.16
Log odds: 0.36

(h) Extreme Monetary vs Health (children)

	Monetary Poor	Monetary Non-poor	Total
Cap. Poor col %	44.05	24.14	28.52
row %	33.98	66.02	100
Cap. Non-poor col %	56.18	75.80	71.48
row %	17.29	82.71	100
Total	22.00	78.00	100
	100	100	100

Cramer's V: 0.18
Log odds: 0.39

(i) Total Monetary vs Combined Capability (adults)

	Monetary Poor	Monetary Non-poor	Total
Cap. Poor			
col %	22.17	19.03	20.73
row %	57.78	42.22	100
Cap. Non-poor			
col%	77.83	80.96	79.27
row %	53.04	46.96	100
Total	54.02	45.98	100
	100	100	100

Cramer's V: 0.04
Log odds: 0.08

(j) Extreme Monetary vs Combined Capability (adults)

	Monetary Poor	Monetary Non-poor	Total
Cap. Poor			
col %	26.60	19.75	20.73
row %	18.39	81.61	100
Cap. Non-poor			
col %	73.41	80.25	79.27
row %	13.27	86.73	100
Total	14.33	85.67	100
	100	100	100

Cramer's V: 0.06
Log odds: 0.17

(k) Total Monetary vs Combined Capability (children)

	Monetary Poor	Monetary Non-poor	Total
Cap. Very Poor			
col%	2.15	1.32	1.77
row %	65.58	34.42	100
Cap. Poor			
col %	20.02	17.71	18.96
row %	57.05	42.95	100
Cap. Non-poor			
col %	77.83	80.96	79.27
row %	53.04	46.96	100
Total	54.02	45.98	100
	100	100	100

Cramer's V: 0.04

(l) Extreme Monetary vs Combined Capability (children)

	Monetary Poor	Monetary Non-poor	Total
Very Poor			
col %	2.46	1.65	1.77
row %	19.91	80.09	100
Poor			
col %	24.15	18.09	18.96
row %	18.25	81.75	100
Non-poor			
col %	73.41	80.25	79.27
row %	13.27	86.73	100
Total Monetary	14.33	85.67	100
	100	100	100

Cramer's V: 0.06

7.8 Conclusions

The empirical investigation carried out in this chapter has demonstrated that different definitions do matter. We have shown that the individuals that are identified as being poor according to one approach are not necessarily the same as those who are poor according to another. In many cases, they do not even share the same socio-economic characteristics.

The choice of indicators to measure poverty has been limited by the availability of data. The rich picture of poverty that arises from definitions involving capabilities, social exclusion or participatory views is not easy to measure, but the exploration of these definitions can help us to reach a better understanding of what poverty is.

Poverty has multiple dimensions that are not captured by one single indicator. When selecting the indicators to be used for identification or targeting of people who are poor, policy-makers should be aware that they may fail to include individuals that would be considered to be poor if other dimensions of poverty were to be considered. For instance, selecting individuals for social programmes based on the fact that their income places them below the poverty line would exclude many individuals who are capability poor from these benefits. Therefore, programmes designed to reduce monetary poverty are likely to be ineffective in reaching all the capability poor or those that would be considered poor by participatory criteria. Programmes aimed at reducing capability poverty should involve less focus on monetary transfers or income generation and more on public education and health programmes.

The participatory exercise suggests that employment creation should be an important element of poverty reduction policies. This is in accordance with the empirical results from the other definitions considered, as it was shown that individuals living in households whose head is employed in precarious conditions or is self-employed in the informal sector are more likely to be poor, either in a monetary sense or in terms of capabilities. This seems to be an element of social exclusion that affects a large proportion of the population.

The indigenous population is also particularly affected by poverty, independently of the definition used. It is therefore suggested that particular policies should be directed towards these groups in order to reverse this situation.

Notes

1. The racial classification was decided by the interviewer, based on the physical appearance of the individuals. As a result, 95 per cent of the population was classified as mixed.

2. Although it would have been possible to adjust the poverty line accordingly and/or using equivalence scales, we took the decision of not doing so in order to get figures for monetary poverty that correspond to the ones commonly used by policy-makers in Peru.
3. The levels of literacy are self-reported, no test was carried out to confirm what the individuals declare.
4. The term 'adults' is used in a loose sense. Children above the age of 5 have been included because measures of malnutrition were not available to measure their level of health poverty. Adults over 59 have been excluded to take into account the fact that many illnesses would in such cases be age-related rather than poverty-related.
5. This is not surprising, because given the way the combined indicator has been defined, both indicators show considerable overlap. Only 3 per cent of the children are malnourished but not stunted.
6. The log-odds ratio can attain its upper bound even under weak perfect association. In our case, considering that the level of monetary poverty is higher than capability poverty, weak perfect association would imply that all the individuals that are capability poor are also monetary poor and the lack of overlap only arises because some of the monetary poor are not capability poor.
7. They included many of the aspects mentioned in the World Bank study *Voices of the Poor* when describing the dimensions of powerlessness and ill-being. Figure 7.3 is adapted from the one used in *Voices of the Poor* (p. 249).
8. *Ayllu* is a term which refers to extended family and local community structures and occupation of space which are part of the Andean tradition.
9. Part of the land is communal. They grow cereals and potatoes there that are either sold or distributed among the population.

8
Destitution in India and Peru

Barbara Harriss-White

Inspired by the research on the many dimensions of poverty presented in this book, this chapter differs from the rest in three respects. First, it is centrally concerned with questions of process, which by the very nature of their databases, the other empirical chapters cannot largely examine. Second, it is concerned not simply with poverty but with the very poorest of the poor: those who 'have' nothing (in terms of assets), 'are' nothing (in terms of political and social status) and contend with ferocious obstacles to the exercise of agency (i.e. can 'do' virtually nothing in terms of realising their capabilities). Although destitution becomes dramatically massed and visible at moments of extreme events such as famine, war and environmental disasters, I will not discuss it through those prisms.[1] I will argue that the mundane condition of destitution is not well conceptualised as extreme poverty, and that the existence of the word suggests that it is a qualitatively different condition. Instead, destitute people are a social category which exists within the territorial boundaries of a society but from which society evidently wishes to rid itself.[2] So third, this chapter is concerned with 'policy' in the sense of society's response. It finds that both state and society are implicated in antagonism towards destitute people, whether they are conceived as problems in social work or in development.

To build this exploratory analysis I have used literature on India and Peru, although because this literature is unsystematic, idiosyncratic and treats the topic obliquely, this chapter – unlike the rest of the book – cannot be rigorously comparative. I have also used my personal field experience with destitute people and NGOs working with them in India in 2002 and 2005.[3] The method of the chapter is to examine economic, social and political processes leading to destitution; then to map destitution onto the approaches to poverty researched in this book; to examine coping relations; and finally to consider the significance of this conception of destitution for policy responses. Since destitution is an economic, social and political phenomenon, each aspect will be examined in turn.

8.1 Economic aspects of destitution

It is useful to begin with insights from development economics. Here, destitution is a twofold kind of deprivation in the 'space' of income or monetary poverty. It involves, first, the absence of any control over assets and, second, the loss of access to income from one's own labour. As a state, it is a contradiction in terms because the complete absence of assets and income spells death. There can be no such thing as long-term destitution. The specification of medium- or long-term destitution then cannot avoid a value judgement of what might constitute a 'nearly complete absence'. One accepted measure is 'a quarter of median rural income' (Hyat 2001), but in fact this threshold is quite arbitrary. It is a convenience for statistical treatment. These economic definitions allude to a process of loss, one which deprives a person of control over assets and income. While loss of assets leads to loss of income from rent or production, loss of income may also be a labour-market phenomenon resulting from the denial or the unavailability of wage work. What deprives people of their control over assets and labour? Economists have focused on hysteresis phenomena – sequences of events in which losses of certain crucial assets are triggered which act as a ratchet, and which trigger other losses in turn, after which things can never return to their previous state. Such events include accidents, profligacy (addictions) and 'natural' disasters as well as health deprivation in the 'space' of capabilities; they are accompanied by debt.[4] People are pitched into increasingly continuous periods with increasingly less assets. The detail of this process of destitution, which is also known as 'coping' or 'survival' is known to vary depending on the quality, lumpiness and complementarity of assets, the timing and the terms of trade of their dispossession, their gendered ownership and their implications for a person's capabilities. A plausible common sequence involves the progressive liquidation of small stock, livestock, consumer goods and eventually the failure to protect from sale the key productive assets, female assets (gold and other moveable collateral) before male assets (land).[5]

Destitution is being conceived of here as an *individual* phenomenon because, by the time a person is destitute, they are usually an individuated remnant of a collapsed household.[6] The process therefore requires the loss of insurance mechanisms – notably savings and credit – with which the members of a household (or a social unit larger than a household) protect themselves from these ratcheting events or shocks to consumption. Insurance may be lost by a change (increase) in the risk of shocks, by a run of uncertain events, by exclusion from a process of rationing both of the means of insurance and the beneficiaries of it, or by the imposition of constraints on the use of specific assets to smooth income or consumption (Hyat 2001). The process of loss of insurance may itself be sequenced – one such sequence would involve a loss of access to non-productive precautionary savings, then to reciprocal, interest-free borrowing, to commercial loans at interest, and to high interest money lenders, then the exhaustion of productive precautionary savings and reduction to a state of extreme vulnerability.

Turning to the loss of control over one's labour, two types of relationship are involved. In one, tactics are deployed by others to force unemployment, for example by preventing entry. The existence of socially regulated wages above a theoretical clearing wage will prevent some workers from being employed. There are specific social rules which determine the particular people who are debarred.[7] Physical condition, being malnourished, disabled or bearing the signs of leprosy may lead to an exclusion which becomes self-reinforcing. Indeed, 'disability' is understood in rural society in terms of a socially defined incapacity for work (Erb and Harriss-White 2002). The second aspect of the loss of control is a culmination of what Sen has called 'unfair inclusion' rather than exclusion (Sen 2001). Forms of labour exploitation become increasingly threatening to the subsistence of labour and so to its day-to-day reproduction. Early on, the right to the asset of one's own labour may be forfeited. This right may be sold (bonded) to others. The concept of dependence may be transformed and the labour of non-labouring dependants sold or bonded. The most extreme tactics do not involve the sale of labour so much as the marketing of the body itself (as in the sale of blood or of organs) or the renting of the body (as in sex-work) (Ram 2002a, 2002b).

8.2   Social aspects of destitution

It has already become evident that destitution is not simply an outcome of market exchange or 'market failure' to be measured in the monetary domain, it is also the loss of enfranchisement or entitlements which are not price-mediated, e.g. the loss of access to 'common' property and public goods and services, the disappearance of political legitimacy and citizenship, i.e. the violation of political rights. It means the collapse of moral units above the level of the individual, the draining away of social support. In India, belonging to a scheduled caste/scheduled tribe, being old and disabled, in Peru, being of Andean indigeneity, migrant, young and out of school, are serious conditions of multiple disadvantage,[8] but not sufficient conditions for the withdrawal of obligation (Rojas and Rey 2002). Rather, categories of people must be recognised as unworthy of exercising social claims and therefore rejected from relationships of accountability. Rather than being passively socially excluded (from a vector of entitlements from which the vast bulk of the population are also excluded[9]) they may be actively socially *expelled*. No less than for assets and labour we have to ask what triggers such losses in customary and moral worth, such extraordinary transformations of social and political status and such an extreme violation of political, economic and social rights.

The transgression of norms of inclusion – of pure, 'clean' practices, 'healthy' sociality, 'normal' sexuality and socially compliant behaviour – will be one kind of trigger for social expulsion.[10] The moral regulation of inclusion has varying plasticity. It will be specific to ethnicities, castes, religions, genders and places. Being social constructs, moral rules are contested and can be changed.

The departure or death of those whose duty is to support, or their failure to support a dependant as a result of desertion/divorce/bigamy (Gupta 2002) or dispute, physical inability and incapacity are other triggers. Other kinds of abuse or neglect of this duty, such as the relations of dysfunctional, reconstituted, violent families when a parent remarries, or the sexual abuse of children result in minors or widows taking to the streets (Speak 2004).[11]

Change to the body is a third. The latter may in turn take several forms. The neglect of actual or perceived or symbolic cleanliness (as happens in addiction); the inability to bear a (male) child; deformity or disability in childhood; signs and symptoms of certain kinds of disease, mental illness or psychological state; even outward signs of extreme malnutrition or starvation may precipitate disenfranchisement. A destitute person is one who is unable to choose to be a *sanyasi* (a spiritual pauper). To have cancer was enough for one Indian woman to be thrown out of her household onto the mercy of abusive police. AIDS is still extremely stigmatising in Peru and may be sufficient for social expulsion (Herencia 2004). Heroin and alcohol-addicted people or those with leprosy will usually be turned away from religious orders and sometimes rejected even as objects of charity from them.

The process of expulsion may involve forcible physical exclusion from the space of a moral unit like a caste or a village. In Andean culture the word for poor is *waqcha*, meaning 'orphan' and drawing attention to the absence of social ties and the instrumental value as well as intrinsic worth of the family (Figueroa 2003). The Hindi word for poverty – *daridhratha* – means 'roving' and implies the breakdown of 'community' (Gopal 2001). It may take the form of uncompensated and unpunished violence to persons, at the extreme (as in the waves of fascistic communal violence in India in 2002), seizure of assets or the complete destruction of property. This expulsion is deemed justifiable and legitimate by those practising it.

However, it also must not be forgotten that expulsion from moral and political society, and exclusion from work or from social protection derived from work or from the preconditions for the day-to-day reproduction of the body or from citizenship are some of the many conditions necessary for the accumulation of wealth by others. This is how destitution enters political economy. It is not simply that the technical requirements for labour processes require some kinds of bodies to be denied access (and with labour displacing growth characteristic of the last decade it is entirely to be expected that exclusive reformulations of the eligibility of the body for labour markets will appear). It is not simply that revenue for social sector spending is simultaneously squeezed, and thus eligibility for social protection by the state will need to be restricted (Russell and Malhotra 2001). It is also that exclusion from exploitation is based on, and legitimated by, culture. The latter entitles society actively to practise oppression. The state is complicit in this process. This theme is revisited later in this essay.

8.3   The state: criminalised poverty and law-induced destitution

Within the territorial boundaries of a state not all people are citizens with the political and economic rights that are slowly being constructed on the basis of citizenship. Lack of citizenship does not only apply to international migrants and refugees. In Peru, despite decades of UN funded projects of incorporation, the formal recognition of native ethnic groups is far from complete: towards the end of the twentieth century 1516 peasant communities and 320 native communities were known not to be titled. This meant that about 27 per cent of these populations lacked any official recognition or rights (Valera 1998;

Figueroa and Barron 2005). But destitution is not simply a serious condition of deprivation of citizenship, illegitimacy and/or invisibility before the state. Under certain conditions (for example those under which the state seizure of land, state-planned, development-induced displacement or state-backed, corporate displacement fail to compensate or 'rehabilitate' evicted people) the law and institutions of development may actively cause destitution (Figueroa and Barron 2005; Barclay 1998; Aroca 1996; Sharma 2002; Dhargamwar et al. 2003). Abuse at school may also force children into destructive street environments (Gigengack 2006). The laws which regulate destitution also exacerbate it. Destitution is also a hard matter of criminalising law.

Vagrancy is a crime. In India, beggary must be 'prevented' under the Act with that name. The state varies greatly in its complicity with beggary. It appears to be most complicit in rural areas and small towns and most intolerant in metropolitan cities. The occupations of destitute people are criminalised – not simply sex-work, or the couriering or peddling of drugs but even mobile trading and squatter trading. An unregistered trading site and the erection of shelters are prosecutable under planning laws, pedestrians' rights and in terms of public nuisance and trespass.[12] Certain kinds of addiction and self-predation are illegal. Children in need of care and protection, children in conflict with the law and child labour fall under the jurisdiction of the judiciary and police.

The enforcement of these laws involves the removal and incarceration of such people. In Peru, many *serranos*, migrants from the Andes, were incarcerated without trial under suspicion of association with *Sendero Luminoso*, the rebel movement, a process which left them destitute on final release (Rojas and Rey 2002; GRADE 2003). In India, targets of preventive detention set for the police require the regular rounding up of homeless and destitute people. Lack of assets, access to law and/or literacy means many fail to secure bail or redress through the courts. Upon release, those not destitute beforehand are destitute after indeterminate periods of detention. The threat of eviction or detention for long periods creates incentives for collusive relations of avoidance involving pay-offs. Institutionalised relations of extortion increase the costs of destitution. These transactions are accompanied by violence. Beating is allowed in law upon apprehension of criminality; and sexual violence on the part of the police is far from being unknown.

In India, recent changes to these laws increase the formal powers of police with respect to destitute people. The Juvenile Justice Act, for example, covers children in need of care and protection and children in conflict with the law. The first category includes street children, child labourers (waiters, garage hands etc.) orphans and the children of beggars and sex-workers. The latter category consists of criminal offenders or children framed for criminal offences. The Act was altered in 2000 after consultation with activists (which ensures that the current Act will be very difficult to amend in future). The upper age of 'children' covered has been increased from 16 to 18, the role of the police enhanced and the destination of preference is segregated institutions. In practice, the older teenagers are harassing younger children; police have institutionalised relations of extortion with juveniles on the streets and part of their operating budgets varies directly with the number of juvenile offences recorded, giving them incentives to harass children. States like Chhattisgarh, already under pressure to reduce and offload social sector spending, are withdrawing from the provision of social security and are eager to have their penal institutions privately run.

The duty of the state to provide shelter (and other economic and social rights) is observed in the breach.[13] In Lima, there appear to be no state-run night shelters for the stream of migrants from the rural *sierra*. A mere Rs 1 crore (around £113,000/$215,000[14]) has been allocated to cater for the needs of homeless people throughout India. In New Delhi in 2002, there were 14 night shelters providing floors or sleeping benches for an estimated 5.6 per cent of the homeless (Menon 2001). In one such, up to 400 men bed down in lines on mats for Rs 6 a night. There is little provision possible for storing belongings. There appeared to be one tap; showers and latrines were in a foul state of maintenance and blankets infested with lice. Lights are kept blazing to prevent conditions conducive to sexual abuse. 'Butterflies' is a grim room for some 50 children, also sleeping in the same conditions of surveillance. Some children are able to store personal belongings in metal trunks. A second shelter, erected after some agitation by workers, is a flimsy temporary tent of polythene and bamboo with no lighting. The Corporation acts as if it needs actively to repel this workforce and between 1998 and 2002, one-third of its shelters had been closed (Singh 2001a; Aashray Adhikar Abhiyan 2002).[15]

Social responses to destitution are contradictory. On the one hand, society follows and develops the assumptions in the law as it is practised. The selective violation of rights is sanctioned by society. It initiates social expulsion, practises notions of justice involving stigma, which permit harsh oppressive treatment outside the law. It condones unpunished illegal extortion, mob justice and the reinforcement of exclusion. It gives a customary licence to harass (including sexually), to abuse, thieve from, be violent towards, push to impure space and not to come to the aid of destitute people. The suspected abuse of entry barriers to accepted and institutionalised kinds of dependence such as (religious/ yogic) begging, public suspicion of deliberate injury or faked disability, and of the deliberate organisation of child beggars by beggar-magnates are comparatively benign devices commonly used to withhold nurture from destitute people (Jha 2002). The justification for such behaviour also involves the fear of criminality – particularly of theft and of the consequences of addiction. It involves views on 'idleness' and its lack of worth, the stigmatisation of occupations as physically dirty, anti-social and illegal (drugs); and notions of ugliness and of destitution as a challenge to modernity.

On the other hand, norms of pity, belief in 'divine credit' (Kamat 1999), charity and kindness motivate selective transfers to destitute people (for example, by rice millers, petty traders, owners of meals-hotels and ticket collectors). The deserving destitute are the old, widows, the sick and disabled; the undeserving destitute are glue-sniffing children, working-age addicts and drug peddlers, sex-workers and the masses of unskilled migrant casual wage labour necessary to the working of every urban economy. The economy of charity fluctuates seasonally due to changes to norms of generosity at the major festivals of each religion. In this pitting of contradictory social forces, the rare but radical assertions of justice for destitute groups must not be overlooked (Figueroa and Barron 2005).[16] In both Peru and India, movements exist for social resti- tution and empowerment and for the reinclusion of disentitled people into the pool of claimants from the state.

It is evident that the exclusivity of the law assuages deep fears of flows of migrant destitute people, protects the economic interests manifest in such fear and prevents the state from providing support to the destitute. In so doing, the state ensures that some categories of people are expendable and expended. The process of destitution is the most extreme manifestation of the process of primary/primitive accumulation in which (while precondi- tions for productive capital are established) labour has to be stripped of its rights to property. But in destitution the stripping of rights exceeds those to property, for labour is stripped of all other rights as well.

8.4 Having almost nothing, not functioning and being expelled – some distinctions

Having characterised economic, social and political aspects of destitution, it becomes possible to map it onto the paradigms of poverty explored elsewhere in this book.[17] Income and capability poverty and social exclusion overlap with destitution in complex ways in which time, place, ascribed social status and language appear to play differentiating roles.

8.4.1 Income poverty

Since long-term destitution is a contradiction in terms, many destitute people will die. Not all destitute people who survive, however, are without income and of those without income not all are unoccupied. The most common occupation reported is 'alms seeking' or beggary. Even though not all beggars are destitute, many destitute people beg. Begging is often the only option for destitute elderly and disabled people, orphaned and abused children, dependants of interned people, those who are mentally ill, people whose sexuality is deemed unacceptable by society, those affected by having had leprosy or having AIDS and addicts. Begging is a negotiated exchange somewhere between a gift proper and a market transaction involving a transient relationship of obligation of giver to receiver in which the beggar has power derived from 'coercive subordination'.[18] Transfers are often in kind rather than cash.

Destitution resulting from the loss of rights to dependent status often leads to self-predatory work. Formerly dependent destitute women are commonly thought to be forced into sex-work. This brings with it a new dependence upon exploitative pimps who 'rescue' them from homelessness.

Mentally ill vagrants have lost dependent status, as have street children and elderly beggars.[19] Although there are norms regulating access to the disposal and recycling of solid waste and a socially regulated labour force may defend its access to recycling (Beall 1999; Gill 2004) many of those who have been deprived of dependence have no alternative but to be occupied in scavenging.

8.4.2 Capability deprivation: not being able to be supported, sheltered, nourished or educated

I have found evidence to relate destitution to two aspects of capability deprivation. The first is not being able to be dependent. Lack of support will result from the absence of support as well as the loss of rights to it. Deprivation in the space of 'being supported' shows up in individuated or collapsed households. These are unusual forms of household in India. NCAER/UNDP data for 33 000 rural households in 1993–4 show that just 1.4 per cent of households are individuated[20] – in which a single person lives without immediate physical and social support. Collapsed households are far from all being destitute in terms of assets and income.

The All India data show that only 17 per cent of such households are income poor – below the monetary poverty line – compared with 35 per cent nationwide. By contrast, in a rural hamlet of scheduled caste people living with leprosy in Chhattisgarh state in 2002, one-third of households were single member and all lived with malnutrition in extreme income poverty. Capability dimensions other than being housed are hardly ever considered in relation to the condition of destitution. The All India data for single member households reveals that they are surprisingly deprived in the capability dimensions of education and health.[21] While 58 per cent of all rural households are capability poor, 86 per cent of those in single member households fall into this category.

The second dimension of capability deprivation is not being sheltered. Not all homeless are destitute but many destitute people are homeless. The evidence for Peru reveals not so much collapsed, individuated households as destitute households, and remnants of households in collapsed houses. *Tugurios* are abandoned, old homes. Together with dilapidated buildings abandoned after earthquakes, they are invaded by homeless migrants. Although there is a state-funded programme of finance for the rebuilding of homes destroyed by earthquakes there is no state support for the shelter of migrant labour (Speak 2004).

Homeless people are another category of those most severely deprived in other capability dimensions. In New Delhi for instance 56 per cent of homeless people are also deprived in education, and illiterate. Sick people have been discovered to have been made destitute by a migration in order to seek health care. A high proportion of homeless people suffer serious respiratory illnesses, acute infections, skin disease and diarrhoea. Those without shelter also have a high incidence of severe mental illness and psycho-sexual disorders (Aashray Adhikar Abhiyan 2001: 27; Desai et al. 2003). Many homeless people have migrated to urban areas where the moral economy is thought to operate according to less restrictive rules than in villages, but just as this signifies freedom, it also means the loss of support. It is in urban areas that destitute people become visible to elites. What does the condition of not having shelter disable people from being and doing? Not having shelter means having no address. Not having an address disentitles people from identity (or food ration) cards which in turn deprives them from eligibility to elementary food security and social protection, and from establishing savings accounts in banks. In turn, this capability deprivation threatens the physical security of their savings. Not having an address disentitles people from eligibility for inclusion in any development projects at a homeless migrant's destination and, because the migrant is usually a male household member it may disentitle his dependants from access to developmental 'rights' in his place of origin.

Not having shelter does not prevent people from working. Homeless migrant male workers live from casual, deskilled (sometimes physically very punishing) labour at unregulated wages in order to remit money.[22] They are forced into homelessness in order to protect their access to employment – by the absence of cheap lodging close to the site of their work or the need to sleep by their equipment to prevent its theft. The loss of access to public goods and services means that the capability sets of destitute people do not include being clean, having clean clothes (or a change of clothes), or being able to wash privately. It means denial of access to defecate in the public spaces customarily given over to such purposes (Mander 2002). In Peru and India, public lavatories are extremely thin on the ground, poorly maintained and not affordable. It may even be difficult to find drinking water. Of course this does not mean that destitute people do not desire personal cleanliness, water and privacy to defecate as 'functionings'.

8.4.3 Not a state of not functioning: social expulsion, exclusion and survival

More than one philosopher of poverty has argued that extreme deprivation robs people of 'dignity', of 'a free human life', 'truly human functioning', 'full humanity' or 'human agency' (Nussbaum 2000; O'Neill 1994). Destitute people have been socially expelled, they have had economic assets and livelihoods, social status and support and political entitlements shorn from them. But, while beggars, scavengers and street children conduct themselves in public space in a way that may appear undignified to others, without wishing to romanticise, in private most are not without personal dignity, a sense of self and stores of courage and kindness.[23] Just as there is a lag of some two months between complete starvation and death, so destitute people survive variable lengths of time before death in conditions of social exclusion. In surviving, people exert a fully human and worthy initiative and agency. They may also construct new social relations.

Destitute people search for new kinds of common property resources and open access sites to which they may gain access in order to sleep. These places may bring them into contact with charity which may help to 'capacitate' them. In urban areas in India, temples, mosques, churches, railway and bus stations provide such space, though the terms of access may be unreliable and arbitrary – and expulsion often practised against them. Destitute people will occupy physically and socially hazardous spaces, for example land adjacent to polluted water and garbage dumps. Here too they may be evicted. Or, as in the case of people living with the disabilities of having had leprosy, the state and society allows them to make socially and physically isolated settlements – 'leper colonies'. It is not only those who 'rove', who have no sites to store possessions and no security for what they possess save that provided by their person, those living in marginal places also lack such elementary security.

Survival requires income or transfers of food, clothing and medicine. Destitute people get these resources from begging, from types of labour which are rejected by the casual wage labour force (very heavy, defiling and dirty work), from access to new common property resources (waste from meals-hotels), theft and work in the illegal distribution of legal and illegal goods, notably hard drugs. In both rural and urban areas destitute people are commonly addicted to alcohol, solvents, narcotics or hard drugs (Desai et al. 2003). Addictions are physically and psychologically destructive therapies for intolerable conditions and costly items of expenditure for people already in severest poverty. While addiction may compromise health irreversibly, both the violence and the theft that figure in public opinion are limited by the physical weakness of socially expelled addicts.

Destitute people have lost the social relations by means of which potential capability is converted to actual functioning (relations which have been neglected in applied research on capabilities and functioning). Yet dependence and solidarity, being and doing, can be reconstituted. The gender division of labour may be changed, most notably when men find water and cook. Although homeless people are rarely female, quasi-families may be created, as when elderly women beggars attempt to care for street children. Street children develop strong bonds with one another.[24] Homeless migrant workers form work-gangs; beggars work in groups which will then develop regulative rules. Groups may refuse to share individual takings, at the same time as they pay a member not to beg but to protect possessions (such as cooking vessels and stoves). Beggars in rural Chhattisgarh have organised routes and territories, particular attire[25] and ways of presenting themselves. In the case of a settlement of leprosy-affected beggars, all disentitled in their villages of origin, although the general pooling of resources from begging was avoided, very small-scale caste-specific credit and insurance institutions had been created. Housing (hovels) was in rationed supply but a combination of the insultingly inadequate state pension and proceeds of begging enabled households with healthier members to accumulate the possessions of abject poverty.[26]

Institutionalised indignity does not necessarily denote lack of self-esteem. Beggars may have pride in their resourcefulness, physical stamina and capacity to fend for dependants – if they have any (Mander 2001). Others have stories explaining their origin, the cause of their condition and their worth. Begging has entry barriers. Further, caste rules of commensality and proscriptions of intermarriage survive the loss of assets and income disentitlement. Beggars and homeless people may organise protection in order to sleep, particularly in the larger towns and cities where savings and possessions are at risk of theft. In Delhi, public spaces (pavements and parks) are privatised at night by *thiyawalahs* or 'bedlords' who erect protective barriers, lay out beds which they rent out – along with bedding – and pay off the police.

In Peru, between 1500 and 2000 children – *piranhitas* – live rough on the streets in gangs which, zealously guarding their territories, parody the private property rights that pervade urban Peruvian society. About 1000 to 1200 are reckoned to live in Lima. Concentrated in public space on the outskirts of the city – *cones* – destitute children occupy rat-infested dumps, wrecked and abandoned vehicles, slaughter house peripheries, garbage deposits from which food can be scrounged, the edges of shopping malls and hazardous spaces adjacent to motorways (Agurto 1998). The occasional doss in a cheap hotel is vital for washing, sex and sleep. The fact that the lives of some are reproducible and a minority of street children have formed real or fictive families and are rearing a second generation has attracted the attention of scholar-activists. For the most part their lives are distinguished by trade in, and addictions to, the solvent *terokal* or to marijuana or cocaine. Glue sniffing gives destitute street children a specific olfactory marker (Gigengack 2006).[27] Roy Gigengack's painstaking ethnographic work has revealed the highly differentiated livelihoods of Latin American street children, stratified by age, gender and place. Over and above drugs, they include other stigmatised extra-legal activity (begging, thieving and prostitution), petty services (bootblacks, squeegees, car minders and protection) and petty trade and production (packing, packaging and chewing gum peddling). Yet, while many may be able to survive, some die of the complications of drug abuse and malnutrition. Of this, Gigengack comments that for a child to perish 'is not that simple. Slowly wasting away is a complicated process. It entails at least the state, the non-governmental bureaucracies and the social production of indifference' (Gigengack 2006: 203). Other children commit suicide and/or kill – mainly over drugs – in what he concludes are tragic processes of destruction, self-destruction and self- and social mockery, the internalised projection of the destruction visited by society and of children's failed attempts to find order (Gigengack 2006; Agurto 2003).

To sum up, destitution is an extreme condition of monetary poverty; destitute people have been socially expelled; most destitute people are extremely deprived in capability dimensions of poverty too. So there is also a high probability that those deprived in all dimensions will be destitute. The state plays an active role in the process of destitution. The process is therefore very hard to reverse. A small minority manages to retreat from destitution to poverty.

8.5   Responses outside political economy?

'Political economy does not recognise the unoccupied worker. The beggar, the unemployed, the starving [and] the destitute are figures which exist not for it, but only for the eyes of doctors, judges, gravediggers and beadles. Nebulous figures which do not belong within the province of political economy' (Marx 1862/1990: 603).

In this chapter we have taken issue with the idea that destitution cannot be incorporated into political economy. Let us now consider Marx's examples of those for whom destitute people exist – meaning that they are visible and cannot be avoided. Very little is known. In both Peru and India, 'doctors' in government hospitals have been observed to refuse and delay treatment. Treatment for mental illness resulting from stress, alienation and insecurity is completely absent (Figueroa and Barron 2005; GRADE 2003; Gigengack 2006; Aashray Adhikar Abhiyan 2002; Desai et al. 2003). Such neglect reinforces the process of expulsion and of denial of rights (Aashray Adhikar Abhiyan 2001). In India, 'judges' – magistrates – are reported as generally satisfied that preventive detention is indeed in the interest of public order and, in enforcing the law, they support the private interests of the police. In Peru and India, 'beadles' (local police) have a predatory and violent 'rent-seeking' relationship with destitute people which may descend to extortion from children. And the 'gravediggers' – at least in Delhi – are alleged to have dumped a body in a drain. Unclaimed bodies are supposed to be reported to the police and disposed of by local authorities. In New Delhi in 2001, 84 per cent of such bodies were of beggars (*Times of India*, 18 September 2001). So destitute people are not 'nebulous', as Marx wrote. Instead they are the object of institutionalised state and social hostility.

8.6 Responses inside political economy?

On the rare instances when they have been consulted, destitute people report basic needs to be dominated by the search for physical security for the body and for possessions, for personal cleanliness and washing facilities, and for access to health (which is a concept including food and drinking water).

A state or political response involves resources, the crucial preconditions for the release of which are twofold. Both are very restrictive. First, destitute people have to have citizenship and voting rights – as they do but rarely in some slums. Second, the negative externalities attributed to them (such as physical pollution,[28] the threat to the security of property and person or fears of such threats) have to threaten the well-being of elites.[29] Responses include eviction on the one hand[30] and infrastructure and rudimentary social transfers on the other. Social interests which profit from the institutionalisation of destitution perpetuate partial and token forms of inclusion which, in being inadequate and rationed, accentuate the disadvantages of the rest.

In Peru, for example, even though *piranhitas* may threaten elite tourists, the anti-poverty response from the state, targeted food for school-age children, excludes those who need it most, since the street children are mostly out of school (Vasquez 2006). In 1999, a Special Solidarity Tax for Abandoned Children (Impuesta Especial de Solidaridad para la Ninez en Abandono) taxed the issue of passports. While $60m had been raised between 1999 and 2003, none was known by the Peruvian Congress to have been invested in street children, one gang of whom camps a mere 100 metres from the Government Palace (Agurto 2003). The state will not tackle the regulation of the glue trade or admit street children to school.

For a further example, the Indian system of benefits for those below the poverty line is not accessible to people without an address. In any case, were destitute people to be made eligible, the old age pension for people under the poverty line, for which All India enabling legislation was enacted in 1995, is about Rs 200 per month (less than £3 or $5),[31] supplemented in some states by a daily meal and clothing, which are now under pressure. Everywhere it is characterised by harsh eligibility criteria and inadequate coverage. The age threshold, at 60, is quite inappropriate. Very few homeless working labourers, let alone destitute people, will reach this age. The life expectancy of manual labourers is lagging one or two generations behind that of professionals or the landed elite. The pension age threshold for poor people is equivalent to age 75 to 80 in OECD countries. In addition, pension beneficiaries who are disabled face non-negligible extra costs due to disability, for which they are not compensated.[32]

By and large, organised civil society is complicit in this neglect. There are nothing more than ad hoc links between destitute people and other kinds of oppressed people or those who for other reasons are unable to earn wages covering their daily maintenance and generational reproduction. There is no solidarity on the part of the latter for the former.[33] In general, aid and development agencies do not see destitution as a development problem they can address. One kind of NGO response is to rehabilitate individual destitute people (particularly street children) or to provide facilities to which they may turn (e.g. shelters for mentally disabled vagrants and sanctuaries for children). Generacion, an NGO with 16 years of experience with street children in Lima, has three such homes, with 105 beds for street children. It also defends them from abuse and has attempted to find livelihoods for some. Instituto Mundo Libre, funded by the US Anti-Narcotics Affairs Office and the Pan-American Health Organisation, has separate homes for street boys and girls.[34]

In India, Aashray Adhikar Abhiyan (AAA) exemplifies an activist, collectivist response. In 2002, having mapped homelessness in the capital and consulted homeless people on their most urgent needs, AAA is supplying health care two nights a week. On another two nights AAA tries to supply affection and encouragement, blankets to the neediest, counselling to addicts,[35] hospital admission and admission to shelters. The underlying long-term objective is to create a cadre of development workers – with skills in health and legal knowledge – from among the street children, beggars and homeless workers themselves. By 2005, it had created street contact points and trained a first generation of para-counsellors, para-lawyers, para-detox advisers and para-medics from among the population of homeless people. It had mobilised two groups of male homeless workers and one group of women collectively to manage two night shelters in the commercial heart of Delhi and one in the school of an evicted village which had encroached onto the bank of the Yamuna river. It was thinking in terms of a federation of homeless people (Aashray Adhikar Abhiyan 2005). Lawyers were being mobilised to scrap the criminalising beggary and vagrancy laws. A small number of elite schools had also been persuaded to allow homeless people to sleep in classrooms and the model had spread to other Indian cities.[36] A rare example of where this might lead can be found in Kolkata, where a social movement of sex-workers is creating new identities and communities.

Politically constructed through ideology, using Freirian conscientisation and education, an egalitarian organisation has been developed in which work is legitimated, solidarity extended to those facing similar forms of oppression and an agenda struggled for. Their political goals include decriminalisation, trade union rights and rights as citizens (Gooptu 2002). All these examples are of unusual NGOs and movements.

All societies have destitute people. The differences in the case of India are their large numbers and their invisibility. Their numbers are thought to be relatively as well as absolutely smaller in Peru. But by definition their numbers cannot be known. The 2001 Indian Census did not attempt to census destitute people and the 2001 count of the capital's homeless is reported as having been severely compromised (Singh 2001a). The 1991 Indian Census estimate of the homeless is 2 million. Those suffering the after-effects of leprosy are thought to be about 4.5 million (Mander 2002). In this chapter, the creation and selective survival of destitute people has been shown to be built into the structure of society, economy and state, and, *pace* Marx, is an integral part of political economy. For the poorest people, anti-poverty policy *is* development. For destitute people anti-poverty policy is not nearly enough. Financial resources for a political response to destitution are entirely inadequate. But funds by themselves are necessary but insufficient conditions for a developmental response to destitution. Even so, they are likely to be easier to come by than a change in the social and political institutions of (un)accountability and expulsion which generate a condition affecting millions of people worldwide.

Notes

1. That conflict can cause destitution and that Peru's civil war was ethnicised is argued in a careful sifting of evidence by Figueroa and Barron (2005).
2. It is evident from Roy Gigengack's research on the self-destructive behaviour of certain street children in Latin America that some destitute children and young adults internalise the process of social degradation and also wish to be rid of themselves (Gigengack 2006).
3. The primary field material introduced into this essay was obtained from two field visits to a settlement of beggars in rural Chhattisgarh state and to homeless people and drug addicts on the streets of New and Old Delhi at night. It was organised by ActionAid, India in January 2002 and by Aashray Adhikar Abhiyan (Movement for Shelter for the Homeless) in December 2005. Angela Ruiz-Uccelli researched the Peruvian material.
4. Work-related accidents and disease are a major cause of adult disability (Erb and Harriss-White 2002).
5. Scholars of the process of impoverishment in times of food scarcity and famine have distinguished coping from survival sequences. In general, coping

sequences are those protecting property while survival sequences are attempts to protect the person – see Vivian (1995).

6. Anthropological field research shows that this not always so – see the work of James Staples (2002) on the organisation of begging in and from Andhra Pradesh.
7. Caste, gender and age can be used to bar people from certain kinds of work.
8. See CONADIS: http://www.conadisperu.gob.pe/ for the condition of disabled people in Peru.
9. See Chapters 1 and 4 in this volume.
10. Despite protective law, the explusion of, and violence against, gay people in Latin America is much more pronounced in rural areas than in urban sites where homosexuality is actually more visible (Rios n.d.).
11. See also Centre of Information and Education for the Prevention of Drug Abuse, Lima, Peru: http://www.cedro.org.pe/activitades.htm; and a large literature on street children critically reviewed by Gigengack (2006).
12. The pincer of urban land rents and planning laws means that poor people are prevented from renting or investing in shelter.
13. The number of shelters has been reduced from 19 to 14 in two years (Singh 2001b).
14. Less than 0.000,000.1 per cent of GDP.
15. See note 13.
16. See also http://www.geocities.com/righttofood/.
17. See Chapter 1 of this volume.
18. The phrase is James Staples' (2002). That societies have strict rules about the acceptability of begging can be deduced from the behaviour of non-government organisations, increasingly corporatised and competitive, which rely on a form of institutionalised and intermediated beggary known as 'fund raising'.
19. One investigation into homeless women found that almost all were mentally ill (Aashray Adhikar Abhiyan 2001).
20. These statistics were calculated directly from the NCAER database. In fact it is not known if destitute people were included in this sample survey.
21. This analysis derives from Saith, Chapter 3 in this volume. Capability poverty is defined as poverty in either the education space or the health space. Education poverty in individuated households where the minimum age is 18 is defined as *illiteracy*. Health poverty is in terms of reported *chronic illness*.
22. According to Aashray Adhikar Abhiyan, 90 per cent of homeless men in New Delhi do such work, 70 per cent of whom are paid under the minimum wage (Aashray Adhikar Abhiyan 2001: 29).
23. See also Gigengack (2006: 173–5).
24. An estimated 4 per cent of homeless people in New Delhi are women – see Aashray Adhikar Abhiyan (2001: ix, 25).
25. About the presentation of self, Kamat writes: 'People who beg ("honourably") in the name of religion have to grow a beard, wear saffron clothes and ash. The fortune teller wears peacock feathers and make up. The transvestites . . . have altogether different yet distinct style. The beggars who use animals for fund raising have to decorate their pets' (Kamat 1979/1999).

26. Deeparapara is a settlement with a well and a water pump. Scheduled caste residents are reckoned by caste lepers in the main village of Premnagar to be nicely segregated there. People live in tiny houses – upwards of unventilated and unlit cells, all of 6ft by 7ft, in which there is a mud stove, earthenware or plastic water pots, a bed, one or two shelves for utensils and for bottles and tins of oil, lentils and salt, lines strung out for a spare set of clothes, bandages, shawls and blankets, and bundles of firewood looped up to the rafters which support the tiled roof. These glorified cupboards become ovens in summer. They have been slowly and painfully constructed and repaired with remittances, and with the returns from begging and occasional wage work. The street is clean and magnificently paved, courtesy of the state. Many of the adults of Deeparapara are severely malnourished.
27. See also, Centre of Information and Education for the Prevention of Drug Abuse – CEDRO: http://www.CEDRo.org.pe/actividades.htm
28. Ignoring the fact that physical pollution is a direct function of wealth and income.
29. This includes the threat to India's competitive advantage in the markets for FDI and tourism.
30. In the 1990s in Peru, Fujimori evicted large numbers of people from squatter settlements in and around Lima, turning them from 'surviving homeless' to crisis homeless (Speak 2004).
31. Contrast this with the minimum wage of Rs 60 per day.
32. For leprosy-affected pensioners the costs of dressing wounds amounts on average to the equivalent of 6 months' disability pension (and bribes take away another month of pension). Disabled workers in South India spend on average the equivalent of 4 months' earnings from one male agricultural labour on the direct and indirect costs of treatment (Erb and Harriss-White 2002).
33. A participatory study of the problems of homeless people revealed this graphically; Aashray AdhikarAbhiyan (2002: 17).
34. See http://mundolibre.tsi.com.pe/ and http://casageneracion.com/
35. And attempts to gain access to de-addiction therapy.
36. In Pune 9000 people are homeless; 60 per cent have been living on the pavements for more than six years (Mishra 2004).

9
Alternative Realities? Different Concepts of Poverty, their Empirical Consequences and Policy Implications: Overview and Conclusions

Frances Stewart, Ruhi Saith, Susana Franco and
Barbara Harriss-White

9.1 Introduction

The elimination of poverty is the overriding aim of those concerned with development. Despite this consensus on the objective, 'poverty' is surprisingly difficult to define. Poverty, of course, represents deprivation: but the critical issues of deprivation *of what* and *by how much* are not agreed. The view that poverty is multidimensional is widely accepted, and policy (as exemplified by the Millennium Development Goals, for example) is also responding to this more comprehensive definition. However, the monetary approach remains the approach most commonly adopted in measurement of poverty. This book analyses some implications of the broader approach to poverty definition, considering some implications of alternative definitions of poverty. We explore differences in poverty estimates arising from alternative interpretations of poverty – through a theoretical review of alternatives and empirically by investigating how far the people identified as being in poverty in India and Peru differed according to the approach adopted. We also devote one chapter to exploring the nature of destitution in India and Peru, examining whether our conclusions hold for the poorest section of the community.

9.2 Findings

9.2.1 Theoretical review

The theoretical review involved an exploration of the evolution of four approaches to poverty – monetary, capabilities, social exclusion and participatory methods. For each, we explored the existing literature and analysed strengths and weaknesses in the approach.

The review of different approaches made it clear that there is no unique, or 'objective', way of defining and measuring poverty. For each approach the identification of poor people depends not only on people's objective situation but also on assumptions which can be quite arbitrary.

- In the monetary approach, substantial differences in poverty result from varying assumptions about calorie needs, diets and prices, the intra-household distribution of income, and adjustments for the composition of the household and within-household economies of scale. More fundamentally, there are questions about the underlying assumption that money income (or utility) is the appropriate measure of well-being rather than the conditions of life people attain. Moreover, monetary poverty generally ignores deficiencies in socially provided goods.

- The major advantage of capability (CA) poverty is that it directly measures individual deprivation in some basic aspects of human well-being. Money income is seen as a means to enhance capabilities rather than an end. But measurement of capability poverty requires assumptions about what basic capabilities are and threshold levels as well as the selection of appropriate indicators. Analysis of CA poverty, like monetary poverty, is usually externally determined, and neglects social dynamics.

- Social exclusion is particularly difficult to define in developing countries, where, with the absence of a functioning welfare state, and a relatively small formal sector, its dimensions differ from the developed country situation. Where the concept has been applied to developing countries, different aspects of SE have been identified in different countries, e.g. those related to caste for India and race for Peru. In common across countries, however, the concept draws our attention to structural and multidimensional causes of poverty, processes and group dynamics.

- Unlike the other approaches, participatory methods allow poor people themselves to define what it is to be poor. Potentially, participatory appraisals (PAs) can provide important inputs into the other methods. Yet there are problems of interpretation, including comparability across PAs, extension to a larger scale and statistical significance.

9.2.2 Empirical findings

A critical issue is whether the various approaches identify different people as poor. If they do, appropriate policies and targeting would vary with the approach adopted. However, if broadly the same set of people is identified as poor by each approach, then any one approach would be a satisfactory proxy for the other approaches including the monetary approach, which is currently the one most frequently adopted. The empirical part of our study investigates this critical question.

The empirical work was carried out in Peru and India, in order to see whether the results were consistent in different environments. For both countries, we used a large existing data set, and a small purposive survey involving participatory methods. We investigated the overlaps and differences in the people identified as poor by the four approaches; whether our findings were the outcome of the particular poverty levels drawn; and the main characteristics of those identified as poor by the various approaches.

To assess the overlap between measures of monetary and capability poverty in the large data sets we constructed contingency tables with appropriate statistical tests (e.g. chi-squared tests of association). We also used multivariate analyses (logit) to differentiate groups most likely to be identified as poor by one or both approaches.

Participatory methods were used to generate well-being rankings among individuals in the area, and to indicate the characteristics of poverty as seen by the people affected. The overlaps between monetary and capability poverty and well-being ranking were then identified. Further individuals were identified as being 'socially excluded' based on criteria traditionally used in the country concerned. We also tried to use inputs from focus group discussions to identify 'excluded' individuals.

For the empirical comparisons, we aimed to adopt poverty thresholds which were to the extent possible (i.e. given data constraints) those commonly used for policy purposes. We did this because we intended to explore the approaches as commonly implemented. Thus monetary poverty was defined as including those with consumption expenditure per capita below the official national poverty line.[1] However, we drew our own poverty lines for the other types of poverty, as there were no official ones. Capability poverty was divided into education and health. Education poverty for children was interpreted as not being enrolled at school,[2] and, for adults, illiteracy in India and failure to complete primary school in Peru. Health poverty for children was interpreted as undernutrition (using 2 standard deviations below the median for Peru and 3 for India), and chronic illness was used as the indicator for adults.

Highlights of the results for the large data set

The level of monetary poverty in India was estimated to be 38 per cent. For capabilities, 52 per cent of adults in the sample were identified as education poor and 26 per cent of children; 70 per cent of children less than 13 years old were undernourished, while 44 per cent were severely undernourished; and 7 per cent of individuals between 7 and 59 suffered from chronic illness. Because of the very high level of undernutrition we used severe undernutrition to identify capability poverty in the later analysis.

In Peru 54 per cent of the population were estimated to be monetary poor, while 20 per cent of the adults and 7 per cent of the children were identified as education poor, much lower than the Indian rate of education poverty despite higher standards being required (in the Peru analysis) for not being classified education poor. Ten per cent of adults were health poor and 29 per cent of the children below 5 years were undernourished. Thus in Peru, in contrast to India, in aggregate, monetary poverty was much higher than capability poverty, indicating that the proportion of people that cannot afford a minimum consumption basket is higher than the proportion of people that are considered to be poor from a capability point of view.

The reason for higher levels of monetary poverty could be two-fold. On the one hand the national poverty line that is used to measure monetary poverty in Peru might have been set at a level that is too high. That would explain why we find levels of monetary poverty in this country that are much higher than in India, even if in both countries the lines are supposed to be set at a value that covers the cost of a basket of basic consumption. This suggests that the 'basic consumption' considered in India is more basic than that in Peru. On the other hand, we can consider the poverty line in Peru truthfully representing the cost of what is considered a basic consumption basket in the country. What we find then is that there is a large proportion of people that, even if they cannot afford that basket, have managed to achieve functionings that situate them in the group of non-poor people from a capability point of view. This contrasts with India, where a higher proportion of people are capability poor, even if the thresholds are in many cases lower (e.g. literacy for education poverty in India and completion of primary education in Peru).

In both countries, the level of poverty varied across socio-economic groups. For example, in India, Muslims, and scheduled castes and tribes had above-average monetary and education poverty, while in Peru, mixed race individuals and native language speakers had above-average poverty by all measures. In both countries, females were poorer in education terms than males.

Individual overlaps.   We found only a limited relationship between those falling below the capability poverty line and those below the monetary poverty line, i.e while the null hypothesis of independence of monetary and non-monetary indicators was rejected for all capability indicators, the association between monetary and non-monetary dimensions was very low (values of Cramer's V < 0.2 for both education indicators and < 0.05 for both health indicators for India, and ranging from 0.03 to 0.16 for Peru).

These weak correlations show that monetary indicators are not good proxies for capturing capability poverty (or conversely), as shown in Table 9.1. These ratios indicate the large omissions of CA poor that would be made if monetary poverty were used as a targeting criterion (and the large inclusions of CA non-poor). For example, in India, the monetary poverty criterion would omit more than half the literacy, undernutrition and chronically ill poor. The overlaps between monetary and capability poverty are a little higher in Peru than in India, although there are still large proportions of CA poor who are not monetary poor. The converse also holds: a significant proportion of those in monetary poverty would not be identified if the capability indicators were used.

Because the total levels of capability and monetary poverty are different, complete overlap obviously cannot be expected to occur. In India, for example, education poverty amongst adults is 52 per cent, while monetary poverty is 34 per cent. Consequently at least 18 per cent of the sample could not overlap. Given that the chosen thresholds for capability poverty are low (in this case adult literacy), however, any lack of overlap arising for this reason is itself a cause for concern. Moreover, the distribution observed is quite different from that expected if there were complete overlap to the extent possible, so that even accounting for the difference in scale of poverty by different measures, the lack in overlap is substantial. For adults in India, for example, the actual lack of overlap (those who are education poor and monetary non-poor) account for 31 per cent of the sample, far higher than the 18 per cent possibly due to the different total proportion in the different types of poverty.

Table 9.1: Overlaps between monetary and CA poverty

Capability poverty measured as		Education		Nutrition/health	
		Children	*Adults*	*Children*	*Adults*
% of CA poor not in monetary poverty	*India*	43	60	53	63
	Peru	32	37	21	55
% of monetary poor not CA poor	*India*	65	38	53	91
	Peru	93	73	66	94

Altering the monetary threshold.   Investigation of the extent of capability poverty for different monetary deciles showed that altering the monetary poverty line would not greatly alter the results. For example, in India, although levels of education poverty were lower in higher deciles, 33 per cent of the richest tenth of the population were illiterate (compared with 64 per cent among the lowest decile). The proportion of health poor in the highest decile is quite similar to that in the lowest decile. Among those with incomes even as high as the seventh monetary decile more than 50 per cent are poor in either education or health. In Peru, 12 per cent of the top decile are education poor among adults, and 5 per cent among children – compared with 32 per cent in the lowest decile for adults and 9 per cent for children. The incidence of child undernutrition is 5 per cent for the top decile of money incomes compared with 9 per cent for the lowest decile. Hence changing the cut-off line for monetary poverty would not eliminate poor overlaps in either country.

Results from the participatory data

Well-being ranking.   The main factors people mentioned differentiating whether a household was classified as of high, medium or low well-being were:

- **Rural:** In India, land ownership; jobs; number of dependants; and adequacy of food. In Peru, the amount of land and cattle owned; the ability to work; and the gender of the household head.
- **Urban:** In India, jobs/source of livelihood; number of dependants; adequacy of food; and resources for providing education to children. In Peru, whether the household head had a job; the fragility of materials used in the construction of houses; and the gender of the household head.[3]

Overlaps.   The overlap between monetary poverty and capability indicators in both small surveys was also not significant, being broadly similar to that between monetary and capability indicators in the big data set. The small survey also showed poor overlap between monetary poverty and people's own perceptions, as indicated by well-being ranking for both countries.

- In India, only around half of those ranked as 'low well-being' were also monetarily poor.[4] Even the highest monetary decile had 34 per cent individuals ranked 'low well-being'. In Peru, in the rural area, 48 per cent of the monetary non-poor were identified as poor according to the well-being ranking, while 39 per cent of the extremely poor, by well-being ranking, were not monetary poor. In the urban area, 49 per cent of the monetary non-poor were ranked as poor while 44 per cent of those ranked as poor were not monetary poor.

- In Peru, a lack of overlap also showed between self-perceptions of poverty and monetary poverty. In the rural area, 29 per cent of the self-declared poor were non-poor according to the monetary indicator, while of the monetary poor, 42 per cent did not believe themselves to be poor. In the urban area, 40 per cent of the self-declared poor were not monetary poor, and 42 per cent of the monetary poor did not state that they were poor.

- Low levels of congruence were also found between capability poverty and poverty by well-being ranking. For example, in Peru, in the rural area, 43 per cent of the capability poor (nutrition) were non-poor according to the ranking, and 33 per cent of those ranked as poor were not capability (nutrition) poor.

It does not appear, therefore, that well-being ranking is any better able to capture capabilities poverty than monetary indicators.

Social exclusion. As we noted in our theoretical review, criteria defining social exclusion depend on the context. Consequently our initial intention was to identify characteristics of social exclusion from the focus group discussions. Racial discrimination and differential treatment which could be considered as part of social exclusion were mentioned in Peru with regard to indigenous people (i.e. people who speak one of the native languages as opposed to Spanish speakers). In India, however, both urban and rural people were insistent on the absence of any form of social exclusion. Although individuals belonging to scheduled castes live in a separate area, neither they nor those belonging to other castes considered them as being excluded from the life of the community. Rather, people pointed to *social boycott* applying to individuals not invited to community events, etc.: this applied in the case of inter-caste, and especially inter-religious, marriages; diseases like leprosy and types of bad behaviour could also lead to social boycott in the rural areas.

Consequently, we used another approach to identify SE, which has been followed by the ILO, i.e. the identification of the groups as being socially excluded in an a priori way, on the basis of analysis of the nature of the two societies. In the Indian case, those belonging to the scheduled castes or tribes were identified as socially excluded. In the case of Peru, people of indigenous origin (who speak one of the native languages) were considered excluded. In the case of Peru, as mentioned earlier, the case study also supported this choice. In both countries there was some correlation between belonging to this 'socially excluded' group and monetary and capability poverty. In Peru, for example, people whose mother tongue is one of the native languages suffer from higher rates of monetary poverty (70 per cent as compared to 51 per cent in the case of Spanish speakers) as well as education poverty in the case of adults (43 per cent of the native speakers have not completed primary education compared to 16 per cent of the Spanish speakers), and health poverty in case of children (51 per cent of the native speaking children are undernourished compared to 25 per cent of the Spanish speaking children). In India, also those belonging to the SC/ST groups are estimated as having a higher likelihood of being monetary 'poor' (around 50 per cent compared to 33 per cent for non-SC/ST) or 'extreme poor' (around 25 per cent compared to 15 per cent for the non-SC/ST group). Adults as well as children belonging to SC/ST households, are more likely to suffer from education 'poverty' compared to individuals belonging to the non-SC/ST groups. In adults around 65 per cent are education 'poor' compared to 46 per cent for non-SC/ST. In children, around 35 per cent are education 'poor' compared to 22 per cent for non-SC/ST.

As with the other results, however, large percentages do not overlap. Consequently, directing developmental benefits directed on the basis of social exclusion alone, cannot be assumed to be addressing other types of poverty. For India, for example, directing benefits to the SC/ST group would mean that a high percentage of individuals in monetary poverty (60 per cent of the total monetary poor) would be left out. Similarly 58 per cent of the educationally poor among children and 69 per cent of the chronically ill adults fall outside the SC/ST category.

Destitution.   The very poorest of the poor are referred to as being destitute. There is no consensus on the defining conditions of those in this situation. Our analysis suggests that while the dimensions of poverty analysed in this book do not map neatly onto one another, among destitute people, for the most part, they *do*. Indeed, falling into every type of poverty could be regarded not only as a defining characteristic of the destitute, but also as a cause of prolonged destitution, since they are prevented from escaping one type of poverty by the iron control exerted by the other types.

Destitution is argued to be a three-fold kind of deprivation in the 'space' of income or monetary poverty, involving first, the absence of assets or of any control over assets; secondly, barriers to insurance mechanisms; and, thirdly, the absence of access to income from one's own labour. The state of destitution arises from a dynamic process of political economy in which a person is pushed into monetary destitution by being deprived of control over assets and income. Physical conditions, e.g. being malnourished, disabled or ill, may lead to an exclusion which becomes self-reinforcing.

Moreover, destitute people generally have deep and comprehensive deprivations in capability spaces, including lack of access to public services and homelessness. This capability deprivation further reinforces the monetary deprivation. The destitute most clearly fall into the category of social exclusion, excluded in particular by their lack of assets, income and capabilities. The focus groups did not include the destitute, but in so far as our poor groups pointed to exclusion it was to these categories of people.

9.3 Comparison of our findings with other studies[5]

Although no other study has attempted to compare the implications of all four approaches to poverty definition, in terms of identifying those in poverty, there have been empirical comparisons of capability and monetary approaches; and of 'subjective' and monetary approaches. Broadly, our findings are consistent with other empirical investigations. That is, for the most part the studies find some correlation between the approaches in terms of levels of poverty across countries or regions and changes in time, and some overlap in the populations identified as poor, but the correlations are quite weak – and there are significant differences in the populations identified as poor by the different approaches, as in our study.

(a) *Studies of overlaps between monetary income and capability poverty*

- For Côte d'Ivoire, Glewwe and van der Gaag (1990) find a substantial lack of overlap between those identified as poor according to capability measures and those according to monetary measures, with, for example, less than half of the people identified as among the 30 per cent with lowest monetary income also being education poor.
- In a sample of poor Italian households, Balestrino (1996) found that nearly half of the population were both income and functioning poor, but a quarter were functioning poor but not income poor and another quarter were income poor but not functioning poor.

- A regional ranking according to income and functionings measures of poverty, within Italy, found that seven of 20 regions were ranked differently by the two measures (Balestrino and Sciclone 2000).
- A study of Chile (Ruggeri Laderchi 1997) found that money income was weakly linked to functioning poverty, defined as education, health and nutrition shortfalls.
- Comparisons of monetary and capability poverty in Jamaica, Nepal, Pakistan, Romania and Vietnam in the 1990s found that household income was positively, but weakly, correlated with capabilities. For households with children, the proportion of households deprived in one of three dimensions (income, education and health) was substantially higher than deprivation in income alone (Appleton and Song 1999).
- Adopting a composite measure of poverty for South Africa, made up of 14 components including basic capabilities and the stated priorities of the population, 30 per cent of the most deprived, according to the composite measure, would not be identified as poor using expenditure measure of poverty (Klasen 2000).
- A provincial ranking of 9 provinces in South Africa, found a significant difference in rankings according to which measure was used (Qizilbash 2002).
- A study of Egypt and Tunisia compares monetary poverty and housing deprivation and finds very large differences (Bibi 2003).
- Baulch and Masset (2003) explore the relationship between chronic monetary poverty and some types of capability poverty at a point in time and over time, using a Vietnam data set. They confirm that for most dimensions of capability poverty that they measure – including child stunting and adult malnutrition as measured by body mass index – there is limited overlap in coverage at a point in time and even less overlap for measures of persistent poverty, with more individuals remaining in capability poverty than in monetary poverty.

(b) *Monetary poverty compared with participatory/'subjective' measures of deprivation*

Studies comparing the identification of the poor using participatory methods with those identified as in monetary poverty have produced mixed results.

- A study by Shaffer (1998) in the Republic of Guinea, found that the incidence of consumption poverty, using national household survey data, was no greater among women than men. In contrast, data from participatory exercises revealed that women were 'worse-off' than men given their excessive work load and lesser decision-making authority. The author concluded that consumption poverty should not be used as the sole guide for equity-based policy intervention.

- In contrast, a study looking at participatory wealth ranking and survey information collected for the same sample concluded that there was a positive correlation of wealth rankings with monetary data (Adams et al. 1997). The study, however, involved some circularity as the socio-economic criteria to be used to classify households into three groups – rich, medium and poor – were suggested to the participants carrying out the wealth ranking.
- In a participatory study in Ladosarai in Delhi, adolescent girls were asked to carry out a wealth ranking in the village based on their own perception of wealth (Mathur et al. 1996). People were classified into three classes – rich, middle class and poor – on the basis of their houses, ownership of consumer durables and cattle, clothes worn and food eaten. A comparison of the wealth ranking with the data collected through a survey showed broad consistency between the wealth ranking and estimates of income obtained by interviews. These results are, however, not very surprising, since the ranking was done based on perceptions of wealth rather than overall well-being.

Data for the 'subjective' approaches are derived from surveys which include questions about people's well-being ('happiness' and, in some cases, whether their basic needs are met). These methods thus differ from our participatory approach, derived from focus group discussions, but are similar in conception, as they aim to find out what the people themselves feel about their situation.

The 'subjective' measures of well-being generally use survey data including questions on the perceived adequacy of their income and well-being more generally. Precise questions vary across studies. Examples of questions that have been used include how much income a family would need to make ends meet; whether the household's consumption of some basic items is less than adequate; whether the household has enough income to meet some basic needs goods that respondents have identified; how far respondents are satisfied/dissatisfied/ happy with their lives. The methodology varies across studies. In general, it differs from our participatory approach, both as to methodology and as to precise questions. Nonetheless, both these measures of 'subjective' well-being (or ill-being) and our participatory measures of poverty derive from the same basic viewpoint – that of getting the people who are poor to say what it is to be poor and whether they consider themselves poor – although our approach also asked the focus groups to rank people in their community – which is not a feature of the measures of subjective well-being. Despite the method-ological differences, therefore, it is relevant to ascertain whether compar-isons of the 'subjective' measures with the monetary measures got similar results to our work. A summary of studies is contained in Table 9.2.

The methodology adopted by the studies in arriving at 'subjective' perceptions varies across the studies, notably in the precise questions asked to ascertain subjective perceptions. The closest correlation with monetary poverty arises when people are asked about the adequacy of their consumption expenditure. When asked about their happiness or about their access to public goods, the correlation is less. Moreover, there seems to be a closer correspondence between the various subjec-tive measures of well-being and monetary measures of poverty, the poorer people are. At upper income levels, there is very little correlation. In general, the studies support our findings using participatory methods among the poor – that there is some, but rather a weak, correlation between how people view their own situation and how it is measured in terms of monetary poverty. The one study that also explored aspects of capability poverty (Kingdon and Knight 2004) found a weak correlation between 'subjective' assessments and capability poverty, as we do.

9.3.1 Some conclusions

Both theoretical and empirical work point to the inadequacy of monetary poverty, as normally measured. Not only is it a fairly artificial construct depending on the methodology adopted, but our empirical work shows that in both India and Peru it fails to capture a large proportion of peo-ple suffering CA poverty, nor does it overlap in any systematic way with poverty as identified by people themselves using participatory methods. It is therefore not very meaningful in itself, and it proved to be an inade-quate proxy for other types of poverty. We found this also to be true when we varied cut-off rates and indicators for monetary and CA poverty. While the existence of a positive correlation between monetary poverty and other types has led some to argue that it is a satisfactory proxy, our findings suggest that relying only on data for monetary poverty would mean that large numbers of people suffering from poverty more broadly defined would not be identified or reached by policy.

A critical question that follows is whether there is *any* value in using a monetary poverty indicator – the indicator which currently dominates measurement, targeting and policy – if it fails to capture adequately any of the conditions we associate with well-being and is not in accord with people's own rankings. We do see some place for it as a subordinate indicator: first, as a means to achieve capabilities, although by no means the only means; secondly, any discrete list of CAs is bound to leave many

Table 9.2: Studies comparing monetary measures of poverty and 'subjective' assessments in developing countries

Country	Authors	Measure of subjective well-being	Data	Findings
Jamaica and Nepal	Pradhan and Ravallion (1998)	Consumption adequacy	Household survey (national)	High overlap with monetary poverty but notable differences in regional and demographic profiles
Nepal	Fafchamps and Shilpi (2003)	Consumption adequacy; health care and schooling; satisfaction with income	Household survey (national)	Income has positive and mostly highly significant effects on subjective well-being
Philippines	Mangahas (2003)	Respondents asked to identify whether they are poor	Social weather surveys (national)	Self-rated poor about twice monetary poor. Trends similar
Ethiopia	Tadesse (1998)	How income and spending had changed since previous survey	Panel household survey (urban)	Different direction of change over time between monetary and subjective assessments and differences in rankings across cities
Ethiopia	Kedir and McKay (2003)	How income and spending had changed since previous survey	Panel household survey (urban)	Subjective and monetary evaluations closer when people are worse off
South Africa	Kingdon and Knight (2003, 2004)	How satisfied households are with lives	Household surveys (national)	Little overlap

Continued

Table 9.2: Continued

Country	Authors	Measure of subjective well-being	Data	Findings
Madagascar	Lokshin, Umapathi and Paternostro (2006)	What minimum income is needed; and consumption adequacy	Household survey (national)	Good overlap for consumption adequacy. Weak for minimum income
Madagascar	Razafindrakoto and Roubaud (2000)	Perception of standard of living, satisfaction of vital needs	Household survey (Antananarivo conurbation)	Limited overlap
Urban sub-Saharan Africa	Razafindrakoto and Roubaud (2004)	Perception of standard of living, satisfaction of vital needs	Household survey (urban)	Limited overlap. Clear distinction between monetary and other typs of poverty
Mexico	Fuentes and Rojas (2001)	Happiness scale	Survey of individuals (urban)	Income explains less than 5% of happiness
Mexico	Rojas (2002)	Happiness scale; satisfaction with 6 domains of life; perceptions of poverty and fulfilment of basic needs	Survey of individuals (rural and urban)	'It seems that the concept of poverty that people make use of is not similar [to] the concept of economists' (Rojas 2002: 16)
Mexico	Lever (2004)	Satisfaction in 11 areas of life	Survey in Mexico city	Little correlation – slightly more among extreme poor
Peru and Madagascar	Herrera, Razafindrakoto and Roubaud (2003)	Minimum income needs; how well-off they feel	Household surveys (national, Peru; urban, Madagascar)	Min. income correlation with monetary poverty is 0.6 for urban Peru, 0.3 for rural Peru, 0.7 for Madagscar

Country	Author	Measure	Survey type	Findings
Peru	Herrera (2002)	Minimum income needed	Household survey (national)	56% of the poor are captured by both monetary and minimum income measures.
India	Jodha (1989)	Living standard assessment (for 1963 to 1966 and again from 1982 to 1984) on the basis of income and quality of life indicators proposed by the villagers themselves	Panel household survey and participant observation (rural – two villages in Rajasthan)	Based on income data, 38% of households had become poorer and poverty incidence increased from 17% to 23%. However, quality of life indicators for these 'poorer' households revealed improvements in the living standard, e.g. reduced reliance on traditional patrons and landlords; reduced dependence on low-pay jobs.
South Africa	Crothers (1997)	Assessment of 'child hunger' by including a question on lack of money to feed children at any time during the previous year (referred to as experiential measure)	Household survey	High correlation between household income, household per capita income and experiential measure. Even the richest income decile households, however, showed 10% of 'child hunger' and amongst the poorest decile, less than 50% were found to suffer from 'child hunger'

aspects of a valuable life out – income provides resources for some of these other aspects (albeit some important capabilities cannot be achieved via expenditure); thirdly, the participatory exercises mostly show that the poor put considerable value on money income.

But we wish to emphasise that the money income indicator can only be justified as a subordinate indicator of poverty. Any serious attempt to measure poverty and identify the poor must make use of indicators of CA poverty and participatory methods. Although it was difficult to give practical interpretation to SE in India and Peru in the same way as the other methods, the participatory exercises and the chapter on destitution suggest it has value, though more for diagnosis and policy than for measurement. These conclusions have important implications for policies (including targeting) and statistics.

One important issue – to which considerable effort is being devoted by some economists – is whether (and how) to produce a composite index of poverty which incorporates its multidimensional aspects.[6] Such efforts can be useful for some purposes, but may also mislead. When poverty is described as multidimensional what is meant is that people can be seriously deprived in many ways – in different material and non-material capabilities, in their self-perceptions, in monetary income or assets, or so on. It does *not* mean that there is a unique measure which can represent all these aspects. In general, most of the different dimensions of poverty are non-commensurable and often not subject to acceptable (or sometimes meaningful) trade-offs with each other. It follows that in most contexts any single index will misrepresent the situation, however sophisticated the effort to produce such a composite index. Of course, it is possible to estimate and present a variety of composite indexes, ranging from some average of the components (arithmetic or geometric), to defining as poor only those who are poor in all dimensions (intersection approach), or defining people as poor if they are poor in any single dimension (union approach). Moreover, one can compare distributions and where one dominates (i.e. in one situation people are poorer in all dimensions than in another), come to unambiguous conclusions that in one situation poverty is higher than in the other. Partial dominance is also possible, permitting some clear conclusions about a range of incomes, or a range of indicators. All these ways of providing some summary measures can be useful, permitting ready comparisons across countries or regions or time. Moreover, to the extent that they induce a move away from an exclusive reliance on monetary poverty lines – in estimation, policy and research – they may represent an improvement. The argument here is similar to that justifying the use of the Human Development Index as a measure of country progress, despite its clear defects. Nonetheless, comparisons using composite indices may be misleading unless the rankings are the same for all the constituent elements, so that one poverty distribution dominates others on all dimensions Whenever a composite or summary index is used, it should be recognised that the way it is put together generally involves arbitrary judgements. Thus if poverty is found to be high according to one approach and low by another, the best way to deal with this is to state it clearly and 'to forgo the luxury of being able to state in aggregate who the poor are and how many of them there are, and instead to draw out the policy implications of each set of indicators separately' (Dessallien 1998: 17).

It has been suggested that the virtue of a monetary measure is that it can act as such a summary index, or a proxy for other types of poverty. This claim depends on there being a close empirical correlation between monetary poverty and other types of poverty. The work presented in this book, and that by others summarised above, shows that a correlation exists between monetary poverty and other types but not a very strong one, so that using a monetary estimate will miss out on large numbers of people who are poor in critically important dimensions.

Policies towards poverty reduction

If the broad goal of poverty reduction policies is reducing deprivation, our results suggest that the emphasis of policies ought to be towards the reduction of capability deprivations directly, although, of course, incomes generally play a role in reducing such deprivation. Aiming at reducing CA poverty involves changes in many of the policies that have been used to address poverty. For example:

- *Targeting* the poor using a money income measure will leave out many in CA poverty (and include some who are not in CA poverty). Therefore targeting policies need to target the capability poor directly.
- Direct transfers directed towards the money poor will only be partially effective in reaching the CA poor, and in promoting CA among those they reach. Other policies needed relate directly to the particular CA deprivation, especially child health and nutrition.
- Policies to promote income generation (e.g. micro-credit) may often be ineffective in reaching the CA poor, since they may lack the capacities to take them up. Again more direct measures are essential. Nutrition, education and health projects are likely to be needed.
- Macro-policies that generate 'pro-poor growth' are widely advocated. Such growth will not necessarily be pro-poor in CA terms. To achieve CA pro-poor growth, the allocation of growth needs to be directed towards the social sectors as well as to the private incomes of the poor.

Policy differences also arise with respect to the other measures adopted. A social exclusion approach often points to structural and group characteristics and causes of poverty, and thus implies the need for policies which address these conditions. To reduce social exclusion, policies therefore may need to be directed towards removing discrimination towards particular groups – possibly including affirmative action policies of various kinds; and to tackling the main causes of such exclusion, such as lack of assets, weak or absent political rights, lack of employment and so on. The particular set of policies needed will vary according to the nature of exclusion in the society in question. Moreover, a social exclusion approach almost unavoidably involves some redistributory policies, since social exclusion is defined as lack of achievement in relation to those obtaining on average in the society. Whereas, using a monetary approach it can be argued that 'Growth is good for the poor' (Dollar and Kraay, 2001), growth without redistribution is unlikely to reduce social exclusion.

The policy implications of participatory approaches must depend on what the poor themselves identify as the most important aspects of deprivation. Judging by our own exercises, a participatory approach requires that policy be directed at the many dimensions of poverty (including security as well as income, lack of assets and employment, problems of accessing water as well as schools). This suggests a much broader approach to anti-poverty policies than commonly adopted, with a particular focus on employment.

In general, this confirms the view that how one poses a problem influences how one goes about solving it. Clearly, as one widens and alters the concept of poverty, a much richer (and different) policy agenda emerges from that suggested by a purely monetary approach.

Statistics

Current statistical systems are geared up to producing information on monetary poverty. Adopting different approaches requires changes in the statistics adopted.

If CA poverty becomes the main measure of poverty, a major effort is needed to improve CA measurement.

- Data, often very weak for CA, need substantial improvement, including systematic collection of nutrition data for adults as well as children, and improved data on health, collected on an annual basis. We were not satisfied with our indicator of adult ill-health; the body mass index would provide a better capability indicator.

- The validity of indicators of CAs needs improvement: e.g. the nature of literacy tests varies hugely. More work is needed in identifying satisfactory capability indicators.
- There is a need for more consideration of appropriate thresholds for CA poverty, including whether and how they should vary between societies with different average levels of achievement.
- Participatory methods have a valuable role to play – particularly in adjusting the elements included in the externally imposed assessments, e.g. defining valuable basic capabilities; drawing poverty lines; defining social exclusion. Lack of comparability and the small samples involved, however, make it unrealistic to expect that PAs can, or should, replace the other poverty assessments.

The problems of definition make it difficult to use social exclusion as the main way in which poverty is measured, on a year-by-year basis. Yet the value of the approach in pointing to structural and dynamic features of poverty, suggest it should be assessed periodically, with the exercise of defining its characteristics itself being a valuable one, pointing to sources of exclusion. For social exclusion, data need to be collected on major aspects of deprivation on a group as well as an individual basis. The appropriate group classification will vary between societies, depending on the nature of identities and sources of discrimination in that society. For example, racial constructions and classifications are relevant to social exclusion in many developed countries; in others, it is indigenous peoples; in others, different ethnic, caste or religious classifications. Since well-being and political mobilisation are partly determined by group membership and status, data to monitor group inequalities are important (see Stewart 2002).

9.4 Conclusions

This review of the different approaches to the identification and measurement of poverty makes clear that there is no unique or 'objective' way of defining and measuring poverty. There is a large element of 'construction' involved in each of the poverty measures (by outsiders generally in the monetary, capability and SE approaches, by a combination of outsiders and the people themselves in PPA). All definitions of poverty contain some arbitrary and subjective elements, often imposed by the outside observer. But this is of most concern with respect to conceptualisation and measurement in the monetary approach, since the precision of the approach, and the very fact that it is expressed in monetary terms, tends to give the false impression that it is the most accurate and objective of the methods, while the judgements made in order to arrive at a measure of monetary poverty are generally not apparent. The fact that it is generally assumed that monetary methods do not involve judgements is indicated by the use of the term 'objective' to describe these measures, as against the use of the term 'subjective' to describe the methods which involve consulting people about their lives. This terminology is quite misleading. All approaches involve subjective judgements: what differs is whose judgements underly the methods. It would be more accurate to differentiate between methods using external judgements and those using internal judgements.

The limited empirical consistency of monetary methods with capability approaches poses particular problems since it means that monetary poverty does not consistently point to failure to achieve certain material objectives, such as adequate nutrition. Yet the monetary poverty line is typically justified as being either food-based or basic needs-based. If nutrition outcomes (or other capability outcomes) are not consistently correlated with monetary measures, then the basic justification of most monetary measures is undermined. In contrast, capability poverty – albeit also subject to relatively arbitrary and subjective decisions – transparently means that people are unable to function in some ways that are universally accepted as important for human development. Capability poverty may not amount to everything we think we mean by poverty, but it definitely constitutes part of it, and the more one extends the basic capabilities which are included, the greater the range of deprivations covered. While participatory methods have a lot to offer – both in helping to make methodological decisions about the other methods, and in providing a valuable (but not exclusive) definition of poverty – i.e. as perceived by the poor themselves – they should not be the exclusive approach as the perceptions of the poor (and even more the expression of these perceptions) are necessarily constrained and conditioned by their circumstances. Moreover, the methods adopted to ascertain these perceptions seem partly to determine the results.

A focus on measuring individual deprivation, whether it is monetary or capability, can neglect, or even draw attention away from, fundamental causes of deprivation. In this respect the SE approach is particularly important. Yet we have found social exclusion difficult to define in the developing country context, but believe the effort to do so is important because it points to processes of impoverishment, structural characteristics of societies responsible for deprivation, and group issues which tend to be neglected in other approaches.

Conceptualisation, definitions and measurement have important implications for targeting and policy. The considerable lack of overlaps empirically between the different approaches to poverty means that targeting according to one type of poverty will involve serious targeting errors in relation to other types. Thus if the monetary poverty is used as the targeting criterion, it will have to be supplemented by other criteria if these errors are not to be very large. Moreover, definitions also have implications for policy. While a monetary approach suggests a focus on increasing money incomes (by economic growth, or redistribution), a capability approach tends to lead to more emphasis on the provision of public goods. Social exclusion draws attention to the need to break down exclusionary factors, for example, by redistribution and anti-discrimination policies.

Both theoretical and empirical work point to the inadequacy of using any one approach and assuming that this serves as a proxy for other dimensions of poverty. At a theoretical level, a comparison of the four different approaches has identified fundamental differences in their historical origins and epistemological and ethical underpinnings. As Dessallien notes, 'Different concepts of poverty assume different causes and manifestations, and are associated with distinct families of indicators, which influence the analysis leading to policy recommendations' (Dessallien 1998: 16). Given the differences in the underpinnings of the approaches, the statement by Shaffer (1996: 33) (in the context of comparison of the participatory and monetary approaches) is relevant: 'In situations such as these no amount of technical tinkering can adjudicate between conflicting results. The problems are philosophical not technical.'

Definitions do matter. Clearer and more transparent definitions of poverty are an essential prerequisite of any development policy that puts poverty reduction at its centre.

Notes

1. In the case of the large data set in India, the poverty line was in terms of income, not expenditure, because of lack of data on consumption expenditure.
2. A combined enrolment and literacy indicator was used for India.
3. Results of other studies which have used wealth or well-being ranking as a participatory tool show that although the criteria used to classify the households are mainly monetary, some non-monetary factors have also been used. Most of these studies show that wealth or well-being is not expressed in the form of cash but in terms of food security (World Bank 2000 for Uganda; GTZ 1998 for Mali; Pritchard 1992 for Thailand).
4. As discussed in Chapter 6, for the participatory data for India, comparisons involving the monetary approach could only be done on urban data.
5. We are grateful to Emma Samman for assistance in reviewing this literature.
6. See e.g. Duclos et al. (2003); Bourguignon and Chakravarty (2003); Atkinson and Bourguignon (1987).

Bibliography

Aashray Adhikar Abhiyan (2001) *The Capital's Homeless* (New Delhi: AAA).

Aashray Adhikar Abhiyan (2002) *Basere ki Kahani: the Problems in the Night Shelters of Delhi, Using Participatory Research* (Delhi: AAA) (www.indev.nic.in/delhihomeless).

Aashray Adhikar Abhiyan (2005) *Update*, vol. 5, no. 18, October.

Adams, A. M., Evans, T., Mohammed, R. and Farnsworth, J. (1997) 'Socioeconomic Stratification by Wealth Ranking: Is It Valid?' *World Development*, vol. 25, no. 7: 1165–72.

Agarwal, B. (1992) 'Rural Women, Poverty and Natural Resources: Sustenance Sustainability and Struggle for Change', in B. Harriss, S. Guhan and R. Cassen (eds), *Poverty in India: Research and Policy* (New Delhi: Oxford University Press), pp. 390–432.

Agurto, G. (1998) 'Mundo Pirana', *Caretas*, no. 1527.

Agurto, G. (2003) 'Saga pirana. Tres "ninos de la calle" siete anos despues historias de supervivencia en el mar del desamparo', *Cateras* no. 1792.

Alkire, S. (2002) *Valuing Freedoms: Sen's Capability Approach and Poverty Reduction* (Oxford: Oxford University Press).

Anand, S., Harris, C. J. and Linton, O. B. (1993) 'On the Concept of Ultra-Poverty', Centre for Population and Development Studies, Working Paper 93.02, Harvard University.

Answer Tree (1999) Version 2.1, SPSS.

Appasamy, P., Guhan, S., Hema, R. et al. (1996) *Social Exclusion from a Welfare Rights Perspective in India*, International Institute for Labour Studies and UNDP, Research Series 106 (Geneva: ILO Publications).

Appleton, S. and Song, L. (1999) 'Income and Human Development at the Household Level: Evidence from Six Countries'. Background paper for *World Development Report 2000/2001*. Available at http://insruct1.cit.cornell.edu/Courses/econ771/papers/appleton_song.doc

Aramburú, C. and Figueroa, A. (2001) 'El desafio d enfrentar las disigualidad de la pobreza extrema in el Perú', in H. Vasquez, C. Aramburú, A. Figueroa and C. Parodi, *Los Desafios de la Lucha con la Pobreza Extrema en el Perú*, Centro de Investigación de la Universidad del Pacifico, International Development Research Centre, Lima, Peru.

Arnstein S. R. (1971) 'A Ladder of Citizen's Participation', *Journal of the American Institute of Planners*, vol. 35: 216–24.

Aroca, Javier (1996) 'Los derechos humanos de los pueblos indígenas', in *El libro derechos humanos y pueblos indígenas de la Amazonía peruana: realidad, normativa y perspectives* (Lina: APEC/CAAP, November).

Arrow, K. J. (1995) 'A Note on Freedom and Flexibility', in K. Basu, P. Pattanaik and K. Suzumura (eds), *Choice, Welfare and Development: a Festchrift in Honour of Amartya K. Sen* (Oxford: Clarendon Press), pp. 7–16.

Atkinson, A. B. (1982) 'The Comparison of Multidimensional Distributions of Economic Status', in A. B. Atkinson (ed.), *Social Justice and Social Policy* (London: Harvester Wheatsheaf).

Atkinson, A. B. (1989) *Poverty and Social Security* (London: Harvester Wheatsheaf).

Atkinson, A. B. (1995) *Incomes and the Welfare State* (Cambridge: Cambridge University Press).

Atkinson, A. B. (1998) 'Social Exclusion, Poverty and Unemployment', in A. B. Atkinson, and J. Hills (eds), *Exclusion, Employment and Opportunity*, STICERD, London School of Economics Discussion Papers Series, CASE/4.

Atkinson, A. B. and Bourguignon, F. (1987) 'Income Distribution and Differences in Needs', in G. R. Feiwel (ed.), *Arrow and the Foundations of the Theory of Economic Policy* (Basingstoke: Macmillan).

Atkinson, A. B. and Hills, J. (1991) 'Social Security in Developed Countries: Are There Lessons for Developing Countries?' in E. Ahmad, J. Dreze, J. Hills and A. Sen (eds), *Social Security in Developing Countries* (Oxford: Clarendon Press), pp. 81–111.

Baker, J. L. (1997) *Poverty Reduction and Human Development in the Caribbean: a Cross-cultural Study* (Washington DC: World Bank).

Bales, Kevin (1999) 'Popular Reactions to Sociological Research: the Case of Charles Booth', *Sociology*, vol. 33, no. 1.

Balestrino, A. (1991) 'Some Suggestions for the Identification of Poverty in a Non-welfarist Framework', *Economic Notes*, vol. 20, no. 2: 335–53.

Balestrino, A. (1994) 'Poverty and Functionings: Issues in Measurement and Public Action', *Giornale degli Economisti e Annali di Economia*, vol. 53, nos. 7–9: 389–406.

Balestrino, A. (1996) 'A Note on Functionings Poverty in Affluent Societies', *Notizei de Politeia*, 12: 97–105.

Balestrino, A. and Petretto, A. (1994) 'Optimal Taxation Rules for "Functioning" – Inputs', *Economic Notes*, vol. 23, no. 2: 216–32.

Balestrino, A. and Sciclone, N. (2000) 'Should We Use Functionings Instead of Income to Measure Wellbeing? Theory and Some Evidence from Italy'. Mimeo, University of Pisa.

Banks, J. and Johnson, P. (1993) *Children and Household Living Standards* (London: Institute for Fiscal Studies).

Barclay, Frederica (1998) 'Perú: Perfil socioeconómico y cultural de los Pueblos Indígenas de la Amazonía'. Documento elaborado para el Banco Mundial. Versión final. PROMUDEH/Banco Mundial, Junio in GRADE, 2003.

Barry, B. (1998) 'Social Exclusion, Social Isolation and the Distribution of Income', CASE paper 12, Centre for Analysis of Social Exclusion, London School of Economics.

Baulch, B. and Masset, E. (2003) 'Do Monetary and Non-monetary Indicators Tell the Same Story about Chronic Poverty? A Study of Vietnam in the 1990s', *World Development*, vol. 31, no. 3: 441–53.

Beall, J. (1999) 'The Role of Households and Livelihood Systems in the Management of Solid Waste in South Asia', *Waterlines*, vol. 17, no. 3.

Bedoui, M. and Gouia, R. (1995) 'Patterns and Processes of Social Exclusion in Tunisia', in G. Rodgers, C. Gore and J. Figueiredo (eds), *Social Exclusion: Rhetoric, Reality, Responses* (Geneva: Institute for Labour Studies).

Bentham, J. (1789) *Introduction to the Principles of Morals and Legislation* (republished Gaunt, incorporated, 2001).

Berghman, J. (1995) 'Social Exclusion in Europe: Policy Context and Analytical Framework', in G. Room (ed.), *Beyond the Threshold: the Measurement and Analysis of Social Exclusion* (Southampton: Hobbs), pp. 10–28.

Bhalla, A. and Lapeyre, F. (1997) 'Social Exclusion: Towards an Analytical and Operational Framework', *Development and Change*, July: 413–33.

Bhalla, A. and Lapeyre, F. (1999) *Poverty and Exclusion in a Global World* (New York: St. Martin's Press; Basingstoke: Macmillan).

Bhalla, A. S. and Lapeyre, F. (2004) *Poverty and Exclusion in a Global World*. 2nd rev. edn (Basingstoke: Palgrave Macmillan).

Bibi, Sami (2003), 'Comparing Multidimensional Poverty between Egypt and Tunisia', paper presented at the 10th Annual ERF Conference, Marrakesh, Morocco. Available at http://www.erf.org.eg/tenthconf/Labor Presented/Bibi.pdf

Bishop, John A., Formby, John P. and Smith, W. James (1993) 'International Comparisons of Welfare and Poverty: Dominance Orderings for Ten Countries', *Canadian Journal of Economics*, vol. 26, no. 3: 707.

Blundell, Richard, Preston, Ian and Walker, Ian (eds) (1994) *The Measurement of Household Welfare* (Cambridge: Cambridge University Press).

Booth, C. (1887) 'The Inhabitants of Tower Hamlets (school board division), their Condition and Occupations', *Journal of Royal Statistical Society*, vol. 50: 326–40.

Booth, D., Holland, J., Hentschel, J., Lanjouw, P. and Herbert, A. (1998) *Participation and Combined Methods in African Poverty Assessments: Renewing the Agenda* (London, DFID Social Development Division, Africa Division).

Bourguignon, F. and Chakravarty, S. R. (2002) 'Multidimensional Poverty Orderings', DELTA Working Paper, 2002–22 (Paris).

Bourguignon, F. and Chakravarty, S. R. (2003) 'The Measurement of Multi-dimensional Poverty', *Journal of Economic Inequality*, vol. 1, no. 1: 1569–1721.

Bowley, Arthur Lyon and Margaret Hogg (1925) *Has Poverty Diminished?: a Sequel to Livelihood and Poverty* (London: P. S. King).

Brandolini, A. and D'Alessio, G. (1998) 'Measuring Well-Being in the Functioning Space', Banca d'Italia Research Department, Mimeo.

Bulmer, Martin (1985) 'The Development of Sociology and of Empirical Social Research in Britain', in M. Bulmer (ed.), *Essays on the History of British Sociological Research* (Cambridge: Cambridge University Press), pp. 3–38.

Burchardt, T., Le Grand, J. and Piachaud, D. (1999) 'Social Exclusion in Britain 1991–1995', *Social Policy and Administration*, vol. 33, no. 3: 227–44.

Burchardt, Tania, Le Grand, Julian and Piachaud, David (2002) 'Degrees of Exclusion: Developing a Dynamic Multidimensional Measure', in J. Hills, J. Le Grand and D. Piachaud (eds), *Understanding Social Exclusion* (Oxford: Oxford University Press), pp. 30–44.

Bürgemeier, Beat (1994) 'The Misperception of Walras?' *American Economic Review*, vol. 84, no. 1: 342–52.

Burgess, R. and Stern, N. (1991) 'Social Security in Developing Countries: What, Why, Who, and How?' in E. Ahmad, J. Dreze, J. Hills and A. Sen (eds), *Social Security in Developing Countries* (Oxford: Clarendon Press), pp. 41–80.

Câmara, Gilberto Antônio Miguel Monteiro, Ramos, Fred, Sposati, Aldaiza and Koga, Dirce (2004). 'Mapping Social Exclusion/Inclusion in Developing Countries: Social Dynamics of São Paulo in the 90's', in D. Jonelle and M. Goodchild (eds), *Spatially Integrated Social Science: Examples in Best Practice* (New York: Oxford University Press), pp. 223–7.

Cartaya, V., Magallanes, R. and DomÃnguez, C. (1997) *Venezuela: Exclusion and Integration: a Synthesis in the Building?* (Geneva: ILO).

Carter, Michael R. and May, Julian (1999) 'Poverty Livelihood and Class in Rural South Africa', *World Development*, vol. 27: 1–20.

Carvalho, Sonya and White, Howard (1997) *Combining the Quantitative and Qualitative Approaches to Poverty Measurement and Analysis: the Practice and the Potential*, World Bank technical paper no. 366 (Washington DC: World Bank).

Cerioli, A. and Zani, S. (1990) 'A Fuzzy Approach to the Measurement of Poverty', in C. Dagum and M. Zenga (eds), *Income and Wealth Distribution* (Berlin: Springer), pp. 272–84.

Chakraborty, A. (1996) 'On the Possibility of a Weighting System for Functionings', *Indian Economic Review*, vol. 31, no. 2: 241–50.

Chambers, R. (1992) 'Poverty in India: Concepts Research and Reality', in B. Harris, S. Guhan and R. Cassen (eds), *Poverty in India: Research and Policy* (New Delhi: Oxford University Press), pp. 301–32.

Chambers, R. (1993) *Challenging the Professions: Frontiers for Rural Development* (London: Intermediate Technology Publications).

Chambers, R. (1994a) 'The Origins and Practice of PRA', *World Development*, vol. 22, no. 7.

Chambers, R. (1994b) 'PRA: Challenges, Potentials and Paradigms', *World Development*, vol. 22, no. 10.

Chambers, R. (1997) *Whose Reality Counts? Putting the First Last* (London: Intermediate Technology Publications).

Cheli, B. and Lemmi, A. (1995) 'A "Totally" Fuzzy and Relative Approach to the Multidimensional Analysis of Poverty', *Economic Notes*, vol. 24, no. 1: 115–34.

Chronic Poverty Report, 2004–2005. Chronic Poverty Research Centre, Institute for Development Policy and Management, University of Manchester, UK. Available at www. chronicpoverty.org

Clark, D. (2002) *Visions of Development: a Study of Human Values* (Cheltenham, Edward Elgar).

Clark, D. A. and Qizilbach, M. (2002) 'Core Poverty and Extreme Vulnerability in South Africa', paper presented at International Association for Research in Income and Wealth conference, Djuhamn, Sweden, August.

Clert, C. (1999) 'Evaluating the Concept of Social Exclusion in Development Discourse', *European Journal of Development Research*, vol. 11, no. 2: 176–99.

Cohen, G. A. (1993) 'Amartya Sen's Unequal World', *Economic and Political Weekly*, vol. 28, no. 40: 2156–60.

Cornia, G. A., Jolly, R. and Stewart, F. (1987) *Adjustment With a Human Face* (Oxford: Oxford University Press).

Cornwall, A. (2000) *Beneficiary, Consumer, Citizen Perspectives on Participation for Poverty Reduction* (Institute of Development Studies, Sussex University).

Cornwall, Andrea, Gujit, Irene and Welbourn, Alice (1993) *Acknowledging Processes: Challenges for Agricultural Research and Extension Methodology*, IDS Discussion Paper 333.

Crocker, D. A. (1992) 'Functioning and Capability: the Foundations of Sen's and Nussbaum's Development Ethic', *Political Theory*, vol. 20, no. 4: 584–612.

Crocker, D. A. (1995) 'Functioning and Capability: the Foundations of Sen's and Nussbaum's Development Ethic, Part 2', in M. C. Nussbaum and J. Glover (eds), *Women, Culture and Development: a Study of Human Capabilities* (Oxford: Clarendon Press), pp. 153–98.

Crothers, C. (1997) 'The Level of Poverty in South Africa: Consideration of an Experiential Measure', *Development Southern Africa*, vol. 14, no. 4: 505–12.

da Cunha, P. V. and Junho Pena, M. V. (1997) *The Limits and Merits of Participation*, Policy Research Working Papers, World Bank.

Dasgupta, P. (1993) *An Enquiry into Well-being and Destitution* (Oxford: Oxford University Press).

Davies, Jonathan, Richards, Michael and Cavendish, William (1999) 'Beyond the Limits of PRA? A Comparison of Participatory and Conventional Economic Research Methods in the Analysis of Ilala Palm Use in South-Eastern Zimbabwe', ODI electronic working paper.

de Graft Agyarko, R. (1998). 'Influencing Policy through Poverty Assessments: Theoretical and Practical Overview of a Changing Process', in PPA Topic Pack, IDS.

de Haan, A. (1999) *Social Exclusion: Towards a Holistic Understanding of Deprivation*, Social Development Department, Dissemination Note No. 2, Department for International Development, London, UK.

de Onis, M., Garza, C. and Habicht, J. P. (1997) 'Time for a New Growth Reference', *Pediatrics*, vol. 100, no. 5. (http://www.pediatrics.org/cgi/content/ full/100/5/e8).

Deaton, A. (1997) *The Analysis of Household Surveys: a Microeconometric Approach to Development Policy* (Washington DC: Johns Hopkins University Press, World Bank).

Deaton, A. (2002) 'Background Paper for the UNDP Human Development Report' (New York: UNDP).

Deaton, Angus and Salman Zaidi (1999) *Guidelines for Constructing Consumption Aggregates for Welfare Analysis*. World Bank, mimeo.

Desai, M. (1995) 'Poverty and Capability: Towards an Empirically Implementable Measure', in *Poverty, Famine and Economic Development: the Selected Essays of Meghnad Desai, Volume II* (Aldershot, UK and Vermont: Edward Elgar Publishing Company), pp. 185–204.

Desai, M. and Shah, A. (1988) 'An Econometric Approach to the Measurement of Poverty', *Oxford Economic Papers*, vol. 40, no. 3: 505–22.

Desai, N., Kaur, P. and Bhardwaje, J. (2003) *Health Care Beyond Zero: Ensuring Basic Rights for the Homeless* (New Delhi: Aashray Adhikar Abhiyan).

Dessallien, R. L. (1998) 'Review of Poverty Concepts and Indicators', *Poverty Elimination Programme* (UNDP).

Dhargamwar, D. (1992) 'The Disadvantaged and the Law', in B. Harriss, S. Guhan and R. Cassen (eds), *Poverty in India: Research and Policy* (New Delhi: Oxford University Press), pp. 433–48.

Dhargamwar, V., De, S. and Verma, N. (2003) *Industrial Development and Displacement: the People of Korba* (New Delhi: Sage).

Dhatt, G. and Ravallion, M. (1998) 'Why Have Some Indian States Done Better than Others at Reducing Rural Poverty?' *Economica*, vol. 65: 17–38.

Dollar, D. and Kraay, A. (2001) *Growth is Good for the Poor*, World Bank Policy Research Working Paper, 2587 (Washington DC: World Bank).

Doyal, L. and Gough, L. (1991) *A Theory of Human Need* (Basingstoke and London: Macmillan Education Limited).

Drèze, J. and Sen, A. (1991) 'Public Action for Social Security: Foundations and Strategy', in E. Ahmad, J. Drèze, J. Hills and A. Sen (eds), *Social Security in Developing Countries* (Oxford: Clarendon Press), pp. 1–40.

Drèze, J. and Sen, A. (1995) *India: Economic Development and Social Opportunity* (Delhi: Oxford University Press).

Duclos, J.-Y., Sahn, D. and Younger, S. (2003) 'Robust Multidimensional Poverty Comparisons', Université Laval – Département d'économique in its series Cahiers de recherche 0115.

Erb, S. and Harriss-White, B. (2002) *Outcast from Social Welfare: Adult Disability and Incapacity in Rural South India* (Bangalore: Books for Change).

Erikson, R. (1993) 'Descriptions of Inequality: the Swedish Approach to Welfare Research', in M. C. Nussbaum and A. Sen (eds), *Quality of Life* (Oxford: Clarendon Press, and reprinted (1999), pp. 67–83, New Delhi: Oxford University Press).

Escobal, J., Saavedra, J. and Torero, M. (1999) 'Los activos de los pobres en el Peru', Grupo de Análisis para el Desarrollo (GRADE), Lima, Peru.

Estrella, Marisol and John, Gaventa (1998) *Who Counts Reality? Participatory Monitoring and Evaluation: a Literature Review*, IDS Working Paper no. 70.

European Commission (2001) *Joint Inclusion Report* (http://ec.europa.eu/employment_social/soc-prot/soc-incl/155223/part1_en.pdf).

European Foundation for the Improvement of Living and Working Conditions (1995) *Public Welfare Services and Social Exclusion: the Development of Consumer Oriented Initiatives in the European Union* (Dublin: European Foundation).

Eurostat Taskforce (1998) *Recommendations on Social Exclusion and Poverty Statistics* (Luxembourg: Eurostat).

Fafchamps, Marcel and Forhad, Shilpi (2003) *Subjective wellbeing, isolation and Rivalry*, Economics Department, Oxford University, Working Paper 216.

Figueroa, A. (2003) 'Poverty Studies in Peru: Towards a More Inclusive Study of Exclusion', WeD Working Paper 05, ESRC Research Group on Wellbeing in Developing Countries, ESRC.

Figueroa, A. and Barron, M. (2005) 'Inequality, Ethnicity and Social Disorder in Peru', Working Paper no. 8, Centre for Research on Inequality, Security and Ethnicity, QEH, Oxford.

Figueroa, A., Altamirano, T. and Sulmont, D. (1996) *Social Exclusion and Inequality in Peru*, International Institute for Labour Studies and United Nations Development Programme, Research Series, 104 (Geneva: ILO Publications).

Forth, J. and Kirby, S. (2000) 'A Guide to the Analysis of the 1998 Workplace Employee Relations Survey', London: WERS98 Data Dissemination Service, National Institute of Economic and Social Research, London, UK (http://www.niesr.ac.uk/niesr/wers98/).

Foster, James (1994) 'Normative Measurement: Is Theory Relevant?' *American Economic Review Papers and Proceedings*.

Foster, J., Greer, J. and Thorbeck, E. (1984) 'A Class of Decomposable Poverty Measures', *Econometrica*, vol. 52, no. 3: 761–6.

Franco, S., Harriss-White, B. et al. (2002) *Alternative Realities? Different Concepts of Poverty, their Empirical Consequences and Policy Implications*, Queen Elizabeth House.

Fuentes, Nicole and Rojas, Mariano (2001) 'Economic Theory and Subjective Well-being: Mexico', *Social Indicators Research*, vol. 53: 289–314. Available at http://mailweb.udlap.mx/~llec_www/documentos/mrojas6.pdf

Gigengack, Roy (2006) *Young, Damned and Banda* (Amsterdam: Amsterdam School of Social Research).

Gill, K. (2004) 'Waste as Work: Measuring and Comparing Poverty and Job-Related Well Being', paper presented to the British Association of South Asian Studies Annual Conference, University of East Anglia. http://www.staff.brad.ac.uk/akundu/basas/basasc04programme.htm

Gillie, Alan (1996) 'The Origin of the Poverty Line', *Economic History Review*, vol. 49, no. 4: 715–30.

Glewwe, Paul and Jacques van der Gaag (1990) 'Identifying the Poor in Developing Countries: Do Definitions Matter?', *World Development*, vol. 18, no. 6: 803–14.

Gooptu, N. (2002) 'Sex Workers in Calcutta and the Dynamics of Collective Action: Political Activism, Community Identity and Group Behaviour', in J. Heyer, F. Stewart and R. Thorp (eds), *Group Behaviour and Development* (Oxford: Oxford University Press), pp. 227–52.

Gopal, G. M. (2001) 'The Challenge of Ending Poverty in India: Towards a New Approach', draft paper to the National Commission for the Review of the Working of the Constitution (NCAER, New Delhi).

Gore, C., with Figueiredo, J. and Rodgers, G. (1995) 'Introduction: Markets, Citizenship and Social Exclusion', in G. Rodgers, C. Gore and J. Figueiredo (eds), *Social Exclusion: Rhetoric, Reality, Responses* (Geneva: International Institute for Labour Studies), pp. 1–40.

Gore, C. and Figueiredo, J. (1997) 'Resources for Debate', in C. Gore, and J. Figueiredo (eds), *Social Exclusion and Anti-poverty Policy: a Debate*, Research Series, 110 (Geneva: International Institute for Labour Studies), pp. 7–34.

GRADE (2003) *Etnicidad, Pobreza u Exclusion Social: la Situacion de la Poblacion Indigena Urbana en el Peru* (Lima, GRADE).

Grosh, M. E. and Glewwe, P. (2000) *Designing Household Survey Questionnaires for Developing Countries: Lessons from 15 Years of the Living Standards Measurement Study*, 3 vols (Washington DC: World Bank).

GTZ (1998) *Poverty Monitoring in Rural Development Projects: the Wealth-ranking Method and its Application in the PRODILO Project* (http://www.gtz.de/forum_armut).

Gujit, Irene and Braden, Su (1999) 'Learning from Analysis: Ensuring Reflection in Participatory Processes', *PLA*, note 34, pp. 18–24 (London: IIED).

Gupta, J. (2002) 'Women, Second on the Land Agenda', *Economic and Political Weekly*, 4 May (http://www.epw.org.in).

Habicht, J. P, Martorell, R., Yarbrough, C., Malina, R. M. and Klein, R. E. (1974) 'Height and Weight Standards for Preschool Children: How Relevant are Ethnic Differences in Growth Potential', *Lancet*, 1: 611–15.

Haddad, Lawrence, Hoddinott, John and Alderman, Harold (eds) (1997) *Intrahousehold Resource Allocation in Developing Countries: Models, Methods and Policies* (Baltimore and London: Johns Hopkins University Press for IFPRI).

Harriss, B. (1992) 'Rural Poverty in India: Micro-level Evidence', in B. Harriss, S. Guhan and R. Cassen (eds), *Poverty in India: Research and Policy* (New Delhi: Oxford University Press), pp. 333–89.

Harriss, B., Guhan, S. and Cassen, R. (1992) *Poverty in India: Research and Policy* (New Delhi: Oxford University Press).

Harriss-White, B. and Hoffenberg R. (eds), (1994) *Food: Multidisciplinary Perspectives* (Oxford: Blackwell).

Hashem, M. (1995) 'Patterns and Processes of Social Exclusion in the Republic of Yemen', in G. Rodgers, C. Gore and J. Figueiredo (eds), *Social Exclusion: Rhetoric, Reality, Responses* (Geneva: International Institute for Labour Studies), pp. 175–86.

Hennock, E. P. (1987) 'The Measurement of Urban Poverty: From the Metropolis to the Nation, 1880–1920', *Economic History Review*, vol. 40: 208–27.

Herencia, E. G. (2004) 'La Epidemia del SIDA: Situacion del peru al 2005, *Rev. Med. Hered.*, vol. 15, no. 4, pp. 179–80 (http://www.redsidaperu.org/Organizacion/LasOrganizaciones.htm).

Herrera, Javier (2002) 'Pobreza subjetiva y pobreza objetiva en el Perú, Extracto del reporte', in J. Herrera, *La Pobreza en el Perú 1001. Una Visión Departamental* (INEI), Lima: Peru. Available at: http://www.paris21.org/htm/workshop/bol2002/herrera.doc

Herrera, Javier, Razafindrakoto, Mireille and Roubaud, François (2003) 'De la pobreza monetaria a los nuevos enfoques de la pobreza: un análisis comparativo de la apreciación subjetiva del bienestar Perú-Madagascar'. Presentation prepared for IRD conference in Lima, October. Available at http://www.dial.prd.fr/dial_evenements/pdf/Razaf16octppt.pdf

Hicks, N. L. (1982) 'Sector Priorities in Meeting Basic Needs: Some Statistical Evidence', *World Development*, vol. 10, no. 6: 489–99.

Hills, John, Le Grand, Julian and Piachaud, David (2002) *Understanding Social Exclusion* (Oxford: Oxford University Press).

Howard, M. and Millard, A. V. (1997) *Hunger and Shame: Child Malnutrition and Poverty on Mount Kilimanjaro* (London, Routledge). Available at http://www.univ-tlse1.fr/ARQADE/ressources/Cahiers/2000/BPtemp27694.pdf

Hulme, D. and Shepherd, A. (2003) 'Conceptualising Chronic Poverty', *World Development*, vol. 31, no. 3: 403–23.

Hyat, T. (2001) 'Essays on Consumption and Asset Mobility in Rural Pakistan', DPhil Thesis, University of Oxford.

IDS (1998) *PPA Topic Pack* (Falmer, Brighton: Institute of Development Studies).

IIIED (1997) *Valuing the Hidden Harvest: Methodological Approaches for Local Level Economic Analysis of Wild Resources*, Sustainable Agriculture Programme Research Series, vol. 3, no. 4. Sustainable Agriculture Programme, London IIED.

Inack, I., Mbida, J. and Bea, P. (1995) 'Ethnic Solidarity and Social Exclusion in Cameroon', in G. Rodgers, C. Gore and J. Figuerido (eds), *Social Exclusion: Rhetoric, Reality, Responses* (Geneva: International Institute for Labour Studies), pp. 229–35.

Jenkins, S. P. and Lambert, P. J. (1993) 'Ranking Income Distributions When Needs Differ', *Review of Income and Wealth*, vol. 39: 337–56.

Jha, S. K. (2002) 'The Beggars of Kathmandu', *The Kathmandu Post* (25 February).

Jodha, N. S. (1989) 'Social Science Research on Rural Change: Some Gaps', in P. Bardhan (ed.), *Conversations Between Economists and Anthropologists* (Delhi: Oxford University Press).

Jonsson, I. (1999) 'Women, Work and Welfare', in P. Littlewood with H. Glorieux, S. Herkommer and I. Jonsson (eds), *Social Exclusion in Europe: Problems and Paradigms* (Aldershot: Ashgate).

Kamat, K. L. (1979/updated 1999) 'The Begging Profession' (http://www.kamat.com/kalranga/bhiksha/begging.htm).

Kanbur, R. (1987) 'The Standard of Living: Uncertainty, Inequality and Opportunity', in G. Hawthorn (ed.), *The Standard of Living: the Tanner Lectures on Human Values* (Cambridge: Cambridge University Press), pp. 59–69.

Kanbur, Ravi (ed.) (2002) *Q-squared: Combining Qualitative and Quantitative Methods in Poverty Appraisal* (New Delhi, Permanent Black).

Kedir, Abbi M. and McKay, Andrew (2003) 'Chronic Poverty in Urban Ethiopia: Panel Data Evidence', paper prepared for International Conference on 'Staying Poor: Chronic Poverty and Development Policy', University of Manchester, UK, 7–9 April. Available at http://idpm.man.ac.uk/cprc/Conference/conferencepapers/kedir&mckay.pdf

Kent, Raymond (1985) 'The Emergence of the Sociological Survey, 1887–1939', in M. Bulmer (ed.), *Essays on the History of British Sociological Research* (Cambridge: Cambridge University Press).

Kingdon, Geeta and Knight, John (2003) 'Well-being: Poverty versus Income Poverty and Capabilities Poverty?' CSAE WPS/2003–16, University of Oxford: Center for the Study of African Economies. Available at: http://www.economics.ox.ac.uk/Members/geeta.kingdon/DiscussionPapers/jdshappinessdec03.pdf

Kingdon, Geeta and John Knight (2004) 'Community, Comparisons and Subjective Well-being in a Divided Society', paper for presentation at CSAE conference, St Catherine's College, 21–22 March.

Klasen, Stephan (2000) 'Measuring Poverty and Deprivation in South Africa', *Review of Income and Wealth*, vol. 46, no. 1: 33–58.

Kozel, Valerie and Parker, Barbara (1999) *Poverty in Rural India: the Contribution of Qualitative Research in Poverty Analysis*, World Bank Working Paper.

Kozel, Valerie and Parker, Barbara (2003) 'A Diagnostic Profile of Poverty in Uttar Pradesh', *Economic and Political Weekly*, vol. 37, no. 4: 385–403.

Laderchi, C. R., Saith, R. and Stewart, F. (2003) 'Everyone Agrees We Need Poverty Reduction but Not What This Means: Does this Matter?' Paper presented at the WIDER Conference on Inequality, Poverty and Human Well-Being, Helsinki, May. Available at http://unstats.un.org/unsd/methods/poverty/Everyone%20agrees%20we%20need%20poverty%20reduction%20by%20Stewart%20may03.pdf

Lanjouw, Peter and Ravallion, Martin (1995) 'Poverty and Household Size', *Economic Journal*, vol. 105, no. 433: 1415–34.

Lavy, Victor, Spratt, Jennifer and Leboucher, Nathalie (1995) *Changing Patterns of Illiteracy in Morocco: Assessment Methods Compared*, Living Standards Measurement Study, Working Paper No. 115, World Bank, Washington DC.

Lenoir, R. (1974/1989) *Les Exclus: Un Français sur Dix* (Paris: Editions de Seuil).

Lever, J. P. (2004) 'Poverty and Subjective Wellbeing in Mexico', *Social Indicators Research*, vol. 68, no. 1: 1–33, August. Available at www.kluweronline.com/article.asp?PIPS=5139350&PDF=1

Levitas, Ruth (1998) 'Social Exclusion in the New Breadline Britain Survey', Chapter 7 in *Perceptions of Poverty and Social Exclusion 1998: Report on Preparatory Research*, Townsend Centre for International Poverty Research, University of Bristol, pp. 39–41.

Lewis, G. W. and Ulph, D. T. (1998) 'Poverty, Inequality and Welfare', *Economic Journal*, vol. 98 (*Conference* 1988): 117–31.

Li, Bingqin (2004) *Urban Social Exclusion in Transitional China*, Centre for Analysis of Social Exclusion (CASE), LSE, Working Paper 82.

Lipton, M. (1983) *Poverty, Undernutrition and Hunger*. World Bank Staff Working Papers no. 597 (Washington DC: World Bank).

Lipton, M. (1988) *The Poor and the Poorest: Some Interim Findings*. World Bank Discussion Papers no. 25 (Washington DC: World Bank).

Lipton, Michael and Martin Ravallion (1995) 'Poverty and Policy', in J. Berhman and T. N. Srinivasan (eds), *Handbook of Development Economics*, vol. III (Elsevier Science).

Lokshin, Michael and Ravallion, Martin (2002) 'Self-rated Economic Welfare in Russia', *European Economic Review*, 46: 1453–76.

Lokshin, M., Umapathi, N. and Paternostro, S. (2006) 'Robustness of Subjective Welfare Analysis in a Poor Developing Country: Madagascar 2001', *Journal of Development Studies*, vol. 42, no. 4: 559–91.

Mander, H. (2001) *Unheard Voices: Stories of Forgotten Lives* (New Delhi: Penguin).

Mander, H. (2002) *Forgotten Lives: Public Policy and Poor People in India* (New Delhi: ActionAid).

Mangahas, Manhar (2003) 'The SWS Survey Time Series on Philippine Poverty and Hunger, 1983–2003', thematic paper for the 2004 Regional Conference on Poverty Monitoring in Asia, 31 December. Available at http://www.rcpm.net/files/pdf/PHI_SWS_Survey_on_Poverty_and_Hunger.pdf

Marshall, Thomas (1981) *The Right to Welfare and Other Essays* (London: Heinemann Educational).

Martinetti, E. C. (1994) 'A New Approach to Evaluation of Well-Being and Poverty by Fuzzy Set Theory', *Giornale degli Economisti e Annali di Economia*, vol. 53, nos 7–9: 367–88.

Marx, Karl (1862/1990) *Capital*, vol. 1 (London: Lawrence and Wishart).

Mathur, P., Sharma, S. and Wadhwa, A. (1996) 'Rapid Assessment Procedures for the Health and Nutritional Profile of Adolescent Girls: an Exploratory Study', *Food and Nutrition Bulletin*, vol. 17, no. 3: 235–40.

McGee, Rosemary (1997) 'Looking at Poverty from Different Points of View: a Colombian Case Study', doctoral thesis, Faculty of Economic Studies, University of Manchester, unpublished.

McGee, Rosemary (1999) 'Technical, Objective, Equitable and Uniform? A Critique of the Colombian System for the Selection of Beneficiaries of Social Programmes, SISBEN', unpublished IDPM working paper.

McGee, Rosemary (2002) 'The Self in Participatory Poverty Research', in Karen Brock and Rosemary McGee (eds), *Knowing Poverty: Critical Reflections on Participatory Research and Policy* (London: Earthscan).

McGee, Rosemary (2004) 'Constructing Poverty Trends in Uganda: a Multidisciplinary Perspective', *Development and Change*, vol. 35: 499–523.

Menon, S. (2001) 'Workers Who Shelter on the Pavement', *Labour File*, vol. 7, no. 6–7: 5–13.

Micklewright, J. (2002) *Social Exclusion and Children: a European View for US Debate* (Florence: UNICEF).

Mishra, P. (2004) *Pune's Homeless: Living on the Fringe*, Pune4change (cyda@vsnl.com).

Morduch, J. (1995) 'Income Smoothing and Consumption Smoothing', *Journal of Economic Perspectives*, vol. 9, no. 3: 103–14.

Mosley, Paul and Dowler, Elizabeth (2003) 'Introduction', Chapter 1 in *Poverty and Social Exclusion in North and South: Essays on Social Policy and Global Poverty Reduction* (London: Routledge), pp. 1–13.

Muellbauer, J. (1987) 'Professor Sen on the Standard of Living', in G. Hawthorn (ed.), *The Standard of Living: the Tanner Lectures on Human Values* (Cambridge: Cambridge University Press), pp. 39–58.

Murray, C. and Chen, L. (1992) 'Understanding Morbidity Change', *Population and Development Review*, vol. 18, no. 3: 481–503.

Narayan, Deepa, Chambers, Robert, Shah, Meera Kaul and Petesch, Patti (2000) *Voices of the Poor: Crying Out for Change* (Oxford University Press for the World Bank).

Narayan-Parker, D. and Patel, R. (2000) *Voices of the Poor: Can Anyone Hear Us?* (Oxford: Oxford University Press).

Narayanan, Pradeep (2003) 'Empowerment through Participation: How Effective is this Approach?' *Economic and Political Weekly*, vol. 8, no. 25 (India. indymedia.org/en/2004/04/209336.shtml).

Nayak, P. (1994) 'Economic Development and Social Exclusion in India', Chapter 2 in *Social Exclusion and South Asia*, Labour Institutions and Development Programme, DP 77, International Institute for Labour Studies (Geneva: International Labour Organisation).

Nolan, Brian and Whelan, Christopher T. (1996) *Resources, Deprivation and Poverty* (Oxford: Clarendon Press).

Norton, Andy and Francis, Paul A. (1992) *Participatory Poverty Assessment in Ghana. Discussion Paper and Proposal* (World Bank).

Nussbaum, M. C. (1995) 'Human Capabilities, Female Human Beings', in M. C. Nussbaum and J. Glover (eds), *Women, Culture and Development: a Study of Human Capabilities* (Oxford: Clarendon Press), pp. 61–104.

Nussbaum, M. C. (2000a) 'In Defence of Universal Values', in *Women and Human Development: the Capabilities Approach*, John Robert Seeley Lectures (Cambridge: Cambridge University Press), pp. 34–110.

Nussbaum, M. (2000b) *Women and Human Development: a Study in Human Capabilities* (Cambridge: Cambridge University Press).

Nussbaum, M. (2000c) 'Women and Work: the Capabilities Approach', *The Little Magazine*, vol. 1, no. 1 (http://www.littlemag.com/2000/martha2.htm).

Nussbaum, M. C. and Sen, A. K (eds) (1993) *The Quality of Life* (Oxford: Clarendon Press; New York: Oxford University Press).

O'Neill, O. (1994) 'Hunger, Needs and Rights', in B. Harriss-White and R. Hoffenberg (eds), *Food: Multidisciplinary Perspectives* (Oxford, Blackwell), pp. 231–2.

Osmani, S. R. (1991) 'Social Security in South Asia', in E. Ahmad, J. Dreze, J. Hills and A. Sen (eds), *Social Security in Developing Countries* (Oxford: Clarendon Press), pp. 305–55.

Patrizi, Vincenzo (1990) 'Sul significato normativo delle misure di poverta', *Politica Economica*, vol. 6, no. 1: 31–76.

Paugam, S. (1995) 'The Spiral of Precariousness: a Multidimensional Approach to the Process of Social Disqualification in France', in G. Room (ed.), *Beyond the Threshold: the Measurement and Analysis of Social Exclusion* (Bristol: Policy Press), pp. 49–72.

Paugam, S. (1996) 'Poverty and Social Disqualification: a Comparative Analysis of Cumulative Social Disadvantage in Europe', *Journal of European Social Policy*, vol. 6, no. 4: 287–303.

Payne, P. R. (1993) *Undernutrition: Measurement and Implications* (Oxford: Clarendon Press).

Phongpaichit, P., Piriyarangsan, S. and Treerat, N. (1995) 'Ethnic Solidarity and Social Exclusion in Thailand', in G. Rodgers, C. Gore and J. Figueiredo (eds), *Social Exclusion: Rhetoric, Reality, Responses* (Geneva: International Institute for Labour Studies), pp. 147–60.

Planning Commission (1993) *Report of the Expert Group on Estimation of Proportion and Number of Poor*, Perspective Planning Division, Planning Commission, Government of India, New Delhi.

Pollak, Robert A. and Wales, Terence J. (1979) 'Welfare Comparisons and Equivalence Scales', *American Economic Review*, vol. 69, no. 2: 216–21.

Pradhan, Menno and Ravallion, Martin (1998) *Measuring Poverty Using Qualitative Perceptions of Welfare*. Policy research working paper 2011. World Bank.

Praxis, Institute for Participatory Practices *PRA Methods Pack: Tools and Techniques*, Patna, India (http://www.praxisindia.org/publications.html).

Pretty, Jules (1995) 'Participatory Learning for Sustainable Agriculture', *World Development*, vol. 23: pp. 1247–63.

Pritchard, M. (1992) 'Wealth Ranking for Participatory Monitoring and Evaluation'. Working Paper No. 19 (Thailand: Aquacualture and Aquatic Resources Management, Asian Institute of Technology).

Qizilbash, M. (1998) 'Poverty: Concept and Measurement', Sustainable Development Policy Institute Research Report Series 12, Islamabad, Pakistan.

Qizilbash, M. (2002) 'A Note on the Measurement of Poverty and Vulnerability in the South African Context', *Journal of International Development*, vol. 14: 757–72.

Quinlan, J. R. (1993) *C4.5 Programs for Machine Learning* (Morgan Kaufmann).

Ram, R. (1982) 'Composite Indices of Physical Quality of Life, Basic Needs Fulfilment and Income: a Principal Component Representation', *Journal of Development Economics*, vol. 11: 227–47.

Ram, V. (2002a) 'International Traffic in Human Organs', *Frontline*, vol. 19, no. 7, 12 March (http://www.flonnet.com/fl1907/19070730.htm).

Ram, V. (2002b) 'Karnataka's Unabating Kidney Trade', *Frontline*, vol. 19, no. 7, 12 March (http://www.flonnet.com/fl1907/19070730.htm).

Rao, V. and Woolcock, M. (2003) 'Integrating Qualitative and Quantitative Approaches in Program Evaluation', in F. J. Bourguignon and L. P. de Silva (eds), *The Impact of Economic Policies on Poverty and Income Distribution: Evaluation Techniques and Tools* (New York: Oxford University Press), pp. 165–90.

Ravallion, M. (1993) *Poverty Comparisons* (Chur, Switzerland; Philadelphia: Harwood Academic Publishers).

Ravallion, M. (1995) 'Issues in Measuring and Modelling Poverty', *Economic Journal*, vol. 106: 1328–43.

Ravallion, M. (1998) *Poverty Lines in Theory and Practice*. LSMS Working Paper, 133 (Washington: World Bank).

Ravallion, M. (2002) *How Not to Count the Poor: a Reply to Reddy and Pogge* (Washington DC: World Bank).

Ravallion, Martin and Bidani, Benu (1994) 'How Robust is a Poverty Profile?' *World Bank Economic Review*, vol. 8, no. 1: 75–102.

Ravallion, M. and Lokshin, M. (2000) *Identifying Welfare Effects from Subjective Questions*. Policy Research Working Papers No. 2301 (Washington DC: World Bank). Available at http://econ.worldbank.org/docs/1055.pdf

Rawls, John (1971) *A Theory of Justice* (Cambridge, MA: Belknap Press of Harvard University Press).

Razafindrakoto, Mireille and Roubaud François (2000) 'The Multiple Facets of Poverty in a Developing Country: the Case of Madagascar's Capital City'.

Paris: DIAL. Available at http://www.dial.prd.fr/dial_evenements/pdf/csae/Chap3_7MadagEng.pdf

Razafindrakoto, Mireille and Roubaud François (2004) 'Subjective Perception of Poverty in Urban sub-Saharan Africa', presentation prepared for the CSAE conference, Oxford, 22 March. Available at http://www.dial.prd.fr/dial_evenements/pdf/csae/razafin_roubaud.pdf

Razavi, S. (1996) 'Excess Female Mortality: an Indicator of Female Insubordination? A Note Drawing on Village-level Evidence from South Eastern Iran', *Politeia*, vol. 12, no. 43–44: 79–96.

Razavi, S. (1998) 'Gendered Poverty and Social Change: an Issues Paper', Discussion Paper no. 94, UNRISD.

Reddy, S. G. and Pogge, T. W. (2002) *How Not to Count the Poor* (New York: Barnard College).

Rew, Alan, Khan, Shahzad and Rew, Martin (2005) 'P3 > Q2 in Northern Orissa: an Example of Integrating Combined Methods through a Platform for Probing Poverties', Q-squared Working Paper no. 8 (http://www.q-squared.ca/pdf/Q2_WP8_Rew.et.al.pdf).

Rios, Roger Raupp (n.d.) *Sexual Rights of Gays, Lesbians and Transgender Persons in Latin America* (http://www.clam.org.br/pdf/rogeringles.pdf).

Robb, Caroline M. (1999) *Can the Poor Influence Policy? Participatory Poverty Assessments in the Developing World* (Washington DC: World Bank).

Rodgers, G., Gore, C. and Figueiredo, J. (1995) *Social Exclusion: Rhetoric, Reality, Responses* (Geneva: Institute for Labour Studies).

Rojas, Bellisa and Rey, I. R. (2002) 'Pobreza y Exclusion Social: una Aproximacion al Caso', *Peruano Bulletin, Institute fr Etudes Andines*, vol. 31, no. 1: 699–720.

Rojas, Mariano (2002) 'The Multidimensionality of Poverty: a Subjective Well-being Approach', paper prepared for the WIDER conference on Inequality, Poverty and Human Well-being. Helsinki, 30–31 May. Available at http://www.wider.unu.edu/conference/conference-2003-2/conference%202003-2-papers/papers-pdf/Rojas%20150403.pdf

Room, G. (ed.) (1995) *Beyond the Threshold: the Measurement and Analysis of Social Exclusion* (Bristol: Policy Press).

Room, G. (1999) 'Social Exclusion, Solidarity and the Challenge of Globalisation', *International Journal of Social Welfare*, vol. 8, no. 3: 66–74.

Rowntree, B. Seebohm (1902) *Poverty: a Study of Town Life* (London: McMillan and Co, 2nd edition).

Rowntree, Seebohm (1918) *The Human Needs of Labour* (London: Thomas Nelson and Sons).

Ruggeri Laderchi, C. (1997) 'Poverty and its Many Dimensions: the Role of Income as an Indicator', *Oxford Development Studies*, vol. 25, no. 3: 345–60.

Ruggeri Laderchi, C. (1999) 'The Many Dimensions of Deprivation in Peru: Theoretical Debates and Empirical Evidence', Queen Elizabeth House, Working Paper Series, QEHWPS29, Oxford.

Ruggeri Laderchi, C. (2000) 'The Monetary Approach to Poverty: a Survey of Concepts and Methods', Queen Elizabeth House, Working Paper Series, WP 58, Oxford.

Ruggeri Laderchi, C. (2001) 'Participatory Methods in the Analysis of Poverty: a Critical Review'. Queen Elizabeth House Working Paper 62, Oxford.

Russell, M. and Malhotra, R. (2001) 'Capitalism and Disability', in L. Panitch and C. Leys (eds), *A World of Contradictions: Socialist Register 2002* (London: Merlin), pp. 211–28.

Saith, R. (2001a) 'Capabilities: the Concept and its Operationalisation', Oxford: Queen Elizabeth House Working Paper 66.

Saith, R. (2001b) 'Social Exclusion: the Concept and Application to Developing Countries', Oxford: Queen Elizabeth House Working Paper 72.

Saith, R. and Harriss-White, B. (1999) 'The Gender Sensitivity of Well-Being Indicators', *Development and Change*, vol. 30, no. 3: 465–97.

Saith, R. R. and Harriss-White, B. (2004) 'Anti-poverty Policy: Screening for Eligibility Using Village-level Evidence', in B. Harriss-White (ed.), *Rural India Facing the 21st Century* (London: Anthem).

Satterthwaite, David (1995) 'The Under-estimation and Misrepresentation of Urban Poverty', *Environment and Urbanization*, vol. 7, no. 1: 3–10.

Schokkaert, E. and Van Ootegem, L. (1990) 'Sen's Concept of the Living Standard Applied to the Belgian Unemployed', *Reserches Economiques de Louvain*, vol. 56, no. 3–4: 429–50.

Scoones, Ian (1995) 'Investigating Difference: Applications of Wealth Ranking and Household Survey Approaches among Farming Households in Southern Zimbabwe', *Development and Change*, vol. 36: 67–88.

Seckler, David (1982) ' "Small but Healthy": a Basic Hypothesis in the Theory, Measurement and Policy of Malnutrition', in P. V. Sukhatme (ed.), *Newer Concepts in Nutrition and their Implications for Policy* (Pune, India: Maharashtra Association for the Cultivation of Science Research Institute).

Selvin, Hannan C with the assistance of Christopher Bernert (1985) 'Durkheim, Booth and Yule: the Non-diffusion of an Intellectual Innovation', in M. Bulmer (ed.), *Essays on the History of British Sociological Research* (Cambridge: Cambridge University Press).

Sen, A. (2002) 'Health: Perception Versus Observation', *British Medical Journal*, vol. 324: 860–1.

Sen, A. K. (1976) 'Poverty: an Ordinal Approach to Measurement', *Econometrica*, vol. 44, no. 2: 219–31.

Sen, A. K. (1980) 'Equality of What?' in S. McMurrin (ed.), *Tanner Lectures on Human Values* (Cambridge: Cambridge University Press and reprinted in A. K. Sen (1982) *Choice Welfare and Measurement*, pp. 353–69 (Cambridge, Massachusetts and London: Harvard University Press).

Sen, A. K. (1982) *Choice Welfare and Measurement* (Cambridge, Massachusetts and London: Harvard University Press).

Sen, A. K. (1985) *Commodities and Capabilities* (Amsterdam: Elsevier, repr. 1999 New Delhi: Oxford University Press).

Sen, A. K. (1987), 'The Standard of Living: Lecture II, Lives and Capabilities', in G. Hawthorn (ed.) *The Standard of Living: the Tanner Lectures on Human Values* (Cambridge: Cambridge University Press), pp. 20–38.

Sen, A. K. (1988) 'The Concept of Development', in H. Chenery and T. N. Srinivasan (eds), *Handbook of Development Economics*, volume 1 (Amsterdam: Elsevier Publishers), pp. 9–26.

Sen, A. K. (1992) *Inequality Reexamined* (Cambridge, MA: Harvard University Press).

Sen, A. K. (1993) 'Capability and Well-Being', in M. C. Nussbaum and A. Sen (eds), *The Quality of Life* (Oxford: Clarendon Press and reprinted (1999), New Delhi: Oxford University Press), pp. 30–53.

Sen, A. K. (1994) 'Well-Being, Capability and Public Policy', *Giornale degli Economisti e Annali di Economia*, vol. 53, nos 7–9: 333–47.

Sen, A. K. (1997) *On Economic Inequality: with a substantial annexe 'On Economic Inequality After a Quarter Century' by J. Foster and A. Sen*, 2nd edition (Oxford: Clarendon Press).

Sen, A. K. (1999) *Development as Freedom* (Oxford: Oxford University Press).

Sen, A. K (2000a) *Development as Freedom* 2nd edn (Oxford: Oxford University Press).

Sen, A. K. (2000b) *Freedom, Rationality and Social Choice: Arrow Lectures and Other Essays* (Oxford: Oxford University Press).

Sen, A. K. (2001) 'Exclusion and Inclusion', *Mainstream*, 28 November (p. 2 on South Asia Citizens Wire: http://www.mnet.fr/aiindex).

Sen, A. K. and Foster, J. (1997) 'Inequality after a Quarter Century', in A. K. Sen, *On Economic Inequality*, 2nd edition (Oxford: Clarendon Press).

Shaffer, Paul (1996) 'Beneath the Poverty Debate: Some Issues', *IDS Bulletin*, vol. 27, no. 1: 23–35.

Shaffer, Paul (1998) 'Gender, Poverty and Deprivation: Evidence from the Republic of Guinea', *World Development*, vol. 26, no. 12: 2119–35.

Shaffer, Paul (2002) 'Difficulties in Combining Income/Consumption and Participatory Approaches to Poverty: Issues and Examples, in R. Kanbur (ed.), *Q-squared: Combining Qualitative and Quantitative Methods in Poverty Appraisal* (New Delhi: Permanent Black).

Shariff, A. (1999) *India Human Development Report* (New Delhi: Oxford University Press).

Sharma, R. (2002) 'Aftershocks: the Rough Guide to Democracy', VHS PAL 66 min (actindia@vsnl.com).

Silver, H. (1995) 'Reconceptualising Social Disadvantage: Three Paradigms of Social Exclusion', in G. Rodgers, C. Gore and J. Figueiredo (eds), *Social Exclusion: Rhetoric, Reality, Responses* (Geneva: International Institute for Labour Studies), pp. 58–80.

Simey, Thomas S. and Simey, Margaret B. (1960) *Charles Booth: Social Scientist* (Oxford: Oxford University Press).

Singh, I. P. (2001a) 'Census of the Homeless: a Painful Farce and Assault', *The First City*, April, pp. 56–59.

Singh, I. P. (2001b) 'Government Policy is Silent on Pavement Workers', *Labour File*, vol. 7, no. 6–7: 34–36.

Sinha, Siddiqui and Munjal (2004) 'The Indian Informal Economy: a SAM Analysis', Mimeo, NCAER and Queen Elizabeth House, Oxford.

Speak, S. (2004) 'Degrees of Destitution: a Typology of Homelessness in Developing Countries', *Housing Studies* vol. 19, no. 3: 465–82.

Staples, James (2002) 'The Body in Society' unpublished chapter of a doctoral dissertation, SOAS, London.

Statsoft electronic textbook (1984–2001) Copyright StatSoft, Inc. (http://www.statsoft.com/textbook/stfacan.html#index).

Stephens, R., Waldegrave, C. and Stuart, S. (1996) 'Participation in Poverty Research: Drawing on the Knowledge of Low Income Householders to Establish an Appropriate Measure for Monitoring Social Policy Impacts', *Social Policy Journal of New Zealand*, vol. 7 (December): 191–206.

Stewart, F. (1985) *Planning to Meet Basic Needs* (Basingstoke: Macmillan).

Stewart, F. (1995) 'Basic Needs, Capabilities and Human Development', *Greek Economic Review*, vol. 17, no. 2: 83–96.

Stewart, F. (2002) 'Horizontal Inequality: a Neglected Dimension of Development', Helsinki, WIDER Annual Development Lecture.

Stewart, F. (2003) 'The Implications for Chronic Poverty of Alternative Approaches to Conceptualising Poverty', paper prepared for IDPM Manchester Conference on Chronic Poverty, April.

Stewart, F. and Wang, M. (2003) 'Do PRSPs Empower Poor Countries and Disempower the World Bank, or is it the Other Way Round?', Queen Elizabeth House Working Paper 108.

Stigler, George J. (1954) 'The Early History of Empirical Studies of Consumer Behaviour', *Journal of Political Economy*, vol. 62, no. 2: 95–113.

Streeten, P. P., Burki, S. J. et al. (1981) *First Things First: Meeting Basic Human Needs in Developing Countries* (New York: Oxford University Press).

Sugden, R. (1993) 'Welfare, Resources and Capabilities: a Review of Inequality Reexamined by Amartya Sen', *Journal of Economic Literature*, vol. 31: 1947–62.

Sukhatme, P. V. (1989). 'Nutritional Adaptation and Variability', *European Journal of Clinical Nutrition*, vol. 43.

Sukhatme, P. V. (ed.) (1982) *Newer Concepts in Nutrition and their Implications for Policy* (Pune, India: Maharashtra Associaiton for the Cultivation of Science).

Sullivan, K. and Gorstein, J. (1999) ANTHRO Software for Calculating Anthropometry, Version 1.02, Y2K Compliant, 29 June.

Svedberg, P. (1991) *Poverty and Undernutrition in Sub-Saharan Africa: Theory, Evidence and Policy*, Institute for International Economic Studies, Stockholm University, Monograph Series No. 19.

Svedberg, P. (2000) *Poverty and Undernutrition: Theory, Measurement and Policy* (New Delhi: Oxford University Press).

Szekely, M., Lustig, N., Meijia, J. A. and Cumpa, M. (2000) *Do We Know How Much Poverty There Is?* (Washington DC: IADB).

Taddesse, M. (1998) 'Perceptions of Welfare and Poverty: Analysis of Qualitative Responses of a Panel of Urban Households in Ethiopia', mimeo, Department of Economics, Addis Ababa University. Unprocessed. Available at http://www.economics.ox.ac.uk/members/marcel.fafchamps/homepage/nepwel.pdf

Tchernina, N. (1995) 'Patterns and Processes of Social Exclusion in Russia' in G. Rodgers, C. Gore and J. Figueiredo (eds), *Social Exclusion: Rhetoric, Reality, Responses* (Geneva: International Institute for Labour Studies), pp. 131–45.

Tesliuc, Emil D. and Lindert, Kathy (2004) *Risk and Vulnerability in Guatemala: a Quantitative and Qualitative Assessment*, Social Protection Discussion Paper Series 0404 (Washington: World Bank).

Thon, Dominique (1983) 'A Note on Troublesome Axioms for Poverty Indices', *Economic Journal*, vol. 93, no. 369.

Tibaijuka, A and Kaijage, F. (1995) 'Patterns and Processes of Social Exclusion in Tanzania', in G. Rodgers, C. Gore and J. Figueiredo (eds), *Social Exclusion:*

Rhetoric, Reality, Responses (Geneva: International Institute for Labour Studies), pp. 187–200.

Times of India 18 September 2001.

Townsend, P. (1979). *Poverty in the United Kingdom* (Harmondsworth: Penguin).

UNDP (1990) *Human Development Report 1990* (New York: Oxford University Press).

UNDP (1997) *Human Development Report 1997* (New York: Oxford University Press).

UNDP (2001) *Human Development Report 2001* (New York: Oxford University Press).

UNDP (2002) *Human Development Report 2002* (New York: Oxford University Press).

Valera, Guillermo (1998) 'Las comunidades en el Perú. Una visión nacional desde las series departamentales', Instituto Rural del Perú, 1ra. Edición, Lima in GRADE, 2003.

van Parijs, Philippe (ed.) (1992) *Arguing for Basic Income: Ethical Foundations for a Radical Reform* (London: Verso).

van Parijs, Philippe (1995) *Real Freedom For All* (Oxford: Oxford Clarendon Press).

Vasquez, E. (2006) *Public Budgets and Social Expense: the Urgency of Monitoring and Evaluation*, Observatory for Infants and Adolescents (http://www.losni-nosprimero.org/portal/index.php?cont=informes).

Veit-Wilson, John (1986) 'Paradigms of Poverty: a Rehabilitation of B.S. Rowntree', *Journal of Social Policy*, vol. 15 no. 1.

Vivian, J. (ed.) (1995) *Adjustment and Social Sector Restructuring* (London: Cass).

Wallace, M. (2001) 'Learning Our Lesson', *The Big Issue*.

Whelan, B. and Whelan, C. (1995) 'Is Poverty Multidimensional?' in G. Room (ed.), *Beyond the Threshold: the Measurement and Analysis of Social Exclusion* (Bristol: Policy Press), pp. 29–48.

White, H. and Masset, E. (2003) 'The Importance of Household Size and Composition in Constructing Poverty Profiles: an Illustration from Vietnam', *Development and Change*, vol. 34, no. 1: 105–26.

White, Sarah (1996) 'Depoliticising Development: the Uses and Abuses of Participation', *Development in Practice*, vol. 6: 6–15.

White, Sarah and Jethro Pettit (2004) *Participatory Approaches and the Measurement of Human Well-Being*, WeD Working Paper 08, UNU-WIDER.

Williams, B. (1987) 'The Standard of Living: Interests and Capabilities', in G. Hawthorn (ed.), *The Standard of Living: the Tanner Lectures on Human Values* (Cambridge: Cambridge University Press), pp. 94–102.

Wood, G. (2001) 'Governance and the Common Man: Embedding Social Policy in the Search for Security', paper prepared for the Social Policy in Developing Countries, Institute for International Policy Analysis, University of Bath Workshop, 1–2 March.

World Bank (1990) *World Development Report* (Oxford: Oxford University Press). (www.worldbank.org/html/dec/Publications/Workpapers/wps2000series/wps 2011/wps2011.pdf).

World Bank (1996) 'Participation in Poverty Assessments', in Appendix II: Working Paper Summaries, *The World Bank Participation Sourcebook* (Washington DC: World Bank).

World Bank (1999) *Poverty and Social Development in Peru, 1994–1997*, World Bank Country Study 0253–2123 (Washington DC: World Bank).

World Bank (2000) 'Consultations with the Poor: Methodology Guide for the 20 Country Study for the World Development Report 2000–01' (Washington DC: World Bank).

World Bank (2003) *The Poverty Reduction Strategy Initiative: an Independent Evaluation of the World Bank's Support Through 2003* (Washington DC: World Bank).

World Bank (2005) *Colombia: the Gap Matters: Poverty and Well-being of Afro-Colombians and Indigenous Peoples* (World Bank Sector Report, 33014).

Yaqub, S. (2000) 'Poverty Dynamics in Developing Countries', *Development Bibliography* 16, April, Institute of Development Studies: Sussex.

Ysander, (1993) 'Robert Erikson: Descriptions of Inequality', in M. C. Nussbaum and A. Sen (eds), *The Quality of Life* (Oxford: Clarendon Press; repr. 1999, New Delhi: Oxford University Press), pp. 30–53.

Yule, G. Udny (1895) 'On the Correlation of Total Pauperism with Proportion of Outrelief', *Economic Journal*, vol. 5, no. 2: 477–89.

Index